S0-BBG-580

IN THE WAKE OF COOK

In the wake of COOK
Exploration, Science & Empire, 1780-1801

David Mackay

ST. MARTIN'S PRESS
New York

© 1985 David Mackay
All rights reserved. For Information, write:
St. Martin's Press, Inc., 175 Fifth Avenue, New York, NY 10010
First published in the United States of America in 1985

Library of Congress Catalog Card Number: 85-40080
Cataloging in Publication Data applied for.

ISBN 0-312-41177-4

Printed and bound in Great Britain

CONTENTS

MAPS

PREFACE

The two decades following the American War of Independence were testing ones for British governments. Traditional sources of executive power were being eroded and the mid-century mechanisms for controlling Parliament were being called into question. Since the Wilkes affairs of the 1760s the workings of government had come in for wider and closer scrutiny: a tendency which was accelerated as the costs of the American War became apparent. Without our advantages of hindsight, many Parliamentary reformers laid the blame for Britain's woes at the feet of those responsible for the spiralling costs of government and the misuse of government offices. After March 1782 this group of economical reformers saw some of their proposals on the statute books, as the Rockingham party sought in legislative form to reverse the destructive processes which in their eyes had been at work since the accession of George III.

The force of these changes had profound repercussions for imperial management. While seemingly intractable administrative problems arose in Canada, India and the West Indies, the resources available to attack these problems had been depleted. The destruction of the third Secretaryship of State left colonial affairs in the control of the over-worked and under-staffed Home Office, which almost seized up under the load. The folding up of the Board of Trade left so great a vacuum that it shortly afterwards had to be almost surreptitiously resurrected in the form of a Privy Council Committee. The momentum of the Rockinghams' campaign against placemen carried through to help destroy Fox's India Bill and even to threaten the Act of 1784.

It was against this administrative and political background that the repercussions of the loss of the American colonies and the discoveries of Captain Cook had to be worked out. One solution to the shortage of government resources and specialist knowledge was to draw on the services of skilled persons outside the ranks of government. Such unofficial recruitment was particularly obvious in colonial affairs, and in matters where scientific advice was required. These two areas were frequently linked, since the traditional mercantilist approach to colonies was under attack both at the theoretical and functional level. Scientific know-how, particularly when applied to the development of tropical cash and food crops seemed to provide possibilities for extending or modifying the mercantilist framework for imperial trade. The exploitation of scientific knowledge in such a context is one of the central themes of this book.

The other central concern here is the impact of the discoveries of Cook and his immediate predecessors on imperial developments. Cook's legacy in particular had a twofold effect. It opened up regions hitherto only vaguely known to European powers. It also provided a model and methodology of scientific exploration which could be drawn upon by subsequent explorers. However, the argument in this book is that the response of the Pitt government to these opportunities was less than systematic; suggestive more of expediency than of coherent and logical policy. While some individuals shared the broad imperial vision described in V.T. Harlow's work, *The Founding of the Second British Empire 1763-1793*, and more recently in Margaret Steven's *Trade, Tactics and Territory*, the hard-pressed administration of William Pitt did not manifest such a vision, much less give it practical expression in terms of policy and action. Those who sailed in the wake of Cook were not conforming to a coherent government plan, but more commonly buttressing traditional imperial structures, stopping gaps, or pursuing individual opportunities for profit.

Those who have kindly assisted in the research and writing of this book will not necessarily share what is a rather cynical view of the vision and operation of governments. I owe a particular debt to Professor I.R. Christie, who some years ago took on the supervision of an unlikely topic and provided meticulous care and attention. A number of people have read and commented on parts of the manuscript, including Mrs Mary Boyd, Professor Glyndwr Williams and the late Dr Averil Lysaght. Valuable assistance has been provided by librarians and archivists in several parts of the world. The staff of the Public Record Office, British Library, British Museum (Natural History), Kew Herbarium Library, India Office Library, National Maritime Museum and Royal Society of Arts in London. In Edinburgh the staff of the National Library of Scotland and Scottish Record Office. In Australia the staff of the State Library of New South Wales and the Australian National Library, Canberra; and in San Francisco the staff of the Sutro Library.

I am grateful for the support of my colleagues in the History Department of Victoria University of Wellington, and to the financial assistance provided by the University's Council and Research and Publications Committees. I also owe a debt to the organisers of the conference on 'Captain Cook and His Times' held at Simon Fraser University, British Columbia in May 1978. This provided an opportunity to redevelop my ideas on the significance of Cook's voyages.

The arduous task of typing and preparing the manuscript was carried out by Margaret Smith and Gwen Wright, and Mrs R. Mita kindly drew the maps. The Editor of *The New Zealand Journal of History* kindly gave permission for reproducing parts of chapters 2 and 5.

ABBREVIATIONS

Add. MSS	Additional Manuscripts, British Library.
A.I.C.	Anderson, J. *An Account of the Importation of the American Cochineal Insects*, Madras, 1795.
A.L.C.	Anderson, J. *Some Additional Letters principally regarding the Culture of Raw Silk*, Madras, 1793.
B.C.H.Q.	*British Columbia Historical Quarterly*.
C.I.C.	Anderson, J. *Correspondence on the Introduction of the Cochineal Insects from America*, Madras, 1791.
C.L.C.	Anderson, J. *The Conclusion of Letters on Cochineal*, Madras, 1799.
D.T.C.	The Dawson Turner Copies of Sir Joseph Banks' Correspondence in the British Museum (Natural History).
H.M.C.	Historical Manuscripts Commission.
H.R.N.S.W.	*Historical Records of New South Wales*, Sydney, 1892–1901.
I.O.	India Office.
Kew B.C.	The Correspondence of Sir Joseph Banks in the Library of the Royal Botanic Gardens, Kew.
L.C.	Anderson, J. *Letters on Cochineal*, Madras, 1788.
L.C.C.	Anderson, J. *Letters on Cochineal Continued*, Madras, 1789.
L.J.B.	Anderson, J. *Letters to Sir Joseph Banks*, Madras, 1788.
M.L. Banks	Correspondence of Sir Joseph Banks in the Mitchell Library, the State Library of New South Wales, Sydney.
N.L.S.	National Library of Scotland.
P.R.O.	Public Record Office, London:
	Adm. Admiralty Papers.
	B.T. Board of Trade Papers.
	C.O. Colonial Office Papers.
	F.O. Foreign Office Papers.
	H.O. Home Office Papers.
	W.O. War Office Papers.
R.S.A.	Royal Society of Arts, London.
S.R.O.	Scottish Record Office.

PART ONE

1 INTRODUCTION: EXPLORATION, SCIENCE AND EMPIRE IN THE LATE EIGHTEENTH CENTURY

On the 19th of January 1801 the Admiralty ordered the Navy Board to register the sloop *Xenophon* on the lists of the Royal Navy as the *Investigator*, to prepare her for an expedition to the South Seas.[1] For a body which usually showed great care, but also a degree of imagination, in the naming of its vessels, the Board of Admiralty had this time made a rather prosaic choice. Other ships sent on voyages of exploration in the reign of George III had had loftier names. *Endeavour, Resolution, Adventure, Discovery* — Cook's ships — all suggested the heroic qualities required of a great navigator: enterprise, striving, determination, fearlessness in the face of the unknown. The middle two had even at the last moment been changed from the *Drake* and the *Raleigh* so as to avoid giving offence to the territorially sensitive Spaniards.[2] *Bounty* seemed an appropriate name for the vessel in which Captain Bligh hoped to carry the breadfruit to a supposedly starving West Indian slave population: the *Providence* and *Assistance* seemed ironically appropriate for the vessels which were to succeed where a mutiny had caused the *Bounty* to fail.[3] The ships concerned in Vancouver's voyage — *Discovery, Chatham* and *Daedalus* — showed less originality in their names, but at least manifested a continuity in style.

Why had the Lords of the Admiralty deviated from a noble tradition in the case of this vessel? It seems that on this occasion they had not themselves made the choice, but had, as it were, farmed it out. The person responsible for the name was Sir Joseph Banks, Bart., KB, Privy Councillor and President of the Royal Society. Shortly after Christmas in 1800 Banks drew up a shortlist of suitable names. They were: Perseverance, Investigator, Searcher, Industrious, Patience, Enquiry, Rival, Diligence.[4] Most of these would have fitted into the pattern of the ships' names outlined above. The *Investigator* seems to stand out. The choice was not without significance.

In terms of equipment and personnel, the *Investigator* was one of the most thoroughly equipped survey vessels up to that time to sail into the seas around New Holland opened up by Captain Cook's voyages. The best sextant by Jesse Ramsden, and chronometers by Arnold and Earnshaw were aboard, as well as a host of other survey-

3

ing and astronomical instruments supplied by the London firm of Edward Troughton.[5] Arrowsmith, the talented cartographer, supplied copies of the most reliable and up-to-date charts. Recent works on voyages of discovery in the South Seas were supplied and Banks lent his own copy of the *Endeavour* log.[6] To enable inland excursions to be made, tents, canteens, fowling shot and a large quantity of trading articles were purchased. On the quarterdeck of the ship a solid greenhouse was constructed for the sheltering of live plant specimens.[7] Putting all this equipment to good use was a skilled group of scientists and their assistants: Robert Brown, one of nineteenth-century England's most distinguished botanists; John Crosley the astronomer; William Westall the landscape painter; Ferdinand Bauer the botanical draughtsman; Peter Good the gardener; John Allen the miner. To be sure, the French survey ships *Le Géographe* and *Le Naturaliste* could boast a zoologist, anthropologist and geographical engineer as well, but with the exception of Cook's second voyage, the *Investigator* could boast a larger scientific party than any other British expedition since 1760.[8]

The instructions to the commander, Mathew Flinders, and to the members of the scientific party naturally emphasised the necessity of accurate observation and measurement. Wherever he touched, Flinders was enjoined to note,

> the winds and weather which usually prevail there at different seasons of the year, the productions and comparative fertility of the soil, and the manner and customs of the inhabitants of such parts as you may be able to explore; fixing in all cases, when in your power, the true positions both in latitude and longitude of remarkable head lands, bays, and harbours, by astronomical observations, and noting the variation of the needle, and the right direction and course of the tides and currents, as well as the perpendicular height of the tides.[9]

If any sizeable rivers gave an opportunity of access to the interior of the country, these were to be fully explored so that further information about natural products and fertility could be gathered. The commander was to ensure that the greenhouse was put to good use, carrying back plants for more detailed examination at Kew Gardens. In their own fields, the botanist and miner were recommended the same dedication to detailed observation and accurate recording.[10]

In terms of the brief it was given, and the technical aids to the fulfilment of that brief, the choice of the name *Investigator* does not, therefore, seem inappropriate. No momentous new geographical discoveries were expected of it; no large continents, or islands, or passages would be added to the charts — the crude outlines of the New Holland coasts were already known. There was still a possibility that a strait might open up southwards from the Gulf of Carpentaria, but most of the aims of the voyage fitted within the confines of Flinders' own phrases — a 'more minute examination of the coast' or 'further knowledge'.[11]

Such 'further knowledge' could and should be of use to England: this was another theme of the instructions and the equipping of the voyage. Coal and salt had already been discovered in New South Wales, and the miner was directed by Banks to study exposed strata closely for signs of mineral deposits — copper and gold would be the most obvious, but many others could be detected by meticulous observation and analysis. Any new or useful products found by the botanist were to be noted; their locations and conditions of growth recorded, and live or dried specimens collected for further investigation. The commander too was to have an eye for 'anything useful to the commerce or manufactures of the United Kingdom', and to watch for valuable harbours and passages suitable for navigation. Hoping that it might also profit from the voyage, the East India Company offered Flinders, his officers and the scientists £1,200 in *batta*, or table money, and as Banks observed to the commander, 'The real reason for the allowance is to Encourage the men of Science to discover such things as will be useful to the Commerce of India & you to find new passages'.[12]

The equipping of the *Investigator*, and the instructions to the commander and scientific staff, manifest an empirical strain which was a strong component of eighteenth-century English science. The debate as to whether empiricism and science are not naturally exclusive does not seem to be worth pursuing at any length in the present context.[13] The great triumph of the seventeenth-century scientific revolution — a triumph only finally accepted in the eighteenth century — was the rejection of knowledge based on teleological or metaphysical explanations. Despite the intuitive and synthetic elements in Newton's discoveries, he had made some methodological contribution by his acceptance that science should be established on the basis of facts derived from close observation and experimental verification. Only in this way could the mechanism of the natural world be made intelligible and submit to rational laws. Not only Aristotle, but Descartes would have to go, although God, in the meantime, could stay. Experiment and theory were both vital aspects of post-Newtonian science.

Empiricism in the sciences suggested a clearly defined and accepted approach to any particular problem: detailed observation of natural phenomena; accurate measurement; study of behaviourial changes; description of phenomena exclusive (in so far as it was possible) of value judgements, and in a mode which was recognisable to and accepted by other scientists; classification and categorisation of phenomena; the formulation from the accumulated data of general principles which were to be checked by experiments or re-examination. Through this process would come understanding and eventually mastery of nature.

The early stages of this process put heavy emphasis on the human senses with the inherent danger that these might introduce subjective impressions. As Alexander Koyré, and more recently, Musson and Robinson, have made clear, the vital aids in this respect were the new scientific instruments which extended and often calibrated the senses.[14] The telescope of Galileo, stripping away the corona around the stars, was the first obvious example, lifting some of the limitations on the power of human vision, and thus revealing the true world. In the course of the seventeenth and eighteenth centuries the instrument makers, working with great mathematical precision themselves, produced other instruments which facilitated greater precision in those who employed them. The microscope, screw micrometer, bubble level and a new range of navigational instruments were crucial aids in the scientific revolution, but also in many senses, products of that revolution.

In both a direct and an indirect way these facets of eighteenth-century science influenced the course of maritime exploration in the reign of George III. The *Investigator* mission was only one of the later and better equipped in this respect. From the time of Captain Cook's first voyage onwards, the planning, equipping and execution of such expeditions were influenced by changes in scientific methods and attitudes. There were, it is true, no revolutionary advances in ship design which owed anything to the scientific revolution, although the introduction of copper sheathing did proceed on an experimental basis. Navigation, however, was becoming a more exact and better equipped science. By the time of Cook's second voyage the practical problems of establishing longitude at sea had been substantially solved as a result of the two-pronged attack represented by the development of a reliable marine chronometer, and the accurate lunar tables published in Maskelyne's *Nautical Almanac* for the year 1767.[15] The calculation and then use of the lunar tables, themselves required close empirical observation and more accurate instruments — Newton reputedly claimed that predicting the movements of the moon was the only problem which made his head ache.[16] Hadley's octant, and the later development of it in the sextant, were the necessary breakthroughs in this area. These navigational advances, important for all shipping movements, naturally in this period had the greatest impact on the course of exploration, and they represent in the words of J.H. Parry, 'one of the few clear instances — at least until recent times — of a direct impact of pure science upon everyday technology'.[17]

Nevertheless, the indirect impact of 'pure' science on technology, and in the present instance on the techniques of exploration, is equally important, for the empirical processes which were vital to eighteenth-century science were just as valuable to the craft of seamanship. Captain James Cook provides a superb example in the present context, and after 1768 provided a contemporary model and standard. His relationship to Maskelyne, Harrison and the theoretical geographers paralleled that of James Watt to Joseph Black, and the qualities he brought to seamanship reflected the new scientific method. He was an astute, curious and yet objective observer — both of rough coasts such as those of Newfoundland and New Zealand, and indigenous peoples, such as the Tahitians or Nootka Sound Indians. He showed unusual but consistent concern for detail and accuracy — the charts he drew of Newfoundland were used well into the nineteenth century. He eschewed conjecture and never firmly laid down a coast which he had not seen or traced; every geographical fact had to be verified and he showed a gentle scorn for the theorising of geographers such as Dalrymple. Cook had a firm scientific interest in new navigational techniques and he experimented determinedly with both Maskelyne's tables and the new chronometers of Harrison and Kendall. His concern for the health of his crew led him to try an exotic range of anti-scorbutics, producing remarkable practical results, although drawing the wrong conclusions from his researches. It was for his efforts in this field that the Royal Society chose to honour him with their Copley Medal. He industriously recorded his observations in his logs, journals and charts in a manner which made them valuable to all who might wish to use them, and although journals of voyages of discovery were not new, with Cook they achieved a greater degree of sophistication. His crews spoke of his powers of instinct and intuition as a seaman: what they actually referred to was that enormous fund of knowledge and experience, collected mainly by the scrupulous application of his own senses, which enabled him to detect a shoal shore, hidden reefs and changes in the weather by observing and assessing the relevant natural phenomena.[18]

Many of these capacities, and the traditions that went with them, were passed on, albeit in lesser degree, to some of Cook's disciples and followers, and they infused the whole era of navigation. King, Bligh, Vancouver, Portlock, Gore and Roberts imbibed and practised his methods, often with considerable distinction. All acknowledged their debt, and when like Bligh and Vancouver they found themselves obliged to correct his errors, they did so with a degree of awe and respect. These men, in turn, passed the tradition on to the next generation of seamen — Broughton, Puget and, of course, Flinders of the *Investigator*.

In one other sense the voyages of exploration which culminated in the *Investigator* voyage were attuned to the scientific empiricism of the age. From the *Endeavour* voyage onwards the ships of discovery carried competent scientific parties intended to augment and extend the observations of the commander. This was not an entirely new development, much less an entirely English one, but from 1768 onwards it became an accepted practice, establishing a tradition running through to Darwin on the *Beagle*, and the $3\frac{1}{2}$-year voyage of the *Challenger* in the 1870s, which established the paradigms of modern oceanography. These scientific parties generally consisted of natural historians, astronomers, landscape painters and botanical draughtsmen, although with the increasing specialisation of science in the late eighteenth and early nineteenth centuries there came additions to this basic complement. All members of such parties were impressed with the need for close observation and the gathering of precise information. All were instructed to keep journals recording their experiences, and to bring back collections or astronomical date for scrutiny in England. Some vessels, such as the *Discovery* and the *Investigator*, carried greenhouses for the collection of live plant specimens. With the qualified exception of Cook's first voyage, these parties were working at the behest of organisations or persons who remained at home, and the very tenor of their instructions often suggested that they were like Galileo's telescope, an extension of their patrons' senses, illuminating what was obscured to the eye.

In its concern to make not only new, but also useful discoveries, the *Investigator* voyage manifests another powerful strain in eighteenth-century science. From the time of Bacon's *New Organon* onwards, the pursuit of science for transcendent goals had slowly given way to the ideology which suggested that the ultimate aim of science was a utilitarian one. Bacon wished scientific activity to move in the direction of recovering dominion over nature and gaining knowledge of natural laws. Once natural forces were understood and controlled, they could be re-directed to benefit mankind as a whole. Bacon's philosophy of science permeated the activities of Gresham College, and was absorbed intact by the Royal Society to be enshrined in its charter: 'The business of the Royal Society is: to improve the knowledge of natural things, and all useful arts, Manufactures, Mechanic practices, Engynes and Inventions by experiment.'[19]

Powerful forces from this point onwards preserved the essentially utilitarian aims of science. The *Philosophical Transactions* of the Royal Society, especially in the first 40 years of its publication, strongly emphasised this concern. Provincial societies — the Gentlemen's Society at Spalding, the Lunar Society of Birmingham, the Derby Philosophical Society — either incorporated such ideas in their charters or strongly exuded such an ethos.[20] In 1754 the Royal Society of Arts, Manufactures and Commerce was formed with the express aim of exploiting scientific knowledge for practical purposes, an objective it pushed forward with generous offers of premiums and bounties.[21] On 9 March 1799, at a meeting at the home of Sir Joseph Banks, the Royal Institution was founded, with the purpose of: 'diffusing the knowledge and facilitating the general introduction of useful mechanical inventions and improvements: and for teaching, by courses of philosophical lectures and experiments, the application of science to the common purposes of life.'[22] Another eighteenth-century facet of this co-operative and public aspect of science, was the enormous increase in the number of works popularising recent scientific developments, and a similar increase in scientific journals.[23]

The Baconian influence was not limited to the institutions of British science, but was apparent in individual scientists and foreign organisations as well. In Brandenburg-Prussia Leibnitz created the pressures which led to the establishment of the Berlin Academy of Science because he believed scientific knowledge should not remain the property of scholars, but be put to practical use. The French Academy of Science showed the same bent and the great tradition of popularising scientific developments, which began with Fontenelle and Réamur, and culminated in the *Encyclopédie*, had as its primary aim the application of scientific knowledge to everyday life. A substantial work by a recent historian of American colonial science emphasises the existence of the same impulse across the Atlantic. The same author questions whether the eighteenth century had any concept of 'pure' science, citing Benjamin Franklin's rhetorical question: 'What signifies philosophy that does not apply to some use.'[24] When introducing his lectures at Glasgow, Joseph Black turned this question on its head: 'Chemistry, like all other sciences, has arisen from the reflections of ingenious men on the general facts which occur in the practice of the various arts of common life.'[25]

That such a Baconian philosophy existed and was the accepted broader aim of science is not widely disputed. However, the actual effect of such a philosophy in terms of practical results, and in particular the question of the direct linkage between scientific developments and the industrial revolution, have of late produced considerable debate. One side of this debate, represented most strongly by Hall, Landes and Ashby, argued that the role of science in the industrial revolution was minimal, and Professor Hall has claimed that the progress of technology in the eighteenth century was regarded as the business of manufacturers and craftsmen: 'Natural philosophy grew by increasing knowledge, invention sprang from ingenuity.'[26] Such a viewpoint tends to elevate the distinction between 'pure' and 'applied' science and to derogate the notion of utility as the ultimate criterion of worth.

On the other side of the fence are those who point to the very close contacts between men of science and men of industry in the eighteenth century, the growing recognition of the need for scientific knowledge and techniques in industry and the interest shown in industrial developments by men of science and scientific societies. These ideas have been supported by Rostow, Ashton and the Clows in their studies of the industrial revolution, and by Schofield, and Hudson and Luckhurst in their studies of scientific societies. More recently, Musson and Robinson have drawn up particularly heavy guns, recording their impression that:

many of the leading scientists and scientifically-minded industrialists were motivated also to a considerable extent by innate
curiosity, by a desire to discover more about how industrial processes worked, by an urge to make improvements, and to be
esteemed by their fellows, not merely for the money they made,
but for their contributions to scientific and technological
advance.[27]

An adjudicating historian has pointed out that the very nature of
the arguments on each side precludes the emergence of any satisfactory proof either way. The semantics involved and the unclear facts
of the situation put grave difficulties in the way of any useful conclusion.[28] In the narrowest sense, those who deny any direct link
between the scientific and industrial revolutions have a powerful
case: the great discoveries of seventeenth-century science were not
productive of any immediate material benefits for mankind: the
most significant achievements of the industrial revolution, and the
most important technical advances, were not, with the qualified
exception of the steam engine, dependent on scientific breakthroughs. But neither science nor industry advanced on such narrow
fronts. It is clear that a number of advances in industrial technique
sprang from communication or collaboration between scientists and
industrialists. The crossfeed between science and industry, and
indeed the feedback in terms of progress in scientific instrument
design, were enormous. No one can read the correspondence
between Watt and Black, printed in the volume by Robinson and
McKie, without getting a most powerful idea of such continual and
fruitful interchange. The Clows and A.E. Musson clearly depict the
same process in their studies of the chemical, bleaching and dyeing
industries.[29]

What this suggests is the importance of the milieu in which industrial, and also agricultural, work went forward. In the eighteenth
century there was enormous faith in the possibility of progress and
technical advance, and the perfectability of manufacturing processes. The scientific revolution had declared man's capacity to
understand, order, control and re-shape nature, and this impulse
was injected into all productive processes. Just as important, the
empirical techniques valuable to the acquiring of scientific knowledge were directly appropriate to agricultural and industrial growth:
close observation and precise measurement, testing by experimentation, and the adoption of instruments which reduced the part which

human fallibility might have in any given process. As has already been suggested in the context of maritime exploration, the prevailing attitudes and methods of science overflowed into other fields of endeavour. Mathias has expressed it more succinctly: 'Scientific procedures and attitudes encouraged by the scientists may have been more influential than the scientific knowledge they dispensed.'[30]

The 'Baconian' influence in botany in a sense pre-dated Bacon. The first accurate observation and description of plants had been done by those who wished to utilise them for medicinal purposes. The Greeks had been the first to do this in any systematic way, and the work of Dioscorides, *De Materia medica*, was still being used in the seventeenth century as a guide to the healing properties of plants. It was the herbalists too — men such as Banckes, Brunfels, Dodoens, Turner and Gerard — who attempted to classify and standardise the names of plants so that their various properties and characteristics could be determined and described in some botanical *lingua franca*.[31] But although in the seventeenth century several men came close to developing a universal system of classifying plants, and the function of stamens was determined, the real breakthrough in this area came from the Swede Carl von Linńe in the 1730s. His comprehensive system, based on the characteristics of the reproductive organs of plants, is no longer important today, but in its time it produced order and reason where undifferentiated and incomprehensible chaos had previously reigned. The development of his system was in itself a triumph of empiricism, based as it was not on *a priori* theory, but upon a minute and objective observation of thousands of plant species. Linńe did botany another great service, one symbolised by the Latin styling he always gave himself (Linnaeus). He introduced an international botanical nomenclature, giving all plants a generic and specific name in Latin and publishing all his own works in that language. More than any other science botany in the eighteenth century exhibited the co-operative and public aspects which Bacon had tried to infuse into all the sciences. Plant collectors travelled the world and communicated widely with their fellows in other countries. Although there were some important exceptions, they generally exchanged ideas and specimens without rivalry, aware that their discipline could best advance through a pooling of knowledge.[32]

One vital adjunct to the growth of botany was the development of the botanical garden. In this area too the demands of medicine acted as a stimulus. Beginning in modern times in Italy, as 'physic' gardens attached to hospitals and universities such as that at Padua, in the sixteenth and seventeenth centuries they spread first to Holland, most notably at Leyden, and then to France, England and some German states. Gradually the functions of these gardens expanded beyond their medicinal origins, although that connection was only slowly broken. They became both scientific institutions in their own right — laboratories where observation and experiment could go forward hand in hand — and centres where new vegetable products could be acclimatised and tried. The first garden to move systematically in this direction was the Jardin du Roi in Paris, which in the eighteenth century came under the sway of Georges Buffon who had unalterable faith in the ability of man to re-direct nature for his own ends. Despite the setting up of the Chelsea Physick Garden in 1673, England was a little slower off the mark in this area, and it required the influence of a Dutch King and the initiative of Sir Hans Sloan before the necessary impetus was found. By the reign of George III, and with the foundation of Kew Gardens, England had caught up, and by the end of the century her plant collectors ranged wider than those of any other country.[33]

The early connection between medicine and botany had a lasting importance which is relevant here. Medical training, particularly in universities such as Edinburgh, Leyden and Göttingen, still incorporated a substantial degree of instruction in natural history. The role of plants in healing was still a vital one and various medicinal drugs featured boldly in lists of European imports from Asia and the Near East.[34] One consequence of this was that many of the plant collectors sent out in this period by Kew Gardens, Sir Joseph Banks, the East India Company, or the British government, were surgeons trained to recognise useful plant species. This interconnection had another practical consequence in that surgeons throughout the world were potential plant collectors, and Banks in particular exploited this to the full — East India Company surgeons in China and India, army surgeons in America or the West Indies, Navy surgeons on foreign stations — all formed part of an international plant collecting network which plied Banks and, therefore, Kew Gardens with specimens and seeds.

It was in fact in the wider imperial context that the productive aspects of botany, and natural history generally, could be exploited to the best advantage. The course of European expansion from the sixteenth century onwards dramatically emphasised this point.

Apart from the Spanish imports of bullion from their South American dominions, the wealth of colonies lay in their tropical vegetable products — spices, sugar, tobacco, dyes and medicinal drugs, tea and coffee, oils. Some of these new vegetable products could be introduced into England; vegetables such as potatoes, tomatoes and spinach to supplement the diet; exotic trees such as the rhododendron, plane and cedar to grace the parklands of the nobility and gentry. In such cases, botanical gardens provided reception centres where plants could be acclimatised, propagated and studied.

Some plants, of course, would not grow in temperate climates, but many could be transferred from one tropical country to another. All European countries with Asian or American empires attempted the interchange of tropical plants to their dominions, the French being particularly active. But in the seventeenth and eighteenth centuries it was for England that it held out the greatest appeal. She had, after all, been something of a latecomer in the scramble for colonies and it often seemed that she had got the worst of the pickings. The Spaniards had the bullion-rich South American colonies which also produced dyes such as cochineal, indigo and logwood, and other cash crops — cocoa, tobacco and sugar. The Portuguese imported enormous quantities of sugar from Brazil, and spices from the East Indies — the font too of Dutch colonial wealth. Even the French had got the most productive West Indian Islands, and until 1759 had the best access to the furs of North America. England, by contrast, had a few small Caribbean Islands and some truculent North American colonies which often competed with the produce of the mother country. How attractive, therefore, was the idea of plant interchange: spices, dyes, coffee, cocoa, cotton could all be introduced into British colonies and distributed to interested planters, eventually supplying the English market and even undercutting European competitors. The gradual assumption of territorial power in India widened such possibilities. Botany could, therefore, have a vital imperial economic function: selecting plants which could be readily transplanted; recommending regions where they might best grow; advising on methods of transporting plants and caring for them at sea; advising on propagating and processing plants; maintaining botanical gardens as reception centres or way stations.[35]

From the middle of the eighteenth century onwards the practice of plant interchange expanded rapidly. The foundation of the Royal Society of Arts, Manufactures and Commerce in 1754 served as a

powerful stimulus. It offered premiums and bounties for the cultivation of indigo, coffee, fine cotton, cloves, breadfruit and cinnamon in the British West Indies or mainland colonies; it encouraged
the culture of cochineal in the Caribbean and Carolinas; it pressed
colonial assemblies (with some degree of success) to establish
botanical gardens which could act as the entrepôts of plant interchange. A parallel development was the appearance of works which
recommended, and gave advice on plant interchange, such as John
Hill's *The Usefulness of Knowledge of Plants illustrated in various
instances* (1759), D. Walker's *Essay on the Translation of Plants
from the East and West Indies*, and a host of narrower works dealing with particular species. Other publications — John Fothergill's
*Directions for taking up Plants and Shrubs and conveying them by
Sea* (1796), and John Ellis's contribution to the *Philosophical
Transactions*, 'Directions for Bringing Plants from the East Indies
and some Additional Observations on the Method of preserving
Seed from Foreign Parts' — were designed for travellers or ships'
crews who showed a willingness to play a part in plant interchange.
The greenhouse on the quarterdeck of the *Investigator* owed some-
thing to the ideas of Dr Fothergill — but it also owed a great deal to
the ideas and influence of Sir Joseph Banks

Reminiscing shortly before his death in 1820, Joseph Banks told
the surgeon attending him that his interest in botany could be
traced back to two episodes when he was a boy of 15 at Eton.
Strolling home after swimming in the Thames one evening, he
encountered a group of women culling 'simples'; common herbs
sold to the druggists for their medicinal and other properties. The
other seminal occasion was his discovery in his mother's dressing
room at Revesby Abbey, the family home, of a copy of Gerard's
famous *Herbal or Historie of Plants* of 1598, in fact an annotated
version of Rembert Dodoens's *Pemptades* of 1583.[36] It is significant that the cullers of simples, Dodoens and Gerard were all concerned with the economic value of plants. The Dedication in the
Herbal reads:

What greater delight is there than to behold the earth apparalled
with plants as with a robe of embroidered worke set with Orient
pearls and garnished with great diversifie of rare and costly jew-
els? Though delight is great, the use is greater and joined to
necessitie.

This 'Baconian' element in Banks' pursuit of botany flowed over into his interest in other sciences, and endured, reinforced occasionally by other early experiences. When his father died in 1761 he moved with his mother to London, living in a house in Paradise Walk, close to the Physick Garden of the Society of Apothecaries. Here, in the garden purchased by Sir Hans Sloan, Banks made the acquaintance of Philip Miller, the remarkable, and by this time elderly, head gardener whose knowledge of exotic plants must have deeply impressed the young Oxford student. In many ways Banks' utilitarian approach to science was connected with his gentry origins. His family had grown and prospered in the early eighteenth century as a result of 'scientific' farm management, the drainage of the fens and careful and innovative husbandry.[37] The improving impulse was continued when Banks came into his inheritance in 1764, the main estates at Revesby being a model which even Arthur Young could hold up to his readers.[38] This interest in agricultural innovation manifested itself in some of Banks' later activities; his introduction of the merino sheep into England and management of the first flocks; his promotion of new strains of wheat and other grains; his further efforts for the drainage of the fens; and his published work on blight in corn.[39]

Banks' interest in exotic plants was given full reign in 1766 when, in the company of an Oxford friend, Constantine Phipps, he sailed to Newfoundland on the *Niger*, a Naval vessel going on the regular patrol of the North American fisheries.[40] Less than two years after his return from that voyage he was again at sea, this time with his own scientific party on board the *Endeavour*, bound for Tahiti and the South Seas, in the company of James Cook.[41]

That voyage had a profound influence on Banks, and shaped and directed his later actions and interests. From his famous commander he learned much of ships and the sea, and not a little of the psychology of seamen. He learned the value of patience, trained observation and accurate recording of data to the science of navigation. His experiences at Tahiti, New Zealand, New South Wales and Batavia left him with an enormous fund of knowledge about the vegetable and animal life of Asia and Oceania, and the value of some exotic products to his own country. His part in the equipping and managing of the expedition, and the scientific staff that accompanied it, gave him unique experience in organising voyages of exploration; experience he was to deploy on numerous occasions in the last 20 years of the eighteenth century.

Although Banks travelled to the Western Isles and Iceland in 1772, and made a short trip to Holland in 1781, his main scientific activities after Cook's voyage were carried on in England. In 1772 he became virtual 'Director' of Kew Gardens, which in subsequent years was employed as the central collecting and distributing point of a vast botanical *imperium*. Elected President of the Royal Society in 1778, he retained that position until his death in 1820, using to the full his powers of patronage to promote the interests of science and scientists. It was in this area that his great strength lay. He published little. His individual contribution to scientific knowledge was insubstantial, although his natural history collections and his Soho Square Library, always open to the dedicated, were rich in material. But in his day Banks was England's greatest promoter and protector of science; he had enormous capacity to generate enthusiasm in others, and the power, wealth and generosity to give that enthusiasm full reign once aroused. Although botany was his first interest, no scientific endeavour was outside the bounds of his curiosity, and therefore beyond his patronage.[42]

In many senses Banks was a conservative figure; nowhere more clearly perhaps than in his attitudes to trade and empire. The free trade ideas of Adam Smith did not appeal to him and he likened them to the principles of the French Revolution, which were founded on unqualified liberty, but not upon reason or experience.[43] He believed that trade in vital commodities such as grain should always be controlled by government, principally in the interests of the landowners. In imperial terms these beliefs translated themselves into an almost unbridled mercantilism. He was concerned about the export of bullion to India and China; he saw no reason why United States shipping should be allowed into the West Indies; he believed the colonies should produce raw materials for consumption by the growing industries of the mother country. He pressed on the government the acquisition of huge slices of West Africa, envisaging:

that in very few years a trading Company might be established under immediate control of the Government, who would take upon themselves the whole expense of the measure, would govern the Negroes far more mildly and make them far more happy than they are now under the tyranny of their arbitrary princes, would become popular at home by converting them to the Christian Religion by inculcating in their rough minds the mild morality which is engrafted on the tenets of our faith and by effecting the greatest practicable diminution of the Slavery of Mankind upon the principles of natural justice and commercial benefit.[44]

Nor did Banks oppose the slave trade. In certain circumstances slavery was fully justified and he believed the religious and humanitarian arguments put forward in favour of abolition were not based on Scripture, logic or practical experience.[45]

Banks' ideas on the economic importance of plant interchange buttressed this philosophy of empire. Scientific knowledge coupled with enterprise and industry could be utilised to augment the biological resources of the British colonies for the aggrandisement of the mother country. Although he saw the application of such techniques as being valuable in all colonies, it was the tropical countries which were likely to benefit most. There were no insurmountable scientific barriers to the trans-shipment of tropical plants, 'few if any instances being known of Plants brought from one intertropical Climate refusing to thrive in another'.[46] Moreover, the promotion in India and the West Indies of vegetable productions which could not be grown in England meant the avoidance of any conflict of commercial interests, as he pointed out to Henry Dundas, the President of the Board of Control, in 1787:

> if we consider for a moment that the merchandises hitherto brought home from India have been chiefly manufactures of a nature which interferes with out manufactures at home, that our cotton manufactures above all, are increasing with a rapidity which renders it politic to give them effectual encouragement, & that a profit of Cent per Cent upon the importation of raw cotton is to be got with certainty, can we too much encourage everything which tends to the cultivation of raw materials in India? Laborers are abundant there: Labor excessive cheap: raw materials of many sorts, dying drugs, Medecines, Spices &c sure of a ready and advantageous market and of producing a most beneficial influence upon the Commerce of the mother country.[47]

By the 1780s Banks' ideas on the value of applied botany to imperial economic development had solidified into a coherent philosophy and he was prepared to promote his opinions with those members of the government and East India Company who were enlightened enough to support him.

In letting Sir Joseph Banks choose the name of the vessel which was to take Flinders to the South Seas, the Board of Admiralty was surrendering one of its own responsibilities to a figure who was outside the government and administration of the day. It is clear, however, that they had permitted him to play a much larger part than this. In 1797 Governor Hunter of New South Wales had asked Banks to press the Ministry for a maritime survey of the coasts of New Holland. Only by such a voyage would the agricultural and mineral wealth of the new continent be fully revealed. Banks, too, was eager that a survey should be carried out, but in his reply he pointed out to Hunter:

> the situation of Europe is at present so critical & his Majesty's Ministers so fully employed in business of the deepest importance, that it is scarce possible to gain a moment's audience on any subject but those which stand foremost in their minds; & colonies of all kinds, you may be assured, are now put into the back ground.[48]

When in September 1800 Mathew Flinders asked Banks to promote such an expedition among government ministers, conditions must have improved somewhat for by November 1800 he had prevailed upon Earl Spencer, First Lord of the Admiralty, to equip a surveying expedition to New Holland and to give Flinders the command of it.[49] From the outset the planning and equipping of the expedition lay in Banks' hands. He appointed the members of the scientific party, stated their salaries and allowances; ordered their equipment; and wrote their instructions and conditions of appointment. He kept regularly in touch with the fitting of the *Investigator* and whenever Flinders required substantial alterations he applied in the first instance to Banks. He negotiated the *batta* money from the East India Company and arranged its distribution. In this latter instance he felt obliged to explain his role, in somewhat understated terms, to the Chairman:

> It may be necessary to explain to you as a reason for my interfering in the last question which seems wholly out of my way that owing to the present heavy pressure of business in the Admiralty

that board have from time to time intrusted me with the execution under their orders of almost every detail of the lesser articles of the outfit of the Ship, hence it is that every part of her affairs are well known to me.[50]

The specialised navigation instruments, charts, accounts of earlier voyages and articles of barter with indigenous peoples were all supplied from lists drawn up by Banks.[51] Those hoping for a place on the vessel knew that it was to him that they could most profitably apply. When in February 1801 Flinders himself was promoted to the rank of commander, he could write to his mentor that this was something 'for which, Sir Joseph, I feel myself entirely indebted to your influence and kindness'.[52] When Banks wrote to the Admiralty asking if his suggestions relating to the fate of journals, and plant and animal specimens from the voyage would be approved, Evan Nepean could reply: 'Any proposal you make will be approved. The whole is left entirely to your decision.'[53] When the time came to draw up Flinders' own instructions, Banks played the major role and subsequently had alterations inserted.[54] The act of naming the *Investigator* was therefore merely symbolic of what was, in effect, the overall direction of the enterprise.

Why had the government, and the Admiralty in particular, entrusted so many official concerns to a civilian? This was not just a whim of the Pitt ministry, or any minister within it, since the change of administration in February 1801 produced no discernible alteration in the management of the enterprise. It would be convenient to accept Banks' own explanation, as given to Inglis: the government was hard-pressed by the needs of war and was happy to have someone else take care of such a subsidiary concern. This may have been in the ministers' minds, and indeed, Banks may have used it as a bargaining counter when stressing the desirability of a voyage in the autumn of 1800. It is clear, however, that his role in the voyage of the *Investigator* was not an isolated case, for Banks had in greater or lesser degree directed all British voyages of discovery in the 20 years after Captain Cook's death, and it is this wider intervention which has to be accounted for.

In so many respects it was his experiences on board the *Endeavour* which equipped Banks to be the general director of exploration in the period under discussion. He became the custodian of the Cook model; the general repository of all the surviving and accumulated knowledge and experience which the great navigator had bequeathed to the world. In developing the overall conceptions of particular voyages, Banks alone retained the respect, level-headedness and boundless geographical knowledge which inspired governmental trust. Alexander Dalrymple, after all, had been tried and found wanting. Despite his vain and foolish behaviour at the time that Cook's second voyage was being organised, Banks was one of the few persons outside the Navy Board with detailed information about the outfitting of ships for voyages of discovery, and from William Bligh's first voyage onwards even the Navy Board came to depend on his advice.[55]

As Cook's own career had illustrated, the question of personnel was of crucial importance for successful voyages of exploration. Here too Banks' influence was crucial. He became the mentor and protector of all those able men and officers who had sailed with Cook: he found them jobs, secured their promotion, helped publish their journals, rescued them from debt and debtors prison, obtained their pensions, looked after their wives, widows and children, and generally maintained their spirits and their skills. His knowledge of these men — Gore, Clerke, Bligh, Matra, Ledyard, Roberts, Vancouver, Flinders, King — made his advice in the selection of officers and commanders invaluable. The men themselves recognised and welcomed his role, aware that he was sustaining a certain *esprit de corps*. In October 1780 Captain James King wrote to him: 'It is with real pleasure & satisfaction that I look up to you as the common Centre of we discoverers.'[56] Almost 40 years later, after a long discussion with an elderly Banks on the subject of Arctic exploration, the young Naval Lieutenant, William Parry, could still feel that he had been close to such a common centre.[57]

Other forces contributed to Banks' power in government circles. He had been elected to the Presidency of the Royal Society in 1778 at the young age of 35 and by the mid-1780s he was the doyen of British applied science. Although natural history remained his greatest love the breadth of his scientific knowledge was enormous and matched by the span of his curiosity. His contribution to the world of science was a managerial — an entrepreneurial one. He was a patron and sponsor; one who knew the right man for the job and did not hesitate to call in specialist opinion. For this reason he was the logical adviser for the government in any enterprise which involved a degree of scientific or technical knowledge.

This also explains his assistance to the government and East India Company in many other areas, some of which are discussed below.

He was virtual director of Kew Gardens, he advised the Board of Trade on the supply of cotton, naval stores, explosives and dye-stuffs. He gave advice on the whaling, fishing and textile industries. He played a crucial role in developing new coinage and in organising supplies of grain in times of dearth. In 1797, in recognition of his hitherto unofficial services, he was made a Privy Councillor so that he could regularly serve the Board of Trade and work on its special-ist committees. Banks was the government's foremost adviser on colonial affairs in the period 1780 to 1800 and became the East India Company's acknowledged counsellor on all matters related to bot-any and vegetable products. No other man outside government in the last 20 years of the eighteenth century exercised such a pervasive influence over such a wide area of government activity.

This formidable power can only partially be explained by the energies and talents of Sir Joseph Banks. Certain fundamental changes in the period after the American War of Independence clearly made such outside assistance acceptable and necessary to government. The American war itself must be held partially responsible. It had been expensive and unsuccessful. The enormous logistical problems of feeding, arming and reinforcing troops 3,000 miles across the Atlantic had exposed inefficiencies, inade-quacies and stupidities in the existing administrative system. The high costs coupled with the lack of success had exposed the govern-ment and the whole system of administration to the sort of criticism which the Economical Reform movement and the Rockingham Whigs expressed most forcefully. The expenses of government had to be reduced; placemen, sinecures and partial government con-tractors had to go; the system of parliamentary representation had to be altered to accord with the best interests of the nation (although there was little agreement on what those interests were). For the benefit of the country as a whole the political system had to be purged of both deadwood and driftwood so that the growing responsibilities of government could be handled scrupulously and efficiently. The Earl of Shelburne, and his disciple William Pitt the Younger, wished to carry these reforms past the House of Commons into the day-to-day running of government departments.

The practical consequences of these impulses were apparent in the 1780s: the early reforms of the Rockingham administration; the Commission for Examining the Public Accounts; the Committee investigations into the affairs of the East India Company and the

Act of 1784; and the host of piecemeal but important reforms affected by Pitt in the Treasury, Exchequer and Customs and Excise.[58] By the end of Pitt's first administration the importance of accurate accounting, professional and disinterested advice and administrative efficiency were coming to be realised.[59]

It was as well that they were, for the period of the American and French Revolutions witnessed other, linked changes. From the early eighteenth century the functions of government were always regarded as being narrow and limited: diplomacy and war, the maintenance of public order, the handling or mishandling of public finance, and the providing of a structure in which the gentry class and aristocracy could exercise power. But in the last third of the eighteenth century there were many pressures forcing ministries to take a broader view of their function. A wider and more articulate political class; the complexity and consequences of rapid industrial growth; the slow move towards England's becoming an importer of food, the vast social problems arising from rapid urban development — all these changes claimed and demanded the attention of government. The quantitative and qualitative changes in legislation before Parliament after 1780 are clear evidence of this pressure.[60]

Despite the reforms of the 1780s this was a period when the tasks confronting government temporarily outstripped the capacity and resources available to handle them. Bodies such as the Home Department, Treasury and Foreign Office had but rudimentary staffs who were not accustomed to taking any initiative or devising policy, but were trained to search for precedents and respond in a pragmatic way to such problems as presented themselves.[61] Faced with these limitations, administrations of the day, and particularly the Pitt Ministry after December 1783, showed a willingness to call on specialist advice and professional expertise from outside the ranks of government. Baker has pointed to Shelburne's consultation of the banker, Baring, and Pitt's discussions with Richard Price on his sinking fund.[62] There are other examples: Pitt's appointment of John Palmer to streamline the Post Office; the consultations and negotiations with Jeremy Bentham over penitentiaries; the government support for Sir John Sinclair's Board of Agriculture in 1793; the acknowledgement of Sir Joseph Banks' role as a one-man department of scientific and industrial research, to be consulted and employed on practically all matters relating to exploration, science and the colonies.

It was in colonial administration that the government faced some of its gravest problems, and was most ready to look for outside advice.[63] The Home Office was inadequately staffed to deal with the new range of problems which came to the fore before and after the American Revolution. The Board of Trade, swept away by Burke's Act, had to be restored via the back door in the mid-1780s and in 1801 colonial affairs were taken away entirely from the Home Office and transferred to the portfolio of the Secretary for War. But in the meantime the existing machinery had to creak on, grappling with new problems of governance and continuing, but ever more complex, problems of imperial trade. The navigation laws, intact but battered, failed to cover new situations created by the loss of the American colonies, the truculence of Ireland and England's own industrial growth. The precedents which had served for the administration of the North American colonies before 1775 were inapplicable in Canada, Ireland, India and in New South Wales.

In the administration of this latter colony the government was at times hopelessly at sea, and in more than the mere metaphorical sense. Unable to devise a suitable administrative and judicial structure for the penal colony, the Pitt ministry launched it as a distant but land-borne naval vessel, with a Naval commander, jurisdiction by Court Martial, and provisioning out of stores. In almost everything else they deferred to the opinion of Sir Joseph Banks, whose conception the colony was; who virtually appointed all governors up to and including Bligh; and who organised its scientific life and further exploration. In that sense too, therefore, the voyage of the *Investigator* was merely one more event in a general pattern of interrelated activities.

Notes

1. *M.L. (Mitchell Library, Sydney) Banks Correspondence*, A79/4, fo. 3; *Adm.* 2/294, 19 January 1801.
2. J.C. Beaglehole (ed.), *The Journals of Captain Cook on his Voyages of Discovery*, II, pp. xxv, 908–9.
3. See below, Chapter 6.
4. The list, in Banks' hand, is in *M.L. Banks*, A79/4, fo. 33.
5. *Adm.* 2/294, 477, 7 March 1801. N. Maskelyne to Banks, 24 December 1800. *M.L. Banks*, A79/4, fo. 11.
6. Flinders to Banks, 8 February 1801, *M.L. Banks*, A79/4, fos 249–51. A list with comments by Banks, ibid., fo. 157. On the *Endeavour* Log, Flinders to Banks, 1 July 1807, ibid., fos 371–3.
7. Flinders to Banks, 29 January 1801, ibid., fo. 243. *Adm.* 2/295, 172–4, 15 April 1801.

8. On Baudin's expedition, J. Dunmore, *French Explorers in the Pacific*, vol. II pp. 9–40. Also Banks' notes on the voyage, *M.L. Banks*, A79/4, fo. 5. Banks was responsible for securing a passport from the English government for the French ships.

9. *Adm.* 1/9800, undated. There is a draft in *M.L. Banks*, A79/4, fos 195–212, May 1801.

10. Banks to R. Brown, 15 June 1801, *Add. MSS.* 32439, fo. 41. Instructions to the miner, *M.L. Banks* A79/4, fos 53–64.

11. Flinders to Banks, 6 September 1800, *M.L. Banks*, A83, fo. 59.

12. Banks to Flinders, 1 May 1801, *M.L. Banks*, A79/4, fo. 187.

13. A.E. Musson & E. Robinson, *Science and Technology in the Industrial Revolution*, pp. 1–9 examine the arguments.

14. A. Koyré, *From the Closed World to the Infinite Universe*, pp. 90ff. Musson & Robinson, pp. 18–19.

15. Advances in navigation are the subject of E.G.R. Taylor's *The Haven-Finding Art*. J.C. Beaglehole, *The Life of Captain James Cook*, ch. 5, puts some of these advances in the perspective of Pacific exploration.

16. F. Hoyle, *Astronomy*, p. 144, quoted in J.H. Parry, *Trade and Dominion*, p. 224.

17. Parry, ibid., p. 228.

18. For these aspects of Cook's career see Beaglehole, *The Life of Captain James Cook*, and A. Villiers, *Captain Cook, the Seaman's Seaman*.

19. Quoted in P. Mathias, 'Who Unbound Prometheus? Science and Technical Change, 1600–1800', p. 61, in P. Mathias (ed.), *Science and Society 1600–1900*.

20. R. Schofield, *The Lunar Society of Birmingham*; Musson & Robinson, *Science and Technology*, pp. 138–42, 190–9.

21. D. Hudson & K. Luckhurst, *The Royal Society of Arts, 1754–1954. Society of Arts, Premiums Offered by the Society Instituted at London for the Encouragement of Arts, Manufactures and Commerce*.

22. H. Lyons, *The Royal Society, 1660–1940*, p. 217.

23. D. McKie, 'The Scientific Periodical from 1665 to 1798' in A. Ferguson (ed.), *Natural Philosophy through the Eighteenth Century*.

24. R.P. Stearns, *Science in the British Colonies of America*, pp. 678–9.

25. J.G. Crowther, *Scientists of the Industrial Revolution*, p. 49.

26. A.R. Hall, 'Science, Technology and Utopia in the Seventeenth Century' in Mathias, *Science and Society*, p. 35. Professor Hall cites Joseph Black as one who 'would never have imagined that the main justification of his work was its utility to manufacturers'. See also D. Landes, *The Unbound Prometheus*, and his contribution to Cambridge Economic History of Europe, vol. vi. Sir E. Ashby, *Technology and the Academics*.

27. Musson & Robinson, *Science and Technology*, p. 8. See also W.W. Rostow, *The Stages of Economic Growth*; T.S. Ashton, *The Industrial Revolution*; A. & N.L. Clow, *The Chemical Revolution*.

28. Mathias, *Science and Society*, pp. 56–9.

29. E. Robinson & D. McKie, *Partners in Science*; A.E. Musson in Musson & Robinson, *Science and Technology*, chs. VII, VIII and IX; Clow, *The Chemical Revolution*.

30. Mathias, *Science and Society*, p. 76. T.S. Ashton, *An Economic History of England: the 18th Century*, p. 104, has made a similar point: 'Englishmen had settled their political and theological differences and were turning their energies to practical ends. The scholarly curiosity of the sixteenth and seventeenth centuries had filtered down to humble people whose forebears can have had little time for speculation or experiment.'

31. On herbals see A. Arber, *Herbals*; E.S. Rohde, *The Old English Herbals*; E.G. Wheelwright, *The Physic Garden*.

32. A point made in a somewhat more general context in Sir G. de Beer, *The Sciences Were Never at War*. For some exceptions, see below pp. 148, 185-6.

33. G.W. Johnson, *A History of English Gardening*; Wheelwright, *The Physic Garden*.

34. For example the list in *N.L.S. (National Library of Scotland) Melville*, 1064, fos 18-19, January 1788.

35. These aspects are discussed below, Chapters 5-7. See also Stearns, *Science in the British Colonies of America*, ch. 9; L.J. Ragatz, *The Fall of the Planter Class in the British Caribbean, 1763-1833*; W.H.G. Armytage, *The Rise of the Technocrats*, ch. 4.

36. The surgeon was Sir Everard Home, who described the episode in February 1822 in his Hunterial Oration, quoted in H.C. Cameron, *Sir Joseph Banks*, Appendix D. On Gerard's notorious act of piracy, see Arber, *Herbals*, pp. 129-35. Banks' copy of the *Herbal* was probably the more reputable Johnson edition of 1632.

37. The record of the growth of the family can be traced in J.W.F. Hill, *Letters and Papers of the Banks Family of Revesby Abbey, 1704-1760*.

38. A. Young, *General View of Lincolnshire*, 1808, quoted in G. Mingay, *English Landed Society in the Eighteenth Century*, pp. 173-4.

39. Sir J. Banks, *A Short Account of the course of a Disease in Corn, called by farmers the blight, the mildew and the rust*, London, 1805. It went through four editions up to 1834. Banks' only other publications also related to agricultural topics, *The Propriety of allowing a Qualified Exportation of Wool, discussed historically*, 1782, and Some *circumstances relating to Merino Sheep*, 1809.

40. The Journal of this voyage, with a wealth of background material, is published in the lush work by A. Lysaght, *Sir Joseph Banks in Newfoundland and Labrador, 1766*. The same work has some biographical information on his companion Constantine Phipps, later Lord Mulgrave, 1744-92, the Naval officer and arctic explorer.

41. The Journal of that Voyage is in J.C. Beaglehole (ed.), *The Endeavour Journal of Joseph Banks, 1768-1771*.

42. His ability to rouse enthusiasm in others is nowhere better illustrated than in his success in persuading botanists and explorers to go to some of the wildest parts of the world: Masson to the Cape, Hove to Gujarat, Hornemann, Ledyard, Park and Afzelius to North Africa, Smith to South East Asia, Caley and Brown to New Holland, Nelson and Menzies to the Pacific, Kerr to China and so on. More important perhaps was his ability to recognise and encourage talents such as those he saw in Robert Brown and Hooker. The latter's first experience of Banks, together with the sustenance he derived from it, is described in M. Allen, *The Hookers of Kew*, pp. 36-45.

43. Banks to Hawkesbury, 28 September 1800, *Add. MSS.* 38234, fo. 165.

44. Quoted in R. Hallet, *The Penetration of Africa*, pp. 321-2.

45. His views on slavery are made clear in a letter to an unnamed correspondent calendared in W.R. Dawson (ed.), *The Banks Letters*, p. 899.

46. Banks to Dundas, 15 June 1787, *D.T.C.* V, fos 184-91. This report also appears in *P.R.O. (Chatham)*, 30/8, 361, fos 34-7; *P.R.O. (Cornwallis)*, 30/11, 112, fos 75-82; and *Windsor Royal Archives*, 6262 + 6263.

47. Ibid., *D.T.C.* copy cited, fo. 186.

48. Banks to Hunter, 1 February 1799, *D.T.C.* XI, fo. 187.

49. Flinders to Banks, 6 September 1800, *M.L. Banks*, A 83, fos 59-62. On Banks' part in Spencer's decision, *M.L. Banks*, A79/4, fo. 3, 12 December 1800, manuscript note on voyage.

50. Banks to Sir Hugh Inglis, 24 April 1801, *M.L. Banks* A79/4, fos 169-70. That volume contains documentation of the other aspects of his intervention mentioned above. In particular the following are important: notes on the voyage, 12/12/1800, fo. 3; Maskelyne to Banks 23 and 24 December 1800, fos 9-11;

instructions for the behaviour of the scientific party, signed 21 August 1801, fos 13–24; Banks to W. Milnes, 20 January 1801, fos 51–2, on the appointment of a miner; Nepean to Banks, 9 February 1801, fo. 253, requesting information on the salaries of the scientific party; Banks' reply to same, same date, fo. 73.

51. Ibid., fos 81–91.

52. Flinders to Banks, 18 February 1801, ibid., fo. 259.

53. Banks to Nepean, and reply, 28 April 1801, ibid., fo. 177.

54. A copy of the instructions, including a rough preliminary draft, is in the Banks papers, ibid., fos 195–212, May 1801.

55. See below, Chapter 6.

56. King to Banks, October 1780, *D.T.C.*, I, fo. 304.

57. W. Parry to his parents, 23 December 1817, quoted in Lysaght, *Sir Joseph Banks*, pp. 284–5.

58. These reforms are detailed in J. Ehrman, *The Younger Pitt*, chs. X & XI.

59. The nature and scope of these administrative changes are perceptively discussed in N. Baker, 'Changing Attitudes towards Government in Eighteenth Century Britain' in A. Whiteman, J.S. Bromley & P.G.M. Dickson (eds.), *Statesmen, Scholars and Merchants*, pp. 202–19.

60. See P.D.G. Thomas, *The House of Commons in the Eighteenth Century*, ch. 3. The average number of Acts passed by Parliament increased from 58 per session in the reign of George I to 254 per session in that of George III, with the proportion of public acts rising as above private acts (Thomas, p. 61).

61. A point I have discussed elsewhere, see D.L. Mackay, 'Direction and Purpose in British Imperial Policy, 1783–1801', pp. 487–501.

62. Baker, 'Changing Attitudes', pp. 216–17.

63. Mackay, 'Direction and Purpose'.

2 THE REDISCOVERY OF THE SOUTHERN OCEANS

Captain Cook's second voyage into the Southern Oceans was arguably his greatest: the commander was at his mental and physical

Map 1 The Atlantic and its Islands

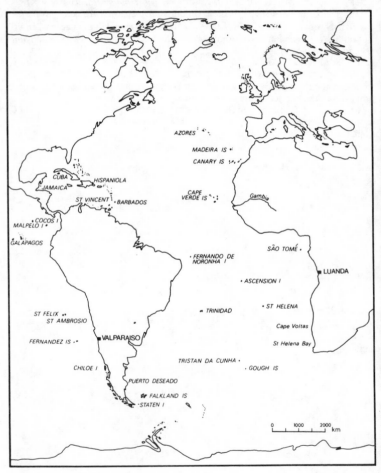

peak; with minor exceptions the ships and men behaved remarkably well in arduous conditions; and as a model of perseverance, dedication and seamanship it has no equal in the annals of navigation. And yet to style it a voyage of discovery is to apply something of a misnomer — at least in terms of the expectations of those who sponsored it. Little was discovered in the tempestuous and tropic seas. Exploration and science had undoubtedly been advanced but the boundaries of empire remained the same. However, in greatly changed circumstances in the 20 years after Cook's death, the navigator's model was employed again and again in traversing the seas which he had found so empty, and the principal aim in each case was to buttress the strategic and commercial foundations of empire.

In 1772 the geographer Alexander Dalrymple attempted to get government backing for an expedition to the south Atlantic, by outlining for Lord North the benefits accruing to Britain from the discovery of *Terra Australis Incognita*. According to early voyagers the Isla Grande was supposed to lie in the middle of the south Atlantic in about latitude 45°S, and Dalrymple proposed that it should be colonised to supply provisions for the West Indies, and serve as a base for ships on their way to India or the south Pacific. This island, he wrote, 'cannot fail of being a very temperate and pleasant Country, in a situation very favourable for carrying on the whale and other Fisheries, and also for the prosecution of any Commerce which may be found in the Countries to the South'.[1] The southern continent itself was reckoned to lie a mere 5° south of Isla Grande and was destined to fulfil the same role as the most flourishing of the North American colonies. Dalrymple published these letters in 1775 as the preface to his *Collection of Voyages* and they represent the last great statement of faith in *Terra Australis Incognita*. The publication was untimely. In July of that year Cook returned from his second great voyage of discovery and the reality of the southern continent was finally denied.

The legend died, but the needs that *Terra Australis Incognita* was to have satisfied persisted, and when the loss of the American colonies became inevitable, these needs were intensified. In the decade of peace after 1784, therefore, the search began for an alternative to the southern continent; a search which was concentrated in the south Atlantic and south-east Pacific.

As Harlow has shown there were two strategic reasons for British interest in the south Atlantic prior to 1783.[2] First, as a result of the great eighteenth-century voyages of discovery, there had developed a need for a gateway into the south Pacific independent of Spanish influence or control. Secondly, there was the traditional problem of securing sea communications with India. The tangled dispute over the Falkland Islands between 1765 and 1774, was the result of one attempt to satisfy the first need, although it had not in fact done so. But before 1780 there had been no serious commercial attempts to penetrate the south Pacific, partly because of the restrictive East India Company and South Sea Company monopolies, and partly because of the deflatory effects of Cook's second voyage. The need for bases and places of refreshment had therefore not arisen, and the various naval expeditions after 1768 were content to use Tahiti, Dusky Sound or other islands for this purpose. With the return of Cook's ships in 1780, on the other hand, the commercial prospects of the Pacific looked slightly more encouraging.

The second point — the need to secure the sea passage to India — involved the shaky independence of the Dutch and control of the Cape of Good Hope. In October 1781 the chairmen of the East India Company wrote to the Secretary of State, Lord Hillsborough, expressing their fears: 'That the power possessing the Cape of Good Hope has the key to and from the East Indies, appears to us self-evident and unquestionable. Indeed we must consider the Cape of Good Hope as the Gibraltar of India.'[3] St Helena was inadequate as a place of refreshment and depended for its own supplies on the Cape. Although there had been attempts under Sir Joseph Banks' patronage to improve the situation in the 1780s, these came late in the decade and before 1795 never looked like making the island a satisfactory alternative to the Cape.[4] These efforts were not unique, for the French government was ominously pursuing an identical scheme, and with more success, on Isle de France and Réunion.[5]

When in December 1780 the Dutch were pressed into war on the side of the French, all Britain's pent-up fears regarding the security of India were suddenly aroused. The result was an abortive attack on the Cape led by Commodore Johnstone in 1781–2, and the French reinforcement of positions there by De Suffren. St Helena was thus cut off and vulnerable to attack. Johnstone offered as a substitute the remote island of Trinidad, on which he had landed a small party to found a base. A subsequent Portuguese claim to the island effectively quashed any hopes in that direction.[6]

Before the news of Johnstone's failure reached England, the government had considered other means of dealing with this predicament. In January 1782 Hillsborough himself summarised the problem for the Chairman of the East India Company: 'The numerous Enemies we now have increase the difficulties and dangers of Navigation and require the utmost attention and foresight: It may therefore be requisite to point out where water and refreshment can be had between England and the Cape.'[7] He suggested that one of the Company's packet vessels should survey the many islands in the south Atlantic and some of the coasts which were unclaimed by other powers. These areas included Trinidad, Ascension Island, Tristan de Cunha, the mythical Isla Grande, and the south-west coast of Africa between the Dutch and Portuguese settlements. When Johnstone returned the vulnerability of the sea lanes became even more apparent and the idea of a surveying expedition was put aside while fresh plans were made for an attack on the Cape.

In the autumn of 1783 the expedition was discussed again and in September the East India Company vessel *Swallow* left England to make the survey. The commander's instructions directed him first to Isla Grande, described by the London merchant Anthoine de la Roche in 1675, sighted by the Spanish merchant ship *Leon* in 1756, and recommended as a place of settlement by Dalrymple in 1772.[8] Supposedly in the middle of the south Atlantic, the island was reported as being large (between six and forty miles long, depending on the source) and fertile. After exploring Isla Grande, the *Swallow* was to continue on to Tristan da Cunha, which was to be charted and searched for water, before she sailed to the African coast. This was to be surveyed from Cape Voltas in about latitude 28°S, northwards to the first Portuguese settlement in Angola. The whole voyage was to be completed in time for the results of the survey to be made available to the East India Company ships sailing from England in the following April.[9]

Although the *Swallow* was renowned as a fast sailer it is clear from remarks made about this voyage six years later, that she was given insufficient time to complete her mission, and that after reaching the coast of Brazil, she was obliged to sail for St Helena.[10]

By the time of the *Swallow*'s return early in 1784, peace had returned to Europe, and it became clear that France did not intend to maintain its garrison at the Cape. For a brief period British anxieties over the passage to India subsided. But by the end of 1785 pressure for a survey of the south Atlantic and its shores had been renewed: there were in the main two reasons for this. The old fears about the Cape were again aroused by the intensification of French intrigues in the United Provinces against the Stadtholder and the Dutch East India Company. Not much need be said about this; it was a traditional fear coming from the traditional direction. The second element was the developing British interest in West Africa as a base for legitimate trade, and as a centre for the transportation of convicts. Here again the effects of the loss of the American colonies are apparent: driving British enterprise towards a search for alternative markets, sources of supply and land bases.

After 1783 the British forts run by the Africa Company came in for a good deal of criticism. They were principally slave trading bases and there had been little effort to develop them as centres for more humane commerce, or as potential colonies producing food or cash crops for the mother country. When the Africa Company gained the right to establish bases on the Gambia in 1784 dissatisfaction increased, and during 1784 and 1785 proposals were submitted to Pitt for settlements on the West African coast. In most cases it was suggested that the initiative should be taken away from the Africa Company, which was generally lethargic, and as a loose body of merchants was not competent to establish and manage a settlement. Hopes were held out for the growing of crops such as cotton, tobacco and indigo, and it was thought feasible to supply essential provisions for the West Indies, thus in some way alleviating the effects of the embargo on the American trade to those islands.[11]

The Pitt ministry was loath to attack another great commercial company at this time, but the idea of using convicts to start a settlement continued to be an attractive one. American independence had meant the loss of valuable penal settlements and as a result the inadequate British prisons were overflowing into the equally inadequate hulks in the Thames and southern naval ports. In the period before substantial penal reform, transportation was regarded as the ideal answer to the problem. This left the question of venue. In April 1785 a Select Committee of the House of Commons was formed to investigate this aspect, and in its report of 28 July 1785 it considered four areas in Africa which had been recommended for settlement.[12] Three of these — the Gambia, Madagascar, and the part of southeast Africa which is now the Province of Natal — were for various reasons rejected, but the fourth, south-west Africa, seemed to offer distinct possibilities. It was a huge and unfrequented tract of land, devoid of European habitation. Its soil was reputedly fertile, and supported thick vegetation and large herds of wild cattle and game. The report stressed the importance of a settlement here to the sea passage to the east, by providing water and refreshments and thus in some way negating the advantages of the French, Dutch and Portuguese settlements. As a last point the Committee mentioned the suitability of a base on the coast as a whaling port, being in a convenient latitude and relatively close to the current fishing grounds off the Brazilian coast.

Despite strong pressure from Captain Blankett and others in favour of Madagascar, the Pitt ministry decided to follow up the Committee's report by an investigation of the African coast from St Helena Bay northwards to Luanda.[13] The expedition was planned in August 1785 and from the outset it was shrouded in secrecy. It was decided that the vessels employed should be two of those regularly involved in patrols on the African coast so as to avoid attracting attention to the preparations. Commodore Thompson, commander of the ships on the Africa station was to lead the expedition in the warship *Grampus*, taking with him the sloop *Nautilus*, under the command of Captain Tripp. After a routine inspection of the African forts, the two vessels would separate, the *Grampus* returning to England and the *Nautilus* undertaking the survey. On 22 August Lord Sydney gave orders for the preparation of the survey, 'in order to fix upon a proper spot for making a settlement upon that Coast, if such a measure should hereafter be judged expedient'.[14] Particular attention was to be paid to the river or bay of Das Voltas, between 28° and 29°S, which was believed to have a good harbour and to abound with copper ore.[15] After charting this bay, the coast contiguous to it was to be surveyed, and the commander was exhorted 'to examine as minutely as Circumstances will admit, the face and produce of the Country, the Character and Disposition of the Inhabitants and in general to use his utmost diligence in gaining every sort of information'.[16]

To enable the country to be properly evaluated, the government decided to send a marine surveyor and a botanist with the expedition. The surveyor, Home Popham, later Rear Admiral Sir Home Riggs Popham, was taken on board the *Grampus* as an additional lieutenant, to be transferred to the *Nautilus* before the survey commenced. Under-Secretary of State, Evan Nepean, wrote to Banks at his Lincolnshire estate of Revesby on the subject of a botanist, and was assured that a suitable one would be found. Initially, it was thought that the Admiralty might have reservations about such an addition to the expedition but on 25 August Nepean received assurances on the matter from Viscount Howe, First Lord of the

Admiralty, who 'very much approves of Sir Joseph's drawing his Instructions, well knowing that they cannot be put into better hands'.[17] Cook's voyages had served to make the scientist a natural and inevitable part of the machinery of survey.

Despite Banks' confidence there was some difficulty in finding a person willing to go on such a voyage, and things were complicated by his absence from London. Eventually, with the assistance of Charles Blagden and the Kew gardener, William Aiton, Banks settled on a young Pole called Au, whom he had formerly recommended to Aiton for botanical training.[18] At first Nepean objected to a foreigner going on the voyage but after reassurances from both Banks and Blagden he was eventually accepted. On 15 September Blagden informed Banks of Au's official appointment:

> Au is literally the only person that offered; & yet fortunately much superior to anyone we could have expected: His education has been far beyond his present station in life; he writes an excellent hand, draws, understands many languages & something of many sciences, has attended many hospitals in London & is, I believe, no despicable practitioner in Surgery; and, with all, is bold, active & animated with the most laudable ambition of being distinguished.[19]

Someone must have suggested to the botanist that he Anglicise his name, for on 19 September Blagden again wrote to Banks: 'The name Au assumes is Howe, which he insists is the true Polish Orthography. May be so!'[20] Was the Pole adopting the name of his noble employer? He eventually settled on the name Hove.

Hove's salary and conditions of appointment were decided by Banks and confirmed by Sydney. On 12 September these details were forwarded to the Admiralty, along with Banks' sketch instructions.[21] Hove's principal task was to assess the fertility of the areas he visited and for this purpose he was to keep a regular journal of his proceedings. If the country was inhabited he was to record the quality of the soil, the types of crops grown and the methods of cultivation. In other regions the landforms, soil, vegetation, minerals and drainage systems were to be observed with care. Wherever the ship touched, he was to collect plant and seed specimens which were to be preserved for Banks' examination on the return to England.[22] On 20 September Hove joined the *Grampus* at Portsmouth.

The haste evident in Hove's appointment was general to the planning of the expedition. On 10 September Blagden informed Banks, 'Mr. Nepean requires the person now to be ready next tuesday: but in reality as Captn. Thompson's instructions are not yet even begun, the whole is in the usual ridiculous hurrying of office, which will spoil the business, without answering any purpose whatever.'[23] Five days later these instructions were ready, and they were delivered to Commodore Thompson at Spithead.[24] They closely followed the Secretary of State's letter of 22 August. Secrecy, speed and accuracy were to be the keynotes of the expedition. With the Commodore's general instructions were enclosed Banks' draft instructions to Hove, which were to form the guidelines for official orders drawn up by Thomson before the *Nautilus* proceeded on the survey. Hove was to be victualled in the same manner as the rest of the ships' companies.

On 28 September 1785 the two vessels weighed anchor and set out for the African coast, but before the inspection of the African forts had been completed Commodore Thompson died of a fever. He was succeeded by Captain Tripp of the *Nautilus*, who in turn, was replaced by the Commodore's son, Thomas Boulden Thompson, second lieutenant of the *Grampus*.[25] After the last fort had been visited, the vessels sailed for the island of São Tomé in the Gulf of Guinea, where they remained for six days while essential stores were transferred to the *Nautilus*. This task suggests the secrecy of the mission, for to prepare and victual the sloop for twelve months in England, as was usual for such voyages of discovery, would have roused unnecessary suspicion particularly with the French, Dutch and Portuguese; she had therefore been normally victualled and stored as for 'African Service'. Having completed the provisioning out of the *Grampus* for a full eight months, the two ships parted on 2 February 1786, the *Grampus* returning to England and the *Nautilus* heading south to begin the survey. In March the *Grampus* reached England where the reports on the African forts were presented, and some seeds and plants were delivered to Banks.[26]

The *Nautilus* put in to St Helena Bay on 25 February, and from there began the three month survey. Little need be said about that three months. The ship cruised slowly northwards a few miles off the African coast, making regular soundings and observations. Home Popham, the surveyor, charted the coast using one of the ship's boats inshore, while at various points Hove took the opportunity to botanise, and scouting parties searched for food and water.

In this manner the survey proceeded north to Das Voltas Bay, Walvis Bay, Pequena Bay and Fisher Bay. Thompson's terse log entries sum up their findings on that desolate coast: 19 April, 'one entire Desert of Rocks & Sand'; 22 April, 'loose sand with high cliffs'; 8 May, 'Land a high barren Sand'; and a cursory entry of 17 May, 'Made sail to Westd. Having completed Survey of Coast from Lat. 32°4' S to Lat. 16° without finding a Drop of fresh Water, or seeing a Tree.'[27] Hove found little to occupy his time. While in Pequena Bay, Thompson recorded: 'Mr. Hove's botanical researches were attended with no success, the only plant growing here being a small Geranium.'[28] On 24 May the *Nautilus* put into St Helena, and by 23 July 1786 the ship was safely anchored at Spithead.

While Hove struggled to get his plant collection past the customs, Thompson was for three weeks closeted with Lord Sydney discussing the results of the survey.[29] The duration of the de-briefing indicated how much the ministry had invested in the south-west coast of Africa, for it was patently unsuitable as a place of settlement, even for convicts. So optimistic had the ministry been that approaches had already been made to the East India Company with regard to the transport of convicts and the establishment of a base.[30] Reluctantly, they were obliged to turn to an alternative site.

In 1779, Banks had suggested to a Committee of the House of Commons that New South Wales would be suitable as a convict colony. Rumours of expeditions to the south Pacific were in the air in mid-1783, and on 28 July James Matra, formerly a midshipman on the *Endeavour*, but at this time unemployed, wrote to Banks asking for information on a proposed settlement in New South Wales. Within a month, probably under Banks' guidance, Matra had mapped out a scheme for a convict colony in New South Wales which would double as a trading entrepôt for the new realm of the Pacific. Matra was later supported by Admiral Sir George Young, and by the testimony of Banks before the Select Committee of 1785. The *Nautilus* expedition marked but another episode in Banks' long and continued association with New South Wales, and he played a critical part in the final decision of 18 August 1786, to send convicts to Botany Bay.[31]

Although by a series of diplomatic coups, and spells of good luck in 1787 and 1788, Pitt had managed to counter French influence in the United Provinces, British fears about the sea passage around the Cape of Good Hope persisted. When France was again in a dangerous mood by the middle of 1789, discussions were resumed. There were new problems to consider. The instructions for the *Swallow* and *Nautilus* expeditions show the surprising inadequacies in British knowledge of the south Atlantic and its shores. For the most part charts were based on information collected during the seventeenth century, and the occasional intelligence gleaned from the logs of East Indiamen which had been blown off course. The need for a more thorough investigation of those seas was obvious, and it complemented similar hydrographic surveys being carried out at the time in the Indian Ocean and south-east Asia.[32]

There were also new commercial objects to consider. Since 1785 the government had shown itself willing to encourage the new 'southern whale' fishery, and was giving the industry determined backing against the monopolies of the East India and South Sea Companies.[33] As has been shown, the advantages of a whaling base on the coast of south-west Africa had been outlined before the *Nautilus* expedition, but the energetic whalers were continually pushing further south and seeking permission to penetrate the Pacific and Indian Oceans. This new fishery differed from the Greenland and Davis Strait fishery in that its prey was the sperm whale, an open-sea mammal which produced more valuable oil.

Before 1775 the southern whale fishery had been dominated by the small Quaker community of Nantucketers, and there had been no attempt to fit out ships from England. During and after the war with America the Nantucketers suffered heavily; cut off from their most lucrative market in England and despite their loyalist pretensions, prey to marauding British ships. In 1776 the British government had taken the opportunity to encourage an indigenous industry by passing an act giving premiums for the five largest cargoes brought back by British ships. Pioneer efforts were made by the firm of Samuel Enderby and Son, but seldom more than three ships were fitted out in any one year, and the total produce of the fishery up to 1785 was only 3,900 tons.[34]

Still shut out of the British market after the war, bands of Nantucketers attempted to shift their industry to British and colonial ports. In July 1785 one of their representatives, Mr Roach, held discussions in London to secure suitable terms for the settlement of some of his fellows in a West Country port. Meeting a generally dull response from Lord Hawkesbury, he crossed to France where he received proposals for the establishment of a whaling base at Dunkirk. The prospects of a rival industry across the Channel alarmed both government and whalers, and in December 1785 the

Board of Trade asked various consuls in European ports to supply information on foreign enterprise in this field. There appears to have been little European competition save from the Portuguese, who operated small vessels off the Brazilian coast.[35]

The whalers still wanted government assistance for their infant industry and early in January 1786 the main firms — Enderby and Son, John St Barbe and Alexander Champion — presented a memorial to the Treasury which was later referred to the Board of Trade.[36] They proposed that a bounty on the tonnage of the ships engaged in the fishery should replace the existing system of premiums given for the largest catch. They also wanted permission to round the Cape of Good Hope and fish in the domains of the East India Company. This last claim was to be characteristic of an industry with a constantly expanding frontier. As each region was worked out, or as the whales became 'wilder' as the memorialists put it, the ships moved to a new region, eventually spanning the Pacific and Indian Oceans. Inevitably the industry began to burn itself out with the depletion of the sperm whale, but not until its ships had scurried into every corner of the vast expanses of ocean opened up by Cook.

The whalers' memorial was read at a Board of Trade meeting on 4 February and the negotiations continued for four months. Throughout this period Hawkesbury received advice from Cook's patron, Admiral Sir Hugh Palliser, a former Governor of Newfoundland, and an avid supporter of the whaling interest. On 15 March the Commissioners of Customs gave their report on the whalers' proposals. They came out against the bounty system, both because of the expense and the lack of incentive it offered. On 17 and 22 March Enderby, Champion and St Barbe were closely questioned by the members of the Board of Trade and were asked to submit further proposals. Although they could come up with no new suggestion, Hawkesbury was in favour of an extension of the existing premium system, which involved a fixed cost and encouraged competition among the whalers themselves. A large part of the negotiations with the whalers was carried out by Palliser, and it was he who eventually persuaded the whalers to accept Hawkesbury's scheme. Both Palliser and Hawkesbury were determined to support the fishery, but they were genuinely convinced that the bounty system dampened enterprise, and they could hold up the ailing Greenland whale fishery as an example.[37]

Their general support became clear in the negotiations with the East India and South Sea Companies for an extension of the whalers' limits. The East India Company Committee of Correspondence reported on the claims of 25 April. They asked for more detailed information on the extensions proposed, but it was plain that the old arguments about the infringements of the Company monopoly were to be raised; illicit trade, the problems of enforcement and the danger to the whalers from heavy seas.[38] These objections were levelled more explicitly by the chairmen of the Company at a Board of Trade meeting on 3 May, but they faced the determined opposition of Pitt and Dundas, as well as Hawkesbury. Their opening defence had been disastrously weak — why in particular should an industry familiar with the icy seas of Greenland be perturbed by the heavy seas of the Indian and Pacific Oceans? Realising what they were up against, they asked to be allowed to refer the intended extensions back to their fellow directors.[39] The sub- and Deputy-Governors of the South Sea Company sought the same indulgence. But the ministry was even less inclined to listen to the pleas of this latter body. George Chalmers, clerk to the Privy Council, drew up a history of the South Sea Company in May, and suggested that an act of George II would 'serve as a precedent for disregarding the Useless claim of the South Sea Company to an exclusive trade, if it should be deemed necessary to propose an express clause to enable the Southern fishers to double Cape Horn'.[40] Perhaps sensing the mood of the times, the Company decided not to raise any objections.

The East India Company grudgingly gave in, but not before some of its objections had been brutally beaten back by the Board of Trade.[41] Although subject to numerous restrictions on their geographical range, the whalers had by 26 May gained the right to proceed into the Indian Ocean. The agreements were ratified by the Act for the 'Encouragment of the Southern Whale Fishery'.[42]

In the next few years the whalers fought to remove more restrictions on their right to fish in the southern oceans. In February 1787 they petitioned for an extension of the time limits which were a part of the conditions attached to their eligibility for premiums, and requested that they should be allowed to take out South Sea Company licences. In the discussions on these points in May both the Board of Trade and Commissioners of Customs showed their willingness to let the whalers have their way. A bill was drafted to accommodate the changes. Later in the same year the whalers pressed for an extension of their fishing limits in the Indian Ocean and consequent alterations in the sailing dates.[43] Hawkesbury forwarded a copy of the proposals to Palliser, pointing out the success of the industry. As more proposals were put forward by the whalers the Board of Trade decided to make the consequent discussions part of a general renewal of the Act of 1786. In December 1787 the Commissioners of Customs were asked to consider whether special premiums should be offered to the ships which doubled Cape Horn. On this occasion the proposals were introduced to the East India Company through the Board of Control, but although the chairmen were called before the Board of Trade in March 1788, they raised no objections. On 7 March the Board of Trade announced to the whalers' representatives that the Act of 1786 was to be amended to give further premiums to vessels fishing around Cape Horn and the Cape of Good Hope, and to alter the sailing and returning dates of ships. Some small encouragement was also to be offered to foreign whalers wishing to settle in England.[44] The Pitt ministry was obviously forcing the East India Company into retreat, and subsidising the penetration of the Pacific and Indian Oceans. As in the breadfruit expedition and the north Pacific fur trade, the commercial possibilities opened up by Cook's surveys were at last being exploited.

As the whalers pushed further south and south-west, doubts arose as to their fishing rights in relation to Spanish claims. Early in 1787 a party of sealers had been dropped on Staten Island by the *Prince of Wales* bound for the north-west coast of America.[45] In July 1788, one of this party, J. Leard, a master in the Navy was back in London seeking government support for such ventures. In letters to Hawkesbury, Pitt, Carmarthen, Chatham and Hood, he pointed out the potential profits from the fishery, and asked for information on Spain's attitude towards British activity off the coast of South America.[46] This question was also in the minds of the whalers themselves, for as they pushed further south the need for bases and places of refreshment became apparent. In 1788 Enderby and Son were preparing their first ship for the Cape Horn Passage, the *Emilia* of 270 tons and, having fears as to her safety, they put a number of questions to the obvious authority on such matters, Sir Joseph Banks:

> What we would particularly wish to know is, whether you can inform us if Juan Fernandez is settled? if settled, whether there would be any risk of our Ship being seized, if she should go to that Place through Distress, or to refresh the Crew in case of Scurvy? or, if there are any other Places where she might derive Benefit

without these Risks? We shall also be much obliged by your informing us, if you know, whether there are any Spermaceti Whales round the Cape & where they are to be met with?[47]

Some of these questions were answered by the case of the two whalers *Sappho* and *Elizabeth and Margaret* which were ordered off the Patagonian coast by Spanish frigates in April 1789, while refreshing their crews and carrying out essential repairs at Puerto Deseado. To add to British anxieties about this particular episode, the Spanish commodore concerned had denied the British right to fish in what he called the 'Public Seas' off the South American coasts. The whalers were clearly alarmed at such a limitation on their mobility and in October 1789 they petitioned both Leeds and Hawkesbury to take the matter up with the Spanish government.[48] In Board of Trade discussions of 20 October the whalers claimed that the Spanish pretensions, if enforced, would be completely destructive to the fishery. In referring the matter back to Leeds in December the Board of Trade gave its opinion:

> The best and latest Writers on the Law of Nations, are of opinion that if there are any Seas, which can be considered in any respects as the Objects of Dominion, or exclusive Rights, they can be either such Parts only, as are near the Land, so that from their proximity to it Dominion can be properly maintained over them, by the Sovereigns of the adjoining Shores, or they are such as are in Part surrounded by the Land being either Roads, Bays, Ports or Harbours.[49]

With characteristic aggression it urged that Britain defend its right to fish in open seas, and to use uninhabited regions for refreshment, although Spain should be assured that ships would not hover or anchor near Spanish territory, nor go within five leagues of their shores.

With these new considerations in mind and with the strategic motive ever present, the British government had decided in the middle of 1789 to send a fully equipped exploring expedition to the south Atlantic under an experienced commander skilled in surveying. And it is in regard to this expedition, planned in the autumn of 1789, that the history of British interests in the south Atlantic and north-west coast of America has become confused. The incidents surrounding the expedition reflect on the commercial thinking of the British government at this time, as it is clear that the interests of the fur traders on the Canadian Pacific coast were regarded by the Pitt ministry as being very secondary to those of the southern whalers. The claim by some historians that the government was determined to underwrite the enterprise of the fur traders before 1790 is based on a misconstruction of events.[50]

In June 1789 Grenville, the new Secretary of State for Home Affairs, reconsidered the objectives of the *Swallow* venture of 1782–3 and reviewed the need for a base in the south Atlantic. By August, it was apparent that a follow-up to that voyage was being planned, for on the 27th Banks wrote to Evan Nepean recommending that Archibald Menzies would be a suitable botanist 'to attend the Voyage now in Contemplation'.[51] Banks referred to an earlier meeting with Nepean on the subject, and there is much to suggest that he played a critical role in the inception of the enterprise and in the events which followed. His involvement was a logical one, since as the planning of the expedition went ahead it became clear that Cook's voyages were to provide the model for those involved, and Banks was the obvious custodian of the model.

On 3 October Grenville outlined the purposes of the expedition to the Lords of the Admiralty, and ordered that a suitable ship be fitted out, as it was expedient that 'certain Island situated in the Southern Atlantic Ocean, and comprised within Cape Horn and the Cape of Good Hope, as well as some parts of the Coast of Africa, should be examined with a view to further operations'.[52] As the season for the sailing of such a voyage was fast approaching, the vessel was to be equipped as quickly as possible.

With this order to the Admiralty, Grenville enclosed draft instructions to the commander of the vessel. Isla Grande was once again the primary concern and the ship was to make traverses eastwards in about latitude 45°S in search of the island. If this island, or any others were found, they were to be thoroughly charted, and the soil, vegetation and water supply were to be examined. This done, the captain was to sail to St Helena and to hand charts and journals to the governor, and then return to the survey. After reaching about 25°W, the ship was to go north and continue its traverses eastwards in the latitude of Tristan da Cunha, which was also to be charted and examined. The same was to be done for the recently discovered Gough's Island, before the ship sailed to survey the coast of Africa from 31°S northwards to the first Portuguese settlements. Charts drawn up by Thompson and Home Popham in 1786 were enclosed with the orders, and the commander was to be instructed to take the same care as his predecessors in searching for wood, water and good harbours. Once this was completed the captain was to return to St Helena, and then refresh his crew and obtain provisions at the Cape. The expedition was to be completed by an examination of the coast of Africa from the eastern limit of Dutch territory to the first Portuguese settlements in Mozambique.[53]

Because the commander of the vessel would not possess the botanical expertise to give an accurate description of the soil and vegetation of the lands visited, Grenville adopted Banks' suggestion that the surgeon/botanist Archibald Menzies should be appointed for this service. Once again a natural historian under Banks' supervision was accredited to an expedition as an integral part of the machinery of survey.[54]

The objectives of this expedition were almost identical with those of the *Swallow* voyage, and it is reasonable to assume that the strategic motive was still uppermost in the ministry's thoughts. By making it a fully-fledged naval expedition, it was hoped that the mistakes of the earlier voyage would not be repeated. The continued interest in south-west Africa is remarkable. The *Nautilus* survey had apparently been thorough, although it had not been continued as far north as Sydney would have wished. Government expectations of this coast must have been high for ministers to have ordered that the same ground be covered again.

On 6 October the Navy Board was ordered to search for a vessel of about 300 tons for the service, and to have a shallop of 40 tons built and put in frame aboard her.[55] Eventually a new ship being constructed in the private yards of Messrs Randall and Brent was purchased. Menzies had expected to sail in November, but by that time the ship was still not finished, and the Navy Board was not able to take delivery of her until 19 December.[56] On 7 December orders were given for the ship to be entered on the lists of the Navy as the *Discovery* — the name of the *Resolution*'s companion ship on Cook's third voyage. The command was given to Captain Henry Roberts, who had been on Cook's second and third voyages.[57] George Vancouver, another Cook veteran, was made her first lieutenant. On 20 December she was launched and towed to Deptford, where work on her fitting out continued and her provisioning was begun. Menzies learned from Evan Nepean that Banks was to draw up botanical instructions but he was also concerned that a suitable place should be set aside on the *Discovery* for the care of plants and seeds. On 7 December the Admiralty ordered that a special plant 'hutch' should be placed on the quarterdeck and on the 12th Banks went down to Randall and Brent's yard to supervise its construction.[58]

It had been decided that the vessel should be fitted, stored and victualled in the same proportions as the ships of Cook's second voyage, since the missions were similar. Her crew was settled at 100 men. As with previous ships on voyages of discovery, a wide variety of nautical and astronomical instruments were supplied to her for the purposes of the survey and she was given the usual, useless selection of anti-scorbutics.[59] By the end of January 1790 the *Discovery* was in all respects ready for sea, but it was to be over a year before she sailed. Towards the end of January the news reached England of the seizure by Spain of English trading vessels at Nootka Sound on the north-west coast of America, and while the Pitt ministry considered expeditions to that coast, the original *Discovery* voyage was suspended.[60]

Throughout the Nootka Crisis of 1790 the government retained its interest in the expedition to the south Atlantic. The crew of the *Discovery* was dispersed through the fleet, and the sloop was used as a receiving ship, but after a declaration with Spain was signed on 24 July, it seemed the expedition could again be got under way. In August Grenville asked Samuel Enderby for information on Tristan da Cunha and the ports of western South America which were likely to be useful for whaling bases.[61] Captain Shields of the *Emilia* had returned from his pioneer voyage to the Pacific in March and was able to supply valuable information and charts. The ministry used this information in its negotiations with Spain over the Nootka matter, and when a convention was signed with Spain on 28 October, the most important concessions gained seemed to be related not so much to the seizure of the *Princess Royal* and *Argonaut* at Nootka, but to the threats made to the *Sappho* and *Elizabeth and Margaret* on the coast of Patagonia, for the southern whalers were guaranteed unrestricted fishing in the South Seas and Pacific so long as they did not go within ten leagues of occupied Spanish territories. Pitt had even wondered if the negotiations might be the appropriate time to raise the question of the opening of the South American trade, and mooted the renewal of discussions over the Falkland Islands.[62]

In November work began on refitting the *Discovery* and the brig *Chatham*, which was now to go with her. At this stage both vessels were bound for the south Atlantic. On 11 December a sudden change occurred: the Admiralty ordered the *Discovery* to be paid off and on 14 December Captain Roberts accompanied his crew to the Pay Office. At the same time the ship received a change of commander, for on 18 December Lieutenant George Vancouver replaced Roberts. With the change in crew came a change in destination: the *Discovery* and *Chatham* were bound for the north-west coast of America.[63]

The most plausible reason for this turn in events was the availability of the ships. An official had to go out to Nootka Sound to accept the restitution of land. Grenville's orders to this effect in December directed the Admiralty to get two ships of a proper class ready for sea, but by this time the *Discovery* and *Chatham* were already in a fit state.[64] Sometime in December the Pitt ministry re-sorted its priorities and decided as the vessels had to go to the north-west coast anyway, it would be a favourable opportunity to carry out a survey, settling once and for all the question of the north-west passage. Archibald Menzies described the change of plan: 'These vessels had been taken up for a different expedition some Months before . . . when the alterations which took place in the destination occasioned a change of Commanders & consequently of Officers & Seamen.'[65]

This did not initially mean that the expedition to the south Atlantic had been abandoned. In a letter to Philip Stephens of 24 December, Roberts requested that several of the men recently paid off, who had entered with him on the *Discovery* for the voyage to the south Atlantic, should be entered on the books of some other ship, 'until such time as another Ship is provided for the expedition'. In June 1791 Roberts was still writing as though the expedition was to be imminently renewed, and he was to be appointed to command it. Menzies, in his *Journal*, claimed that Roberts was detained to go out in another vessel in the spring of 1791. Menzies himself, bored with 18 months' indecision, stayed with the *Discovery*.[66]

It was clear that the government's intention was merely to postpone the expedition. There was certainly sufficient pressure to keep the project alive, for the southern whalers had taken advantage of their privileged position to push further into the Pacific, making continuous assaults on the East India Company monopoly. During 1790 the issues raised by the *Sappho* and *Elizabeth and Margaret* came to the fore again when similar treatment was meted out to the vessel *Astrea*, which was ordered off the Patagonian coast in March.

Both the *Astrea* and the *Elizabeth and Margaret* were owned by the firm of Lucas and Spencer, which estimated a total loss of £5,000 on the two ventures.[67] The owners petitioned the Board of Trade for redress of their grievances.

The convention with Spain presented an opportunity to air this and other problems connected with the southern whale fishery. On 8 January 1791 a Bristol whaler and fur trader. Sydenham Teast, approached the Board of Trade for advice on the rights and privileges of whalers since the signing of the convention. Time was crucial as the season for the sailing of vessels around Cape Horn was fast approaching. Teast wanted to know where on the Spanish American coast he was allowed to fish; if there was any place around Cape Horn where the whalers might refit, refresh and carry on a seal fishery; and if they were permitted to carry articles of trade to those areas or to Nootka Sound. His letter was referred to the Duke of Leeds, who avoided the issue and bounced the ball back into the Board of Trade's court by suggesting a general investigation of the southern whale fishery and the trade to the north-west coast of America.[68]

Hawkesbury saw this as an opportunity to edge back the East India Company monopoly a little further, and where he went on such matters it was likely that Pitt would follow, more especially since Dundas and Grenville were inclined towards Hawkesbury's views. Writing to the Lord Lieutenant of Ireland on 13 January, Grenville confided: 'Our general idea (but that must not on any account be opened in Ireland) is to enable any persons to carry on that trade under certain licences, to which are to be annexed as conditions such regulations as are, *bona fide*, necessary to secure the East India Company's monopoly of the tea-trade to these kingdoms, the only one of the objects under the charters I have mentioned that is of real importance.' Westmoreland was concerned to quell the anxieties of Irish merchants who feared that they might be excluded from a new and lucrative area of trade.[69]

When the negotiations began on 20 January, the Board of Trade raised the question of the fur trade with the whalers present.[70] The latter had asked for the right to fish on both sides of continental South America without having to take out East India Company or South Sea Company licences, but they were not prepared for the Lords' question on the profitability of participating in the fur trade. Although their representatives asked for more time to consider the matter, it was obvious what the answer would be. Enderby and Son had made healthy profits on the *Emilia* voyage and an extension of the fishery northwards combined with the advantages of an occasional dabbling in the fur trade was an attractive proposition. On 21 January, Enderby, Champion and St Barbe submitted the appropriate answer to the Board of Trade. A summary of the discussions was sent to Leeds with the suggestion that the proposed changes be incorporated into legislation.[71]

On 8 February Pitt, Grenville, Hawkesbury and Dundas met to consider the whale fishery and the maritime fur trade. They decided that the whalers should be allowed to fish anywhere in the Pacific and to carry on a trade with the north-west coast of America, although they would not be permitted to range as far as China or the East Indies. Unless in distress, the prohibition against fishing within ten leagues of Spanish territory was to stand. This draft scheme was formulated as a set of propositions which were sent to the Court of Directors on 14 February, and it was stressed that all illicit trade would be controlled. To this end ships going as far as Canton would be obliged to stop at that port and give an account of their proceedings to the Company supercargoes.[72]

When the Company raised the now familiar objections to such a wholesale invasion of its monopoly, the ministry decided on the direct but unusual step of asking the Company to form a committee of directors able to negotiate directly across the table with the ministers. The discussion continued for a month, but by 10 March a compromise had been worked out which allowed the whalers freedom of the Pacific while protecting the Company trade with China and India. When the scheme was shown to the directorate as a body a new set of objections were raised, but the Board of Trade refused to alter the arrangement of 10 March.[73] Although the Attorney General and Solicitor General were called before the Board of Trade to assist in drawing up the bill, the matter was eventually put off because of increasing opposition within the Company.[74] In April Hawkesbury saw a way out of the dilemma and he informed Pitt:

Lord Hawkesbury presents his compliments to Mr. Pitt and sends him inclosed copy of a letter he has just received from Mr. Enderby, by which Mr. Pitt will see that the Business of the South Sea Fishery may be put off by the consent of the Parties on condition of two favours which appear to Lord H. to be reasonable.[75]

These were the relaxation of the impressment of apprentices, and the end of the duty on salt which was used for preserving seal skins.

The whalers' most urgent need was still for bases to refresh their crews and carry out repairs, as they were not welcome in Spanish ports, and the Cape of Good Hope and St Helena were now too far away from their Pacific fishing grounds. The number of ships in the trade had risen from four in 1783 to 53 in 1791, and an increasing proportion of these were going around the Horn into the Pacific. In March 1793 discussions on the problem of bases were resumed and on 10 March the Lords of Trade put to Enderby and Champion several questions on the length of the time ships were at sea and the losses of men through scurvy.[76] It was also suggested that they should name any islands which would be suitable for bases. The whalers were able to present a devastating case. Ships rounding the Horn had been severely crippled by scurvy and their cargoes had suffered as a result. On the *Aurora*, which had left England in September 1790 with a crew of 22, seven men had died from scurvy, and when the ship arrived at Rio de Janeiro on her return voyage, the remainder of the crew was so debilitated that the captain had hired Portuguese sailors to navigate her back to England. It was not thought that any of the original crew would be able to go to sea again. At one stage the vessel was at sea for $11\frac{1}{2}$ months. Other vessels had similar records. With this account Enderby and Champion enclosed a statement on suitable places of refreshment. Juan Fernandez was their first preference, but they gave five other possible ports.[77]

A memorial stating the whalers' case had already been sent to Grenville, the new Foreign Secretary, and on 17 March it was presented with the whalers' evidence to the Board of Trade. Pitt, Grenville, Dundas and Hawkesbury discussed the matter on 8 April and agreed that it would be necessary to send a vessel to survey the Pacific coast of South America outside the limits of Spanish settlement. Captain Vancouver's instructions had directed him to explore this area and the Isla Grande on his return voyage, but only if he had sufficient time. In January 1792 Samuel Enderby Jnr had even suggested that one of his firm's vessels would search for Isla Grande if the government 'would grant any Encouragement on the Discovery of this Island'. However, the ministry drew on previous experience in deciding to send out a fully-fledged naval venture.[78]

The parties concerned gathered at the Board of Trade on 14 April to work out some plan of action, and the geographer Alexander

Dalrymple was called to give evidence on suitable islands for whaling bases off the Pacific coast of Spanish America. Reporting six days later, Dalrymple suggested that the Cocos, Galapagos, St Felix and St Ambrosio Islands should be examined, as well as the island supposed to lie 750 leagues west of the coast in latitude 8°S. The government might consider sending a skilled officer in one of the whaling vessels to carry out such a survey. At a Board of Trade meeting on 20 April Hawkesbury acquainted the whalers that the government intended to send a ship to the Pacific expressly for the purpose of carrying out such a survey. The following day the recommendations were passed on to the Home Office.[79]

Early in June Dundas requested that the Admiralty Lords order the fitting out of a vessel to conduct the survey, but during July he began to have second thoughts about the plan which he believed was too extensive, and after discussions with Dalrymple he concluded that it would be sufficient if one of the regular whaling vessels were used for the purpose and given a naval commander skilled in surveying. The whaling firm concerned would receive a gratuity of £500 for their troubles. Such a scheme had in fact been put forward by the firm of Joseph Lucas and Sons some months earlier, but it was now rejected by the whaling firms involved on the grounds that no suitable ship was available. In the end a compromise was settled upon. A naval sloop was to be lent for the purpose and temporarily converted for whaling. An able naval officer would command her and have the assistance of a whaling master. In September the Navy settled on the sloop *Rattler*, which was undergoing a refit at Woolwich, and the vessel was removed to a private yard for conversion.[80]

Unfortunately it was discovered that, once converted, the sloop would no longer be of use to the Navy. When this was made clear to Enderby and Son, the whaling firm concerned, they agreed to purchase the vessel, and an order for delivery was made out, leading to the anomalous situation of a joint naval and commercial venture. The conversion of the *Rattler* was supervised by one of the Navy's assistant surveyors, and by 11 November 1792 she was ready for sea and lay waiting at Portsmouth for the commander's instructions. On 5 November Lieutenant James Colnett, recently returned from the north-west coast of America, was appointed to command her.[81]

Until the end of December the departure of the *Rattler* was held up while the various departments of government quibbled over the drawing up of the Captain's instructions. In November, Lord

Chatham, the First Lord of the Admiralty, asserted that as the expedition had originally been planned by the Board of Trade, the instructions were its responsibility, and should therefore be drawn up by the Secretary of State.[82] Eventually the Admiralty was prevailed upon to draw up Colnett's instructions, and they were submitted to Grenville in the second half of November. They closely followed Dalrymple's memorandum of 19 April. Colnett was to survey the coast in the vicinity of the Island of Inchi (now Tenquehuen Island on the Chilean coast), and if the terrain was suitable to sow seeds of various edible plants. He was then to move north along the coast, examining Juan Fernandez, Más Afuero (or Alejandro Selkirk Island, also in the Juan Fernandez group), St Felix, the Galapagos and the Cocos. The Islands of St Felix were to be claimed for Britain. On the return voyage the Isla Grande was to be located and surveyed. A list of specialised nautical and astronomical instruments was to be supplied.[83]

Grenville was alarmed at the orders to take possession of several of the islands, and to leave men upon them. On 23 November he sent Hawkesbury a modified version of the instructions, warning that the formation of a settlement as originally proposed 'would in fact necessarily form such a depot for smuggling with Peru as must drive Spain into a War the first moment she finds it possible'.[84] Hawkesbury agreed that no islands should be claimed in the southern oceans 'especially by Direction of Government', but it was necessary that they should be thoroughly surveyed so that the situation could be reviewed by the ministry on the vessel's return. Pitt and Dundas were shown the instructions in their altered state, and both expressed their approval, but Grenville was still plagued by doubts:

> I could have wished that more consideration could have been given to the whole idea but as the time is said to press I have made such alterations as seem to me the best supposing the plan itself to be right which I am greatly inclined to doubt. When it is so very clear that no settlement or resort of our Ships can take place without first offence to Spain I see no use in survey or examination except to raise useless Jealousy — And therefore I wish it to be understood by Mr. D. that the alterations I have made by no means imply my approbation of the general plan, which on the contrary I must wish him to reconsider before he gives sanction to it.[85]

The delay caused by these divisions within the Cabinet was severely vexing to Enderby and Son, and on 20 December they wrote to the Admiralty asking for some decision. They had heard that the whole plan was to be reviewed by the ministry, which would mean the *Rattler* would miss her rendezvous with other whaling ships at Rio de Janeiro. The whalers put forward a suggestion of their own: 'If their Lordships think proper to send Lieut. Colnett in the ship without Orders, to avoid giving cause of Jealousy to the Spaniards, we shall have no objection as it is our Interest and wish to discover an Island which is capable of refreshing the Crews of the South Whalers at, in the Pacific Ocean.' This provided the opening the ministry needed, and the following day, Dundas accepted the Enderby proposal. Samuel Enderby himself drew up Colnett's instructions along the lines of the Admiralty draft.[86]

On 24 December Colnett joined his ship, and ten days later the *Rattler* made her way down Channel. The voyage is interesting in that it indicates the gradual swing of interest since the peace of 1783. It was principally a venture for the benefit of the whalers and, as such, showed more interest in the south-west Atlantic and eastern Pacific. From the instructions, and from Colnett's own comments on the voyage, the ministry evidently hoped that information might be incidentally gained which would locate an offshore base for Britain as a centre for possible commercial or military attacks on the Pacific coast of Spanish America.[87] But its main importance lies in the fact that it pointed to the first sustained attempt to exploit the commercial possibilities of the Pacific in the 20 years after Cook's death.

After touching at Rio de Janeiro, the *Rattler* finally proved the non-existence of the Isla Grande on which so many hopes had been pinned. In his journal Colnett noted that the discovery of the island 'was to have been the first service I understood the orders of The Right Honourable, The Lords Commissioners of the Admiralty were to have directed my attention to'. Vancouver later followed up Colnett's search for the island.[88] The next objective was to find a suitable island base close to the western side of South America, and with this in view the *Rattler* cruised northwards up the Pacific coast charting and examining Wager Island, Mocha Island, the islands of St Felix and St Ambrosio, Isla St Lawrence, Lobos le Mar, the Galapagos, Isla Plata, Malpelo Island and Cocos. After touching at Socorro, the California peninsula, and several small islands off the Mexican coast, the *Rattler* returned to England via the Galapagos,

Cape Horn and St Helena. A few of the islands examined by Colnett were suitable as rendezvous points and places of minor refreshment, but only the Cocos, Socorro and Galapagos were in any way suitable as bases. The latter group of islands greatly impressed Colnett. Their fertility, good harbours and proximity to Spanish America, made them ideal for a free port, or as a base for offensives against the mainland. They were, he wrote, 'one of the most desirable Spots under heaven to our Country'.[89] Almost the entire voyage had been devoted to surveying, partly because Colnett had an eye towards promotion in the Navy. As a result few whales were caught, and the *Rattler* returned with a mere 50 barrels of oil. Shortly after her return another ship, the *Providence* under Captain Broughton, left England with the intention of surveying the coast Colnett had just abandoned. In the event Broughton invoked a discretionary clause in his instructions to switch his interest to the north Pacific in the belief that Vancouver was to survey the South American coast.[90]

By the time the *Rattler* reached England on 3 November 1794, its original purpose, and indeed the various objectives of the expeditions planned since 1782, were close to being met. In April 1795 two squadrons sailed from England with 6,000 men and the Cape fell into British hands. Henceforth British fears for the security of India were shifted elsewhere.[91] New South Wales had solved the convict problem, and after renewed pressure on the government in 1797 and 1798, the whalers were able to make use of that settlement, New Zealand and the Sandwich Islands for the refreshment of their crews and refitting of their ships.[92] Bligh's second attempt to carry breadfruit and other esculent plants from the Pacific to the West Indies had avoided the misfortunes of the first, thus partially fulfilling yet another of Dalrymple's designs for *Terra Australis Incognita*.

British interest in the southern oceans in this period was related to a number of specific needs — some traditional, some new — but it did not form a part of any co-ordinated imperial policy. Government activity in the area, normally taking the form of exploratory expeditions, was usually initiated in response to immediate problems such as strategic or penal deficiencies, or to outside pressure such as that from the southern whalers. Any discernible pattern emerging from this activity is, therefore, indicative of the continuing appeal of traditional remedies for old and new problems, and not of any great vision and purpose in those who were responsible for British imperial administration in the decade after the American War of Independence.

Notes

1. A Dalrymple, *A Collection of Voyages Chiefly in the Southern Atlantick Ocean*, p. 6.

2. V.T. Harlow, *The Founding of the Second British Empire 1763-1793*, vol. I, ch. IV. These strategic arguments are also analysed in A. Frost, *Convicts and Empire: A Naval Question*.

3. Chairmen to Hillsborough, 25 October 1781, in V.T. Harlow & F. Madden, *British Colonial Developments, 1774-1834*, p. 6.

4. See below, Chapter 7.

5. See, for example, Banks to Sir G. Yonge, 15 May 1787, *D.T.C.*, V, fos 160-1.

6. Harlow, *Founding of the Second British Empire*, Vol. I, pp. 108-20. Trinidad: not to be confused with the Caribbean island of that name.

7. Hillsborough to Chairman, January 1782, *C.O.* 77/25, in the memorandum of 17 June 1789.

8. For La Roche, see Beaglehole, *The Journals of Captain Cook on His Voyages of Discovery*, vol. II, p. 617n.

9. Instructions to the Commander of the *Swallow*, September 1783, *C.O.* 77/25.

10. Memorandum on the *Swallow* voyage, 17 June 1789, ibid.

11. For such proposals, E. Morse to Pitt, 24 November 1784, *P.R.O. (Chatham)*, 30/8, 363, fos 76-7. Also Lieutenant Clarke's report, 17 March 1785, ibid., fos 56-67.

12. An undated copy of the report is in *H.O.* 42/7.

13. For Madagascar, *P.R.O. (Chatham)*, 30/8, 363, fos 78-81, about 6 June 1785. Some of Blankett's correspondence is in *H.O.* 42/9. Blankett was later a strong advocate of a British presence at the Cape, and in 1795 he led one of the squadrons which took the Cape: see Harlow, *Founding of the Second British Empire*, vol. I, pp. 133-5. Colonel William Dalrymple put forward a scheme in September 1785 for a settlement east of Plettenberg Bay, South Africa. The proposal was put before Pitt and Dundas, and had the support of the East India Company. It was probably rejected because of the proximity of the location to the Dutch settlements, see *Scottish Record Office, G.D. 51 (Melville)*, 3, 17, 1-3, September-October 1785.

14. Sydney to Lords of Adm., 22 August 1785, *H.O.* 28/5, 118-20.

15. This was Alexander Bay at the mouth of the Orange River.

16. Sydney to Lords of Adm., 22 August 1785, *H.O.* 28/5, 118-20.

17. J. Ibbetson to Nepean, 25 August 1785, *H.O.* 28/5, 121. Ibbetson had been secretary to the Board of Longitude, and appears at this time to have been acting as a clerk to the Admiralty.

18. Blagden to Banks, 3 September 1785, *Kew B.C.* I, 201. Blagden to Banks, 10 September 1785, ibid., 203.

19. Blagden to Banks, 15 September 1785, ibid., 204. Blagden, later Sir Charles Blagden, the eminent physician. He was Banks' most regular and prolific correspondent.

20. Blagden to Banks, 19 September 1785, *D.T.C.* IV, fo. 172.

21. Nepean to P. Stephens, 12 September 1785, *H.O.* 29/2, 22.

22. Heads of Instructions, 15 September 1785, *Adm.* 2/1342.

23. Blagden to Banks, 10 September 1785, *Kew B.C.* I, 203.

24. Secret Instructions to Thompson, 15 September 1785, *Adm.* 2/1342.

25. T.B. Thompson to Stephens, 30 January 1786, *Adm.* 1/2594 (Captains' Letters).

26. Tripp to Stephens, 24 March 1786, *Adm.* 1/2594. Tripp to Home Popham, 1 February 1786, *H.O.* 28/61, 114-17, Instructions for survey. Hove to Banks, 31 January 1786, *Kew B.C.* I, 223.

27. Log of the *Nautilus, Adm.* 51/627.

28. Thompson's Journal, *Adm.* 55/92, fo. 26. Endorsed in Stephens' hand 'Rd 24 July 1786'.

29. Hove to Banks, 1 August 1786, *Kew B.C.* I, 236. T.B. Thompson to Stephens, 15 August 1786, *Adm.* 1/2594.

30. Pitt to Grenville, 2 October 1785, *H.M.C. (Dropmore)*, 30, I, p. 257.

31. *Commons Journals*, 1778-80, XXXVII, col. 311. Matra to Banks, 28 July 1783, *Add. MSS.* 33977, fo. 206. *H.R.N.S.W.*, I, ii, pp. 1-8. Matra's part in the choice of New South Wales can be exaggerated. He had previously been a secretary to the embassy at Constantinople, but in 1783 he was in London, unemployed, and a supplicant for Bank's favours. Banks eventually arranged his appointment as consul to Tangier. It is unlikely that his scheme would have been noticed but for support from Banks. On Banks and Australia, J.H. Maiden, *Sir Joseph Banks: the 'Father of Australia'*; G. Mackaness, *Sir Joseph Banks. His Relations with Australia*. On the choice of Botany Bay see Frost, *Convicts and Empire* and G. Martin (ed.), *The Founding of Australia*.

32. H.T. Fry, 'Early British Interest in the Chagos Archipelago and Maldive Islands', pp. 343-56 and *Alexander Dalrymple and the Expansion of British Trade*.

33. The term 'southern whale fishery' applied to all fishery carried on below the latitude of Britain in the Atlantic or, in fact, in any latitude in the Pacific, the sense being that vessels had initially to proceed south.

34. *Add. MSS.* 38346, fo. 75.

35. Harlow, *Founding of the Second British Empire*, vol. II, ch. V. Cottrell to Carmarthen, 16 December 1785, *B.T.* 5/2, 176-7. Consuls' reports in *B.T.* 6/93, especially R. Walpole to Carmarthen, 18 March 1786, from Lisbon.

36. Memorial of Messrs Enderby, St Barbe and Champion, *B.T.* 6/93.

37. *B.T.* 5/3, 55-6, 4 February 1786; ibid., 132-8, 17 & 22 March 1786; *B.T.* 6/93, 15 March 1786. Palliser to Cottrell, [?], 9 April 1786, *B.T.* 6/93.

38. Report of Committee of Correspondence, 25 April 1786, *B.T.* 6/93.

39. *B.T.* 5/3, 192-3, 3 May 1786.

40. Collections as to the South Sea Company, 26 May 1786, *B.T.* 6/93.

41. See Resolutions passed by the Court of Directors, 10 May 1786, ibid.

42. *B.T.* 5/3, 199. 26 May 1789. *26 Geo. III, cap. 50.*

43. Memorial of Messrs Enderby, St Barbe and Champion, 14 February 1787, *B.T.* 6/95. Report of Commissioners of Customs, 8 May 1787, *B.T.* 5/4, 139. Champion to Hawkesbury, 30 October 1787, *B.T.* 6/95. Hawkesbury to Palliser, 1 November 1787, *Add. MSS.* 38310, fo. 9. 'I rely much on your Judgement in this Business.'

44. *B.T.* 5/4, 209, 21 December 1787. Morton to Cottrell, 10 April 1788, *B.T.* 6/95. Some bonds were included in the Act to prevent infringement. *B.T.* 5/5, 25-8, 7 March 1788.

45. See below, Chapter 3.

46. Leard to Hawkesbury, 16 July 1788, *B.T.* 6/95. The same to Pitt is in *P.R.O. (Chatham)* 30/8, 151, fos 1-4. To Chatham, ibid. 30/8, 368, fos 1-4.

47. Enderby and Son to Banks, 26 August 1788, *Kew B.C.* I, 319.

48. Affadavit of Captain Middleton of the *Sappho*, 25 September 1789, 6/95. Memorial of whalers to Duke of Leeds, 16 October 1789, ibid. Enderby and Champion to Hawkesbury, 2 October 1789, ibid. Discussions, *B.T.* 5/5, 195-6, 20 October 1789.

49. Fawkener to Leeds, 8 December 1789, *B.T.* 3/2, 134-53.

50. See Harlow, *Founding of the Second British Empire*, vol. II, ch. VII, particularly pp. 438-41. On the fur trade and Vancouver's expedition, see below Chapters 3-4.

51. Grenville memorandum, 17 June 1789, *C.O.* 77/25. Banks to Nepean, 27 August 1789, *H.O.* 28/6, 314.

52. Grenville to Lords of Adm., 3 October 1789, *Adm.* 1/4154, 43, also *H.O.* 28/6, 304-5.

53. Enclosure in *Adm.* 1/4156. Heads of Instructions, 3 October 1789, *Adm.* 1/4155, wrongly dated 3 October 1790. Also in *H.O.* 28/6, 306–12.

54. Grenville to Lords of Adm., 3 October 1789, *Adm.* 1/4154, 43. For Menzies see below, Chapters 3–4.

55. *Adm.* 3/106, 48, 6 October 1789. On the shallop, ibid., 27 October 1789.

56. Menzies to Banks, 8 October 1789, *Kew B.C.* I, 362.

57. *Adm.* 106/2631, 9 December 1789. On the launching, ibid., 21 December 1789. The total cost of the *Discovery* on launching was £5,410 12 5d, *Adm.* 106/2632, 8 February 1790.

58. Menzies to Banks, 8 October 1789, *Kew B.C.* I, 362. *Adm.* 3/106, 96, 7 December 1789. *Adm.* 106/2631, 9 December 1789. *H.O.* 28/6, 382.

59. *Adm.* 3/106, 96. *Adm.* 2/265, 332, 19 January 1790. *Adm.* 106/2632, 25 January 1790. The anti-scorbutics were those supplied to Cook on his voyages, and to Bligh in 1787. They included portable soup, juice of wort, essence of malt, sauerkraut and elixir of vitriol — all useless in combating scurvy, see C. Lloyd and J.L.S. Coulter, *Medicine and the Navy: 1200–1900*, vol. III, ch. 18.

60. For the events surrounding the Nootka crisis, see below, Chapters 3–4.

61. *Adm.* 3/107, 113, 7 May 1790. Enderby to Nepean, 16 August 1790, *H.O.* 42/16, with enclosures.

62. Leeds to Pitt, 21 November 1790, *Add. MSS.* 28066, fo. 348. During the crisis of 1790 Pitt had considered forcing open that market, see Harlow, *Founding of the Second British Empire*, vol. II, pp. 645–8.

63. *Adm.* 106/2635, 16 November 1790; 11–18 December 1790.

64. Grenville to Lords of Adm., December 1790, *H.O.* 28/7, 392–9.

65. A. Menzies, 'Journal of Vancouver's Voyage', *Add. MSS.* 32641, fo. 1.

66. Roberts to Stephens, 24 December 1790, *Adm.* 1/2395. Roberts to Stephens, 23 June 1791, ibid. Menzies, ibid., fo. 1.

67. Lucas & Co. to Hawkesbury, 23 November 1790, *B.T.* 6/95.

68. Teast to Board of Trade, 8 January 1791, ibid. Fawkener to Leeds, 11 January 1791, *B.T.* 3/3, 198. For the discussions on the fur trade see below, Chapter 3.

69. Grenville to Westmoreland, 13 January 1791, *H.M.C. (Dropmore)*, 30, vol. II, p. 14.

70. The discussions are in *B.T.* 5/7, 8–11, 20 & 21 January 1791.

71. Fawkener to Leeds, 21 January 1791, *B.T.* 3/3, 205–8.

72. Pitt to Hawkesbury, 5 February 1791, *Add. MSS.* 38192, fo. 79. An undated draft of the proposals is in *P.R.O. (Chatham)*, 30/8, 341, fos 113–17. *B.T.* 5/7, 26–7, 14 February 1791.

73. *B.T.* 5/7, 32–3, 3 March 1791; 47–8, 21 March 1791.

74. The discussions are in *B.T.* 5/7, 55–62. Cottrell to Attorney General, 9 April 1791, *B.T.* 3/3, 284–6.

75. Hawkesbury to Pitt, no date, *B.T.* 6/95.

76. *B.T.* 5/7, 197–8, 10 March 1792.

77. Enderby and Champion to Hawkesbury, 16 March 1792, *B.T.* 1/2, 271–5, also in *Adm.* 1/4156, enclosure 3.

78. *B.T.* 3/4, 26–8, 17 March 1792. Pitt to Hawkesbury, 7 April 1792, *Add. MSS.* 38192, fo. 87. Instructions to Vancouver, 11 February 1791, *Adm.* 1/4156, 14.

79. *B.T.* 5/8, 4–5, 14 & 20 April 1792. Dalrymple memorandum, 19 April 1792, *Adm.* 1/4156. *B.T.* 5/8, 8–12, 20 April 1792. Cottrell to King, 21 April 1792, *B.T.* 3/4, 51–3.

80. Nepean to Stephens, 1 August 1792, *H.O.* 28/8, 274–5. Also *Adm.* 1/4156, 104. Lords of Admiralty to Navy Board, 1 September 1792, *Adm.* 2/269, 35–7.

81. J. Colnett, 'A Voyage for Whaling and Discovery', *Add. MSS.* 30369, fos 8–9.

82. Chatham to Nepean, November 1792, *H.O.* 28/8, 272.

83. The instructions are in *Adm.* 1/4156.

84. Grenville to Hawkesbury, 23 November, ibid.

85. Hawkesbury to Grenville, 30 November 1792, ibid. Pitt to Hawkesbury, no date, ibid. Grenville to Hawkesbury [?], 9 December 1792, ibid.

86. Enderby and Son to Stephen, 20 December 1792, ibid. Stephen to Nepean, 19 [20?] December 1792, ibid. Colnett, 'Voyage', fo. 10.

87. Colnett, ibid. log entries on Islas Tres Marias and the Galapagos.

88. G. Vancouver, *A Voyage of Discovery to the North Pacific Ocean and Round the World*, vol. III, p. 469.

89. Colnett, 'Voyage', fo. 228.

90. See below, Chapter 4.

91. For an analysis of the place of the Cape of Good Hope in British policy throughout this period, and a more detailed discussion of some points about the Cape which have been raised here, see, L.C.F. Turner, 'The Cape of Good Hope and Anglo-French Rivalry, 1778–1796', pp. 166–85.

92. See discussions on the extensions of the whalers' limits in *B.T.* 1/15, 259–72, October 1797 to January 1798. *B.T.* 3/5, 341–9, for the same period.

3 FUR TRADERS IN THE NORTH PACIFIC

There are difficulties in assessing the influence of Cook's voyages upon imperial developments in the two decades following the great navigator's death. Expansion seldom followed a predetermined or systematic course. Although Cook clearly played a part in pushing forward the imperial frontier, many other forces helped to determine the exploitation of his discoveries, often obscuring his own imprint. Sometimes, indeed, that imprint was less clear than it might have been, confusing those who followed in his path. This was the case with the third voyage which had been incomplete, partly because of shortcomings in Cook's instructions, and partly because of the tragic and untimely death of the commander himself.[1] British interest in the area was distorted by the failure to destroy the great remaining geographical myth of the north-west passage to China, and while the credibility of De Fuca and De Fonte remained intact, there was always the hope that the narrowest inlet might open into an expansive seaway, providing a valuable link with the markets of the East. In the minds of men like Dalrymple the passage itself seemed to become the El Dorado; the means triumphed over the end.[2]

Not only had Cook's third voyage failed to destroy a myth, but it had directly created another, lesser one. Since Bering's voyages in the first half of the eighteenth century, Russian traders had been gathering the luxuriant furs of the sea otter (*Enhydra lutris*) off the Pacific coasts of Siberia, and the string of islands stretching through the Kurils and Aleutians to Alaska. Most of these furs were taken back through Petropavlovsk, Yakutsk and Irkutsk to the frontier town of Kyakhta, where they were sold to Chinese merchants from Peking. Although the dangers and rigours of this trade were many, the profits for the fortunate were fabulously high, and provided sufficient incentive for its continuation. Remarkably, little knowledge of the trade percolated through to Western Europe.[3] The first suggestion of Russian activity probably came after a revolt at Bolsheretsk in Kamchatka in 1771, when the mutineers overthrew the garrison commanders and fled in one of the largest ships to America by way of Macao, Madagascar and France.[4] It was Spain which first reacted to Russian enterprise in the north Pacific, after learning of a

Map 2 The North Pacific

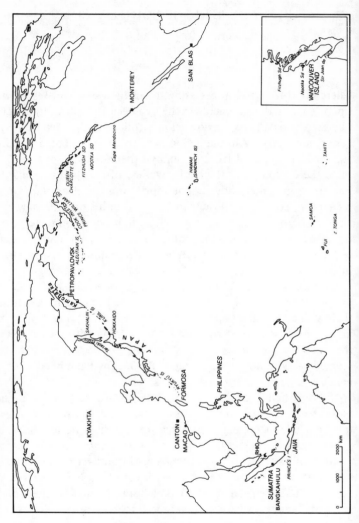

report on the fur trade to the Russian government by one Krenitzin who had recently returned from Siberia seeking government support. More interested in the territorial than the commercial implications of this, the Viceroy of Mexico ordered two expeditions to the north-west coast of America in 1774 and 1775. Neither expedition got any further than latitude 58°N.[5]

With the return of Cook's ships in 1780 knowledge of Russian expansion became general. More specifically, interest centred on the commercial side of the Russian undertakings, that being the aspect that had impressed the crews of the *Discovery* and *Resolution*. In his journal Captain Clerke reported conversations with Russians in the Aleutians, in which he was told of sea otter furs reaching up to 100 roubles a piece in China.[6] David Samwell, surgeon on the *Resolution*, recorded: 'One of our Gentlemen bought as many Sea Beaver Skins for half a dozen blue Beads as sold afterwards for £40 at Kamchatka.'[7] Armed with thousands of blue beads, small groups of adventurers set out for the north Pacific in the years after 1784 in search of quick profits. But this bonanza itself proved to be a myth, and within ten years its British aspect withered and virtually died. It had never been profitable. Nevertheless, the lure of a quick route to the East and a quick passage to fortune provided their own fascination and, for Britons, gave the north Pacific an inflated importance for a short period after 1780.

With the private expeditions to the north Pacific in the 20 years following the death of Captain Cook, much of the interest lies in the way in which the entrepreneurs concerned endeavoured to model their enterprises on the voyages of the great navigator. Undoubtedly this was to some extent lip service designed to attract the patronage of men like Sir Joseph Banks and Dalrymple, but it also reflected a genuine faith in the validity of the model. It was not thought incongruous that science and commerce should go hand in hand; indeed the employment of scientists on such voyages suggested a faith in the discovery of new commercial possibilities as the fruit of such co-operation. All of the private voyages fell far short of the model, but this scarcely invalidates its importance to them.

From 1783 onwards, London was rife with rumours of impending voyages to the Pacific. Sir Joseph Banks was supposedly involved in such an undertaking, with the co-operation of Lord Sandwich and Lord Mulgrave, and ships under the command of Lieutenant Gore who had been on Cook's first and third voyages, and had travelled to Iceland with Banks in 1772.[8] This was a likely sort of combination, and it was the general view that any such voyage would be in the hands of members of the Cook circle. In fact, the prospects for such an enterprise at that time were unlikely. Sandwich was completely out of touch with the Admiralty and he even felt obliged to use Banks as an intermediary in the publication of the Cook voyages.[9] Banks was heavily involved in the disputes over his authority in the Royal Society, and although these may have re-enlivened the lure of Tahiti for him, he was not the sort to run away from such problems.[10]

Towards the end of 1783 a concrete proposal for an expedition to the north Pacific came from a seaman who had been on Cook's third voyage. Joseph Billings had been rescued from debtors' prison by Banks in January 1783, and while languishing in King's Bench he had formulated a scheme and submitted it to his benefactor.[11] During 1783 Billings had discussions with the East India Company and private merchants, but meeting no favourable response he applied through the Russian Ambassador in Paris, Simolin, for permission to join the Russian Navy.[12] He left for St Petersburg early in 1784. After a year of argument and persuasion he caught the ear of Banks' correspondent Peter Pallas, who recommended to the Empress an overland expedition to eastern Siberia. The news of the departure of La Pérouse's expedition acted as a spur to Russian activity, and at the beginning of November 1785 Billings headed east from Moscow. Banks was offered the opportunity of sending a botanical collector, but he seems to have turned it down.[13]

In August 1784, another Cook veteran approached Banks with schemes for an expedition to the north-west coast of America. George Dixon suggested a land crossing of America along the string of lakes westward, using the skill and labour of 30 or 40 Indian guides. Three scientists would direct this venture, and it would be equipped with an initial capital of only £1,500 provided by 30 subscribers. At the end of the enterprise the profits would be split between the three scientists and the subscribers. Dixon had interested others in his plans for he told Banks that David Nelson, assistant-surgeon on the *Resolution*, and William Ellis, another surgeon, would accompany the expedition as botanist and draughtsman. Dixon himself would take command and do the astronomical work.[14]

He had several meetings with Banks to get support but the latter remained sceptical. If America had still been dependent on Britain, or even if relations between the two countries had been on a sound footing, he would have encouraged the venture. But while the unsettled state of things 'furnishes excuses for every act of irregularity' such a scheme would be futile. He anyway believed that just such a plan was being considered by Congress.[15] But Dixon was only temporarily disappointed, and Banks was otherwise generally interested in the idea of a maritime expedition to the north Pacific.

Towards the end of 1784 Dixon became involved in just such a voyage planned by the Imperial Asiatic Company of Vienna. The main figure in this plan was the Dutch adventurer William Bolts who had been deported from India by the East India Company, and had gone bankrupt in 1773. He had planned an expedition to the northwest coast of America in 1781 under Austrian colours, but the scheme had been wrecked by his fellow directors in the Imperial Company of Trieste for the Commerce of Asia. In 1784 Bolts was supervising the construction of a ship at Marseille for a second attempt, and approaches were made to Dixon. It was presumably this ship, the *Imperial Eagle*, which was seized by creditors in Cadiz, thus wrecking Bolts' plans. By the end of 1784 he was again bankrupt.[16] At this juncture he offered his services to the French. Whether he had any connection with the voyage of La Pérouse is open to doubt.[17]

At the time that La Pérouse's expedition was being planned in Paris, moves were afoot in London to promote two quite separate voyages to the north-west coast of America. With Banks' support George Dixon had been searching for a merchant prepared to risk a British voyage. Early in March 1785 one Richard Cadman Etches, a shipping merchant and dabbler in the whale fishery, became interested in the plan, and on 13 March he discussed the organisation of such a voyage with Banks. Banks readily gave his advice. The initial subscription to the undertaking should be very large so that the fitting of the ships, and the development of the trade, would not be handicapped. Etches agreed to this and proposed that the nominal capital should be £200,000 divided into £100 shares.[18]

On the direction of the trade, Banks had important and misleading advice to offer. In 1776 and 1777 the Swedish botanist Carl Thunberg had been in Japan as physician to the Dutch governor, and he had an opportunity to collect plants and examine the country. On his return to Europe in the autumn of 1778 he met Banks in London and discussed his travels.[19] From his conversations with Thunberg Banks believed that the Japanese market might be opened to British traders. It was this hope which he held out to Etches and his partners, and he promised to write to Thunberg in Uppsala to obtain further information.

Whether Etches himself believed that this was a profitable avenue to pursue is open to doubt, nevertheless he continued to enthuse about the prospects in subsequent letters to Banks. It was certainly a useful lever to apply in what was to be the most difficult step in getting a voyage underway: obtaining a licence to trade in the domains of the East India Company.

A vital prerequisite here was some degree of government support. This ground had already been explored by George Taswell, a master attendant for the East India Company at Madras, who, early in 1785, was on furlough in England. On 23 March Taswell outlined his plans to Lord Sydney. He intended to trade as an individual on the north-west coast of America, and sell his furs through the East India Company at Canton. Although Sydney took the trouble to forward the letter to the Company, nothing developed from Taswell's initiative.[20]

Etches and his associates enjoyed more success, and this was partially due to the interest which they had cultivated in ministerial circles. The ubiquitous Lord Mulgrave gave his support, doubtless introduced to their activities through his friendship with Banks. Mulgrave was invariably interested in projects of this nature, and his membership of the Board of Control would be invaluable to Etches. George Rose, Secretary to the Treasury, was another adherent to the venture, and he later used his influence to get the merchants a licence from the South Sea Company. Finally the merchants had attracted the support of Sir John Dick, a diplomatist who in 1786 became Commissioner for the Enquiry into Fees in Public Offices. Dick had a considerable knowledge of Russian expansion, and was mentioned by Captain Portlock as one of the main promoters of the Etches enterprise.[21]

In April 1785, the King George's Sound Company, as it was then constituted, obtained government permission to trade between the north-west coast of America and Japan and Korea, conditional upon the approval of the East India Company. Armed with this recommendation the merchants took their proposal to the Court of Directors, which met and considered the propositions at the end of April.[22] Naturally the merchants framed their case to give the greatest appeal. The prospect of opening the Japanese market was dangled like a carrot: 'The Japanese Islands would be our grand object, to open a friendly intercourse with which, we have every possible hope of attaining from holding out so great a temptation as the Sea Otter Skins.'[23] The specie acquired by such transactions would be deposited in the East India Company treasury at Canton and save valuable remittances of bullion from Europe. That the Japanese market could be opened was beyond doubt, as the merchants had,

> received the most flattering encouragement from conversation of Gentlemen of the greatest eminence and abilities (for Knowledge of Japan) that should our attempt meet with success, it may open a very extensive and valuable source of Commerce to this Country.[24]

This was an obvious reference to Banks.

The merchants pursued another useful tack by stressing the scientific value of such a voyage in following up Cook's researches — a prospect which they had wisely laid before Banks. Great stretches of the north Pacific remained unexplored, and even the sounds in the vicinity of Cook Inlet and Prince William Sound had not been fully investigated by the great navigator. Yet the depth of the water in some of these inlets, their general direction, and the testimonies of the natives, all suggested the possibility of a navigable communication to Hudson Bay or Baffin Bay.[25] The Etches consortium would similarly follow Cook in utilising the Sandwich Islands as a place of rendezvous and refreshment, with the ultimate possibility of their becoming a grand 'emporium of Commerce'.[26] Finally they were able to assure the Company that the command of the ships would be in good hands, because although Dixon had been offered the command of a French expedition, they believed 'his predeliction for this his Native Country', might enable them to entice him into their own service.[27]

The East India Company referred the matter to the Committee of Correspondence, which was to meet on 6 May with Etches giving evidence before it.[28] It was finally recommended that the Company should encourage the scheme so far as to licence two ships by way of experiment, subject to various conditions related to the Company monopoly. As Harlow pointed out, these hindered the merchants from the outset, but they were not the sole cause of the failure of the expedition.[29] The agreement assumed that the greater part of the merchants' trade would be with Japan, Korea and islands north of Japan, and that only the proceeds of such sales would pass through

East India Company hands. That the fur traders were eventually obliged to sell their furs at Canton was not the fault of the Company. Etches and his associates were hoist with their own petard. Nor were the rates at which the ships were to be freighted back to England disastrously low. In the first voyage they were certainly higher than the rates obtained by the convict ships from New South Wales which returned to Europe via Canton.[30]

Immediately these negotiations were concluded Etches purchased two ships of 320 and 200 tons and began overhauling them in the Thames. By 8 July they were out of dry dock and were being stored and provisioned at Deptford.[31] Some time in June the merchants approached another Cook veteran, Nathaniel Portlock, and offered him overall command of the expedition.[32] It was not until the ships were virtually ready for sea that Etches 'accidentally discovered' that the north-west coast of America was within the limits of the South Sea Company charter. This oversight might be forgiven him but it was nevertheless necessary to obtain a licence from that Company.[33] George Rose approached the Deputy and Sub-Governor privately on the merchants behalf, but was advised that it would be necessary to go through the proper official channels.[34] At beginning of August Sydney was stirred into recommending that the Directors of the South Sea Company dispense with their privilege under charter, and grant a licence to Etches and his associates.[35] On 4 August this request was granted and a licence was forwarded to Etches with the Company seal attached.[36]

Immediately before the two ships put to sea on 29 August, a party was held on board them at which Mulgrave, Banks and Rose were present. Rose named the largest of the vessels the *King George*, the other was named by Banks the *Queen Charlotte*, and Portlock confidently observed that they were of the 'size and burden which Captain Cook after adequate trials, recommended as the fittest for distant employments'.[37]

As Portlock and Dixon were on the point of sailing, another expedition was being organised in India. Early in 1785 one James Strange of the Madras establishment had approached Banks with plans for an expedition to the north-west coast of America. Presumably Banks gave the same advice that he had given to Etches, and with this information, Strange sought out a patron for his enterprise. He was to be fortunate. David Scott, a country merchant in the trade to China, was about to return to England in 1785, determined to attack the restrictions imposed by the East India

Company monopoly. Strange's scheme fitted in with his own plans for the development of Britain's trade to the East, and Scott immediately threw his weight behind it. Before leaving India he drew up a series of instructions for Strange, which were later submitted for Banks' consideration. Banks was also asked if he wished to issue Strange with instructions of his own.[38]

As with the Etches venture it was to consist of two ships, and supposedly to be a mixed commercial and scientific voyage. The vessels would proceed with a cargo to Macao as soon as fitted out, and leave for the north-west coast of America in the early spring of the following year. After touching at Nootka Sound, they would proceed north to latitude 56°N before continuing along Cook's track to Kamchatka and the coast of China.[39] Once the approval of the Bombay government had been obtained, Strange purchased two ships, which were named the *Captain Cook* (350 tons) and *Experiment* (150 tons). They were coppered and fitted out in line with the precedents laid down by Cook, and were well equipped with nautical and surveying instruments.[40] The command of the largest vessel was given to a Captain Laurie, the smaller to Captain Guise, although Strange was to go with the ships as the overall director of the enterprise.[41] Strange's instructions emphasised that the ships were specifically chosen and equipped for the purposes of discovery, and this was to be the prime concern of the voyage. The establishment of a channel of commerce with the north-west coast was professed to be a secondary consideration. However, Scott observed that because of the heavy costs of fitting the ships 'we recommend to you more strongly, the Subject of Commerce, than otherwise we thought We shou'd have occasion to do'.[42] In the event they were to succeed at neither.

Unbeknown to either Etches or Strange, someone was already on the north-west coast of America gathering furs. Captain James Hanna had made two voyages to the coast between 1785 and 1787. The first, in the 60 ton *Harmon*, had been relatively successful; the cargo of 560 skins selling for 20,000 Spanish dollars.[43] This was a good price, and the East India Company supercargoes at Canton wrote optimistically to the directors that the trade might 'prove of great Benefit to the Company Affairs here, by opening another Channel of Supply which in the present increasing State of their Investment they stand greatly in need of'.[44] Encouraged by this success, Hanna equipped a larger vessel, the 120 ton *Sea Otter*, but when he returned from his second voyage in February 1787, he brought with him a proportionately smaller cargo of 100 skins and 300 oddments which sold for only $8,000. James Strange had also returned to Macao by this stage and the supercargoes were able to make a cooler appraisal of the situation:

> We are sorry to observe that the hopes entertained of deriving some considerable Supply from the Fur Trade to the North West Coast of America are likely to prove delusive: there is no demand here for a large Quantity, & they appear to have been chiefly indebted to their Scarcity for the value which has sometimes been put upon them.[45]

Nothing would happen in the following eight years to change the supercargoes' opinions.[46]

Portlock and Dixon had mixed success. In their first season on the coast they arrived too late and in too high a latitude, thus shortening the season available for trade. Trade was further restricted by their inability to make a harbour in the region of Nootka Sound, and Portlock's plan of wintering on the coast and building a small schooner for inshore work had to be abandoned. On their return from the Sandwich Islands the second season, the two commanders persisted in searching for trade in the areas where Cook's ships had gathered the most furs, but they did take the sensible step of separating. By November 1787 both ships were at Canton, where the furs were sold through the East India Company. In February 1788 the *King George* and *Queen Charlotte* sailed for England with cargoes of tea and chinaware.[47]

Despite the boasted equipage of his two ships, James Strange seems to have been poorly prepared. Scarcely had he left Indian waters than the *Experiment* was holed as a result of inept seamanship, and both vessels 'were obliged to go to Batavia for repairs.[48] Nor did the medical stores and anti-scorbutics provide much protection, for the crews were debilitated by malaria and scurvy before they reached the American coast on 24 June 1786. Once again vessels had arrived on the north-west coast with much of the trading season over. After calling at Nootka, where he left a surgeon with the Indians, Strange headed north to Prince William Sound, before being driven from the coast by a gale in September. With scant regard for what was stated to be his primary aim — geographical discovery — the irresolute navigator headed for China, badly short of provisions, and with his crew incapacitated by scurvy. The

Experiment, which had been dispatched from Prince William Sound to find Copper Island, mentioned in Coxe's *Russian Discoveries*, arrived at Macao in December 1786, having failed to make her objective.[49] Back in India, Strange attempted to interest Sir Archibald Campbell in the development of the fur trade. One is left to speculate as to what inducements he offered.[50]

While on the north-west coast, these two expeditions had met with an even less fortunate venture organised from Bengal. James Meares, a lieutenant in the Navy, and Captain Tipping, had left Bengal in March 1786 in the *Nootka* (200 tons) and the *Sea Otter* (100 tons). Despite the usual reverent homage to Cook and his method, these were the most poorly-equipped vessels to fit out for that inhospitable coast. Short of stores and provisions, without a carpenter or boatswain between them, the two ships separated and headed for the coast hoping to effect a rendezvous in the region of Cook Inlet. Strange met the *Sea Otter* near Prince William Sound on 5 September 1786, and noted that both ship and crew were in poor condition.[51] Tipping was never to make the appointed rendezvous and his ship was not heard of again.[52]

Meares and his crew in the *Nootka* suffered a fate only a little less disastrous. In the middle of August they reached the north-west coast in the region of Unalaska. It was clearly ludicrous to arrive in such a high latitude so late in the season. On 20 September, with winter setting in, beset by gales and snow, and with his crew in a mutinous state, Meares decided to winter in Prince William Sound.[53] Eight months later Portlock and Dixon discovered Meares's vessel locked in the ice, with half the crew dead and the other half weak from hunger, scurvy, and an excessive resort to spirits for nourishment.[54] Although Portlock and Dixon gave some assistance, Meares gave them deliberately misleading advice about the fur trade and later castigated the two commanders for their lack of generosity.[55]

Undeterred by his setbacks, Meares obtained the support of two merchants at Macao for the equipment of another expedition after he had returned from the coast in October 1787. These men, John Cox and Daniel Beale, were under investigation by the supercargoes for being illegally in China, and although Beale managed to stay on as Prussian consul at Canton, Cox was later ordered out of China despite his pleas that deportation might be deferred as he had a 'variety of accounts unsettled'.[56] By 20 January 1788 the merchant proprietors, as they were called, had two ships fitted out and ready for sea. Wary of the exclusive rights given to the King George's Sound Company, it was decided that the two vessels, the *Felice* (formerly the *Nootka*) and the *Iphigenia*, should be given Portuguese registration and fly the Portuguese flag. They were nominally registered in the name of a local Portuguese merchant. Once again special attention was given to the fitting of the ships and the provision of anti-scorbutics. Once again the oceans provided the final test of preparedness; scurvy, mutiny and leaks in the ships had all taken their toll before they reached Nootka.[57] There a small schooner was built, while the two ships searched for furs. On 24 September the *Felice* returned to Macao via the Sandwich Islands with all the furs collected during the summer, and the *Iphigenia*, and the schooner, *North-West America*, left for Hawaii at the end of October, intending to winter there and return to the coast the following season.[58]

Meanwhile in England, Banks had become involved in another expedition being planned by Etches and his associates. Although no information had come through from Portlock or Dixon, Etches had decided in 1786 to fit out two more ships for the 1787 season. In July 1786, he approached Lieutenant James Colnett (who had been a midshipman on the *Resolution* during Cook's second voyage) with the offer of the command of a vessel to go to Nootka.[59] Once the permission of the government and the East India Company had been obtained, Etches purchased a ship of 171 tons and a schooner of 65 tons, which were inevitably named the *Prince of Wales* and *Princess Royal*.[60] During August the ships were repaired, provisioned and generally made ready for sea. To provide overall supervision of the Etches' concerns in the north Pacific, it was decided that John, brother of Richard Cadman Etches, should go with the *Prince of Wales* as supercargo. The pre-conditions for a crisis had been established.

On Banks' recommendation Etches agreed to appoint a surgeon with a knowledge of botany to the expedition. Initially this position was to go to a John Melvill, but late in August Melvill fell ill and Etches began looking for a substitute.[61] Banks was quickly able to provide one. Since May 1784 he had been corresponding with Archibald Menzies, a Navy surgeon who had received training in botany from Dr John Hope, a professor at Edinburgh. While on station at Nova Scotia and in the West Indies, Menzies had collected plant specimens for Banks' herbarium, and acquired a reputation as an able and energetic young man.[62] On returning to England in

August 1787, Menzies heard of the Etches expedition, and wrote to Banks: 'Should I be so happy as to be appointed Surgeon of her [*Prince of Wales*], it will at least gratify one of my greatest earthly Ambitions, & afford one of the best opportunity [sic] of collecting Seeds & other objects of Natural History for you & the rest of my friends.'[63] Banks was happy to oblige, and a fortnight later Menzies wrote again: 'I am happy to acquaint you that I am appointed Surgeon to an Expedition round the World.' He asked Banks for a set of instructions.[64]

Finding himself hampered by the restrictions which Etches had imposed on the crew with regard to private trade, Menzies asked Banks to intervene so that he might barter for plant and animal specimens. Etches was eager to conciliate so powerful a patron, and indicated that he would dispense with the restrictions in Menzies' case, 'so far as can have any tendency to be beneficial to science in general'.[65] He also mentioned to Banks the proposition put to him to carry a gentleman and his servant to Tahiti, and wondered if Banks knew of anybody else wishing to take such an opportunity. Nothing more came of this plan, but the ships did take another party on board. A Lieutenant Marshall of the Navy wished to be landed at Staten Island with a party of 15 men to start a seal and sea lion fishery. These men, with their equipment and stores were received on board the already crowded ships.[66]

The *Prince of Wales* and *Princess Royal* dropped down Channel on 16 October and headed for Cape Horn. At Staten Island Marshall and his crew were landed with their stores, and Menzies took the opportunity to wander around the island botanising. The two ships left Staten Island a fortnight later, and after rounding the Horn, headed north towards Nootka, making the coast off the Sound on 5 July.[67] This was a remarkable voyage. From their departure from Staten Island to their arrival at Nootka, the ships were at sea for a total of five months. There were, of course, the usual outbreaks of scurvy on board, but not a man died from its effects during the passage. All this in one vessel which was 36 years old, and another of only 65 tons, manned by 15 men.[68]

Colnett was surprised to find another vessel anchored in Friendly Cove; the *Imperial Eagle*, formerly the *Lowden*, which had been fitted out in the Thames in 1786, and had then registered at Ostend under Austrian colours.[69] Colnett showed a rather naïve indignation at the presence of a ship with an English captain (William Barkley) and crew, trading under foreign colours in an area in which the King

George's Sound Company had an exclusive trading right. But a part of his anger was due to the fact that Barkley had arrived at Nootka on 13 June 1787, and depleted the area of its fur supplies.[70] Three weeks after Colnett put into Nootka, Barkley headed south along the coast towards the Strait of Juan de Fuca before putting off for Macao.[71]

On clearing the Sound himself in August, Colnett sighted the *Queen Charlotte* about to make her passage to Hawaii and China. On Dixon's advice, Colnett decided to spend another season on the coast, and to centre his operations around the Queen Charlotte Islands where Dixon had been so successful. Returning from the Sandwich Islands in March 1788, Colnett headed for the higher latitude of Prince William Sound. During the passage from the Sandwich Islands he had separated from the *Princess Royal*, and although they both spent much of their time trading in the vicinity of the Queen Charlotte Islands, they did not meet up with each other until their return to Hawaii the following September.[72] It was in the region of the Queen Charlotte Islands that Menzies saw Indians with

a short warlike Weapon of solid Brass, somewhat in the shape of a Newzeland [sic] Pata-Patoo, about fifteen Inches long . . . embellished on one side with an Escutcheon inscribing Jos. Banks Esqr. — The Natives put a very high value on it, for they would not part with it for considerable offers; — The inscription & Escutcheonal embellishments, were nearly worn off, by their great attention in keeping it clean.

To commemorate the discovery Banks' name was given to a cluster of islands in the region.[73]

By 13 November 1788 both the *Prince of Wales* and *Princess Royal* were at Macao. There, while the supercargoes were arranging the sale of the furs, Colnett and John Etches came under the spell of the beguiling Meares, and his recently acquired partners. Doubtless influenced by the low prices the furs were reaching at Canton, Colnett and Etches entered into a combination with the merchant proprietors.[74] Meares obviously hoped to benefit from the East India Company licence. Under the terms of that licence the *Prince of Wales* was obliged to return to Europe in freight, but the *Princess Royal* had the right to return to the north-west coast to continue the trade and carry stores to any settlement there.[75] The new consortium then purchased a 120 ton snow (two-masted merchant vessel, rigged as a brig) for 9,000 Spanish dollars, and began fitting her out in the Typa. The share of Carvalho, the Portuguese partner in the Meares enterprise, was bought out, and henceforth all vessels in the consortium were to fly English colours and operate under the licence granted to Etches.[76] The new ship, named the *Argonaut* was to be commanded by Colnett, but as Captain Duncan wished to return to Europe, command of the *Princess Royal* was given to Thomas Hudson. Before these two ships sailed there were hints of the trouble to come. Hudson indicated that he would not be amenable to Colnett's instructions, and Colnett himself was dissatisfied with the instructions issued to him by Meares.[77] The *Argonaut* left Macao on 25 April 1789, the *Princess Royal* some weeks earlier.

The *Prince of Wales* had in the meantime been loaded with a cargo of tea and chinaware, and sailed from China on 1 February. She arrived in England in July 1789, after what Menzies described as a 'tedious Voyage round the Globe of near three years'.[78]

Save for the small building erected in Friendly Cove by Meares in the summer of 1788, there was no attempt by the traders to establish a permanent factory on the north-west coast of America, although such an establishment had been provided for in the 1785 negotiations with the East India Company.[79] The *King George* and *Queen Charlotte* had been equipped with extra stores and men for the establishment of a factory at Nootka, but Portlock and Dixon found themselves unable to carry out this aspect of their instructions owing to the contrary winds in their first trading season, and the failure to achieve a rendezvous in the second. Although Colnett was surprised to find there had been no base established when he anchored in Nootka Sound in July 1787, Etches himself does not seem in the first place to have been annoyed over this failure. He told Banks in July 1788 that Portlock and Dixon had not established a factory as 'their Powers of Government were not competent to the task — nor cou'd they form any Establishment with a certainty of it ever being prosperous, because they had not Powers to form any real Government for the regulating the People, consequently all wou'd soon have been Anarchy and Confusion'.[80] Later, in 1790 and 1792, Etches severely criticised the two commanders for their failure in this direction, but then he had a much greater axe to grind.[81] Nor did Strange establish a base, although he did land the surgeon, Mackay, later to be picked up by Barkley, and it was his intention initially to return to Nootka.[82]

In the summer of 1788 Etches had several discussions with Banks on the subject of forming a permanent settlement on the north-west coast of America. He obviously had in mind the convict colony being established at the time in New South Wales, and he must have been aware of Banks' central role in the foundation of that settlement. When the first accounts of Portlock's and Dixon's voyage reached England, Etches realised the disadvantages he was under compared to those men such as Barkley, who fitted out under foreign colours, or Strange and Meares, who operated under the auspices of the East India Company country trade. On 17 July 1788 Etches pointed out these deficiencies to Banks and sought his approval for a scheme which he believed would ameliorate their position. He suggested the establishment of a factory on the Queen Charlotte Islands, which Dixon had found to be particularly abundant in furs. This would serve as a place of annual rendezvous, and a base for four small shallops which would trade the length of the coast. It would be serviced by larger vessels running between Canton and the coast, bringing provisions for the settlement and carrying each season's supply of furs to market. Such a settlement would require some administration and protection, and it was on this point that Etches wished to solicit Banks' 'future endeavour to complete our Views — Protection from Government is what we presume to hope for'.[83] He suggested that Banks draw up a scheme which could be embodied in a memorial to the government. As the Pitt ministry had just established a colony in New Holland, Etches wondered if a similar convict settlement could be established on the north-west coast of America. If such a plan were approved he would undertake to freight out the convicts and stores, and hoped for a monopoly of the commercial aspect for such time as the government thought fit.

In the next two days Etches met Banks to discuss the above plan. Although happy to assist, Banks saw one great objection to the idea of establishing a convict settlement: the government would not be prepared to foot the bill. Etches remained enthusiastic, and on 20 July he put more suggestions to Banks. If the government would give him authority over the colony, costs could be kept to a minimum. Failing this a small armed vessel might be stationed permanently on the coast, carrying out surveys of the unexplored regions, and keeping a watchful eye on the convicts. As there was plenty of timber and provisions could be procured from Canton, the settlement would be easily maintained, and would serve as an admirable base for the fur trade. Once fully established it would increase the prospects of opening the Japanese market.[84]

In the following week Etches talked to some of the crew of the *Imperial Eagle,* who had just returned from Macao, and although he abandoned the idea of a convict settlement, the information he collected reinforced his plans for the establishment of a trading factory. On 30 July he again outlined his schemes to Banks. The *Imperial Eagle* had found a strait to the south of Nootka which tended north-eastwards towards the interior of the continent. This proved the validity of the accounts by De Fuca and De Fonte, and indicated that the whole coast 'is nothing but Islands'. Etches was here pursuing another, more subtle tack. In the same area Barkley had collected a profusion of furs. Etches again stressed the utility of forming small factories on the coast, and stated his willingness, 'To rely on Your kind assistance in the adopting any measure that can be conducive to permanent securing of the Commerce.'[85]

A week later Etches sought Banks' advice on another issue — the old chimera of the trade with Japan. In his letter of 20 July he had pointed out that Portlock and Dixon had been unable to try the Japanese market 'owing to the Season being too far advanc'd'.[86] However, his brother John had indicated his intention to take some furs to Japan should he return from the coast while the trading season at Canton was closed. Etches questioned Banks' on the chances of opening that market as he was about to write to his brother by the next ship to Canton. All the merchants in the maritime fur trade professed an interest in opening a trade with Japan. None effected it. Portlock and Dixon never mentioned the possibility in their journals, nor did Colnett in his voyage in the *Prince of Wales.* After his release by the Spaniards in 1790 Colnett did attempt to trade with the Japanese when he found the Canton market closed. He had no success. Of course while the opening of that market remained a possibility, the merchants continued to make much of it for propaganda purposes. This was especially the case during the negotiations with Spain over the Nootka crisis, when both Meares and Etches claimed the opening of the Japanese market had been imminent at the time of the seizure of their ships. Such claims were finally destroyed by Broughton's voyage in the *Providence* from 1795 to 1798.[87]

The brunt of the problem after 1790 was that it was wiser to make claims on Spain on the basis of potential, rather than actual losses, because, as the supercargoes in Canton had pointed out in 1787, the fur trade with China was a losing affair. There was, first, a geographical problem. The north-west coast of America was a great distance from Europe and India, and difficult to reach. Outfitting of the ships was, therefore, an expensive and troublesome business. For those like Strange and Meares who did not fit out their vessels adequately, the coast proved an inhospitable and brutal environment in which to trade, making the commerce a strictly seasonal matter.

Nor was the gathering of furs an easy task. The Indians with whom the merchants traded only collected furs for their domestic needs, and were not easily stimulated into hunting for them on a commercial basis. The usual pattern of the trade, therefore, was that in response to the merchants' offer of trinkets the Indians would disrobe, and hand over their clothes. Such a trade was made more difficult by the rise in Indian expectations once Western goods were introduced among them. Very soon the market became saturated with beads, and nothing but horsemen's caps and medals would suffice. The next season they would demand copperware and axes in return for their furs.[88] In his season on the coast in 1788, Colnett encountered just such difficulties, and noted in his journal that the 'Price commonly paid for skins was a piece of Iron three foot long & three Inches broad with beads and other trifling articles, but till they have found out some new want; I think few skins will be collected which we had convincing proof of this year, for not an Indian that had got his long knife & spear of Iron was at the pains to have kill'd single Otter, Capt Dixon last year procur'd Six or Eight hundred & Captain Duncan & self did not get one hundred.'[89] There was no way of regularising the supply of furs and the merchants were forced to seek out new regions each trading season.

The disposal of the furs in China was an even more difficult problem. Whether obliged to sell their furs through the East India Company or not, the merchants were prey to the vicissitudes of the Chinese market. Entry to that market was difficult, and to the European mind the methods of Chinese commerce were arbitrary and unfair. Colnett's experiences provide another example. When he returned to China in May 1791, after being released by the Spaniards, he found that the Chinese had imposed a total prohibition on the importation of sea otter skins, as it was believed that all such skins were purchased initially from the Russians, and those two countries were at the height of one of the periodic disputes which have marked their relationships to the present day.[90] Colnett decided to pursue the object that Etches had outlined as his main intention in 1785 — the opening of the trade with Japan. On 26 July he pulled out of the Typa and headed north.[91] By November he was back at Macao with a sad story. Not only had his attempts to trade with Japan been unsuccessful, but his ship had lost its rudder, and was falling apart with rot.[92] So unsound was she that Colnett was forced to run her aground lest she sank.[93] Knowing that the ship had been fitted out at Macao, the supercargoes asked for Colnett's authority to trade under the British flag, and demanded he produce his licence. The unfortunate commander still had his Admiralty licence, issued in respect of the *Prince of Wales*, but he had no certificate of registry. This was due, he explained, to the fact that he had not originally intended to return to China — a blatant lie. The rest of his papers had been kept by the Spaniards. The supercargoes accepted his story.

There remained the problem of the furs. A few had been disposed of at Chusan, but the bulk of the cargo remained, and as the prohibition on the sale of furs was still in force at Canton, Colnett threw himself on the mercy of the supercargoes. At the beginning of December it was decided to ship the furs back to England, and the whole cargo was loaded on the *General Coote*, East Indiaman, as part of the captain's private trade.[94] Colnett was to go along as a passenger.[95] In England the furs were offered to the East India Company at what Etches thought was a reasonable China price — $80 a skin (about £20). When it was found that the Company intended to buy the skins at an English price and ship them to China to make a profit, Etches and Meares expressed their indignation to Dundas, and appealed for government intervention.[96] The Company was in fact loath to take the skins at all and only acquiesced under pressure from Grenville, who wished to settle the long-standing affair. Eventually the cargo was purchased for £9,660, an average of eight guineas a skin — under half the price Etches and Meares expected.[97]

Certainly the Company was correct in assuming they would make a loss on the furs. They had paid the merchants almost twice the average price that Portlock and Dixon obtained in China. Etches' demand of $80 was clearly farcical, and perhaps based on his suggestion that the furs would make an ideal ingredient for Lord Macartney's gift-pack for the Emperor of China.[98] Ironically, when the Court of Directors attempted to dispose of the furs, along with others bought from the Hudson's Bay Company, they suggested to the supercargoes that they should be offered to the Hong merchants as a trial run. They expected no profit on the skins, but claimed that they had been induced to buy them 'with a view of facilitating the operations of Govt. in adjusting their claims with the Court of Spain'. Trade was now serving the ends of diplomacy. The wheel had turned full circle.[99]

But the basic weakness of the China market was that it was very limited. Cook's crew, even Hanna on his first voyage, had achieved good prices, but they had extremely small consignments. Thereafter the price of furs steadily declined, especially for large cargoes such as those offered by Portlock and Dixon. During the Nootka crisis of 1790, the subject of fur prices became a matter for debate. Meares, anxious to recoup his losses, inflated the average price obtained by each ship. Dixon and Dalrymple, each with his own axe to grind, gave figures closer to the truth.[100] In the final analysis even Meares grudgingly admitted that the trade had brought few advantages to the merchants, but this he claimed was the result of misfortune and bad management, and had meant that 'a very false idea has arisen, that the trade to the North West Coast of America is an unproductive business'.[101]

More information on prices is available for those cargoes which were sold through the East India Company, but the troubles of those concerned are not uncharacteristic of the trade as a whole. Portlock and Dixon offered their cargo of 3,020 furs to the supercargoes for $121,630. When the Hong merchants inspected the furs, however, their highest bid was only $50,000. Although the commanders had the option of leaving the furs in the care of the supercargoes to await better prices, they chose to accept the offer, although they observed that it was 'very inadequate to our expectations'.[102] As both vessels were pronounced fit to carry tea back to Europe, the Etches Company made something on the freight, and also a small amount on private sales of furs by the commanders. Portlock and Dixon benefited from the usual indulgence of private or 'privilege' trade granted to the captains of East Indiamen. The supercargoes took no commission on the sales, although duty was deductable.

Colnett fared little better in the 1788–9 season, although his initial bid was not as ambitious as that of his colleagues. He asked $79,713 for the total consignment of furs and cloaks, averaging about $40 a piece.[103] On offering the furs to the Hong merchants, the highest bid of $56,000 came from Shy Kinqua, who had taken Portlock's cargo. This was a better bid than that made to Portlock and Dixon, but it was still below expectations, and Etches and Colnett only grudgingly accepted it.[104] $9,520 obtained from small lots of furs sold on

Colnett's own initiative went towards the defraying of expenses at Canton and refitting the ship.[105] The *Prince of Wales* was freighted back to Europe at £11 per ton, and although Colnett did not accompany her he was granted an allowance of private trade.[106] £10,520 was granted to the merchants by the Company for fitting and victualling the ship, and this was deducted from the total profits which were advanced in bills on the Court of Directors.[107]

Although Hanna, Strange, La Pérouse and Barkley averaged higher prices, their gross return was low because of the small size of their cargoes. Their figures also disguise other losses. The cost of fitting the *Captain Cook* and *Experiment* was high and their crews large.[108] Meares had lost the *Sea Otter* with its cargo and crew, and lost part of his own crew. Although Hanna fitted out a much larger ship for his second voyage, his takings were under half those of his first. Barkley had one of the largest ships in the trade, with a large crew, and he suffered heavy losses when his vessel was hastily sold at Calcutta in 1788. Another voyage which he made in the ship *Halcyon* in 1791 and 1792 was also a loss.[109] La Pérouse was not officially on a commercial undertaking, and the able and unfortunate navigator later lost his ships, and his life, in the Pacific.

Ironically, the only ones to make a profit in the trade were the Russians. In rickety and ill-equipped ships their tough hunters crossed from Kamchatka to the Aleutians, gradually working their way across to the Alaskan mainland. With little interest in discovery or science, these men only progressed as far as was necessary to their commercial interests, and wherever they went they enslaved the local Indian or Eskimo populations, and compelled them to hunt for sea otters. Accustomed to Arctic conditions, they wintered in the field, and lived the sparse life of the natives themselves. In such a mode of operations, capital costs were kept relatively low and a constant supply of furs was maintained. Although the Russians too were subject to changes in the Chinese market, they had a different inlet, through the frontier town of Kyakhta, south of Lake Baikal, and a direct link from there with Peking. The home market provided a useful back-up to this trade.[110]

Although a few British ships participated in the trade after 1791, it was for the most part engrossed by the Americans and Russians. Even for them it declined after 1795 with the rapid and tragic slaughter of the sea otter.[111] One expedition after 1791 serves as a symbolic epitaph to the British aspect of the trade. Sydenham Teast, a Bristol merchant, sent the 74 ton *Jenny* on two voyages to the north-west coast of America between 1791 and 1794. On the first voyage she found the Canton market closed and returned to England with her furs; on the second no profit was made, and the East India Company refused to provide freight for the return to England. Undeterred, Teast in 1794 sent the 101 ton *Ruby* to the coast under Captain Charles Bishop. In Canton in 1795 Bishop found that the price of furs was low, and the cost of stores high, and the voyage turned into a total loss. After a more successful trade with Amboina in the period after its capture by the British, Bishop sold the *Ruby* and purchased another ship, the *Nautilus*, in which he again attempted to reach the north-west coast. On this occasion the attempt was abandoned because of contrary winds. Thus deterred, Bishop found his way to Tahiti, and later to New South Wales where he carried on a variety of trading enterprises. He appears to have been a somewhat naïve and irresolute seaman, and his erratic global meanderings could hardly be said to epitomise direction or intent in British imperial policy in this period. Bishop searched for profits on the north-west coast of America, but a variety of factors — low prices, storms and his own indecision — drove him to South-east Asia, Tahiti and New South Wales. It was New South Wales that seemed to offer the greatest promise, and it is perhaps more significant that Charles Bishop ended his imperial career as a farmer in the convict colony, than that he began it as a merchant adventurer in the north Pacific.[112]

Notes

1. On the instructions, which required Cook to survey only that part of the coast north of latitude 65°N, where, according to the prevailing theorists the passage was supposed to originate, see Beaglehole, *The Journals of Captain Cook on His Voyages of Discovery*, vol. III, i, p. lxvi. Also G. Williams, *The British Search for the Northwest Passage in the Eighteenth Century*, pp. 157–211.

2. On De Fuca and De Fonte, the legendary voyagers of the sixteenth and seventeenth centuries, see Beaglehole, ibid., vol. III, i, pp. xxxvii-xlvii, Williams, ibid., pp. 35-6, 81-2; W.L. Cook, *Flood Tide of Empire: Spain and the Pacific Northwest*, pp. 21–41.

3. For an account of the trade based on Russian sources, see H. McCracken, *Hunters of the Stormy Sea*. Also S.R. Tompkins and M.L. Moorehead, 'Russia's Approach to America', pp. 55-6, 231-55.

4. McCracken, ibid., p. 93.

5. Ibid., p. 98. Barrington, 'Journal of a Voyage of 1775', *Miscellanies*. Cook, *Flood Tide of Empire*, p. 81.

6. Beaglehole, *Journals of Captain Cook*, vol. III, ii, p. 1338. 100 roubles = about £20.

7. Ibid., p. 1108. He is, of course, referring to the sea otter.

8. Pallas to Banks, 3–14 September 1783, *Add. MSS.* 8097, fos 234–5. J.M. Matra to Banks, 28 July 1783, *Add. MSS.* 33977, fo. 206.

9. Sandwich to Banks, 16 September 1782, *D.T.C.* II, fo. 186. 'It would be deemed officiousness in me if I was to put myself forward in this matter, without your interference, as a middle man.'

10. Blagden to Banks, 22 December 1783–6 April 1784, *D.T.C.* II & IV.

11. Billings to Banks, 8 January 1783, *Kew B.C.* I, 122.

12. A.I. Alekseev, 'Joseph Billings', p. 235.

13. Pallas to Banks, 2/13 June 1785, *Add. MSS.* 8096, fos 148–9. M.A. Sauer, *An Account of a Geographical and Astronomical Expedition to the Northern Parts of Russia.* G.A. Sarytschew, *Account of a Voyage of Discovery to the North-East of Siberia, the Frozen Ocean, and the North-East Sea.*

14. Dixon to Banks, 27 August 1784, *D.T.C.* IV, fos 47–8.

15. Banks to Dixon, 29 August 1784, *D.T.C.* IV, fo. 49.

16. N.L. Hallward, *William Bolts. A Dutch Adventurer under John Company*, pp. 193–5.

17. *I.O. Home Misc.* 494, p. 366.

18. Etches to Banks, 14 March 1785, *Kew B.C.* I, 195.

19. J. Deutz to Banks, 18 February 1777, *Add. MSS.* 8094, fo. 143. N. Burman to Banks, 24 November 1778, fo. 139, C. Thunberg to Banks, 16 May 1779, ibid., fo. 261. On Thunberg's travels, C.P. Thunberg, *Travels in Europe, Africa and Asia.*

20. Taswell to Sydney, 23 March 1785, *I.O. Home Misc.* 190, pp. 617–18. c.f. V.T. Harlow, *The Founding of the Second British Empire 1763–1793*, vol. II, p. 420. Taswell had no connection with Etches.

21. N. Portlock, *A Voyage Round the World; but more Particularly to the North-West Coast of America*, p. 69.

22. *I.O. Home Misc.* 494, p. 359. Harlow, *Founding of the Second British Empire*, vol. II, pp. 421–4.

23. *I.O. Home Misc.* 494, p. 363.

24. Ibid., p. 365.

25. Ibid., p. 360.

26. Ibid., p. 362.

27. Ibid., p. 366.

28. Ibid., p. 369.

29. Harlow, *Founding of the Second British Empire*, vol. II, pp. 423–4.

30. *I.O. Court's Letters to China*, R/10, Vol. I, 13 December 1786. The convict ships were freighted back with tea at £10 per ton. The rates for Etches' vessel were initially £13, later falling to £11 on the *Prince of Wales.*

31. Portlock, *Voyage*, p. 5.

32. It was rumoured that Gore was to take command, see Broussonet to Banks, 16 June 1785, *Add. MSS.* 8096, fo. 51.

33. Etches to South Sea Company, 21 July 1785, *Add. MSS.* 25521, fo. 49, South Sea Company Papers.

34. Rose to South Sea Company, 28 July 1785, ibid., fo. 51.

35. Sydney to South Sea Company, 4 August 1785, ibid., fo. 52.

36. A copy of the licence is in *Add. MSS.* 25578, fos 134–40, Register of Instruments Under Seal. Also in *H.O.* 42/7.

37. Portlock, *Voyage*, p. 5.

38. Scott to Banks, n.d. 1785, *Add. MSS.* 33982, fo. 329. Scott to Banks, 1785, ibid., fo. 330.

39. *I.O. Home Misc.* 494, pp. 417–20.

40. Strange to Banks, 3 December 1785, *Kew B.C.* I, 215.

41. Instructions to Strange, *I.O. Home Misc.* 494, p. 420, dated at Bombay, 7 December 1785.

42. *I.O. Home Misc.* 494, p. 424.

43. G. Dixon, *A Voyage Round the World; but more Particularly to the North-West Coast of America*, xvii, 316–17.

44. *I.O. China Consultations* R/10, Vol. 15, p. 8, 1 March 1786.

45. Ibid., p. 43, 24 March 1787.

46. A Journal of Hanna's first voyage appears to have been circulating in England in 1786, see C. Blagden to Banks, 24 September 1786, *Add. MSS* 33272, fo. 12. According to Meares Hanna died in 1787, J. Meares, *Voyages Made in the Years 1788 and 1789 from China to the North West Coast of America*, p. lii.

47. See Portlock, *Voyage* and Dixon, *Voyage*.

48. J. Strange, 'Narrative of a Voyage', in *I.O. Home Misc.* 800. As they had been forced to call at Batavia, the original plan of calling at Macao was abandoned.

49. Copper Island: one of the two Kommandor Islands east of Bering Island. It was reputedly thick with copper ore. Guise was to take on a cargo.

50. Harlow, *Founding of the Second British Empire*, Vol. II, p. 431.

51. Strange, 'Narrative of a Voyage'.

52. This was the second English vessel lost in the trade. In July 1786, the snow *Lark*, Captain Peters, left Macao for the coast via Kamchatka. She was wrecked on an island in September 1786. Dixon, *Voyage*, p. xviii. Harlow confused the *Sea Otter* of Tipping with that of Hanna, and wrongly stated that Tipping made Macao, Harlow, *The Founding of the Second British Empire*, vol. II, p. 43, p. 432n.

53. Meares, *Voyages*, p. xii.

54. Ibid., p. xxxvi. Dixon, *Voyage*, pp. 154–7.

55. Dixon, ibid., p. 156. F.W. Howay, (ed.), *The Dixon-Meares Controversy*. Portlock asked the supercargoes to ensure that Meares discharged the men lent to him to navigate the *Nootka* to Macao, as it was possible Meares would attempt to retain them, an indication of the distrust between the two parties, *I.O. China Consultations* R/10, vol. 16, p. 150, 21 October 1787.

56. *I.O. China Consultations* R/10, vol. 16, pp. 440–3, 1 & 2 April 1788.

57. Meares, *Voyages*, pp. 25–6.

58. Ibid., pp. 104–15, 255, 334.

59. J. Colnett, 'Log aboard the Prince of Wales', *Adm.* 55/146, fo. 6.

60. Etches to Nepean, n.d. 1786, *H.O.* 42/7. *I.O. China, Court's Letters* R/10, Vol. I, 19 January 1787. Colnett, ibid., fo. 6.

61. Melvill to Banks, 21 October 1786, *Kew B.C.* I, fo. 248. Melvill claimed he was appointed by Lord Mulgrave on Banks' recommendation, a further example of the latter's participation in the affairs of the Etches consortium.

62. Menzies to Banks, 30 May 1784–8 June 1786, *Kew B.C.* I, 163, 175, 221, 234.

63. Menzies to Banks, 21 August 1786, ibid., 239.

64. Menzies to Banks, 7 September 1786, ibid., 243.

65. Etches to Banks, 29 September 1786, ibid., 246.

66. Colnett, 'Log', fo. 7. Menzies to Banks, 11 February 1787, *Kew B.C.* I, 259. Staten Island or Islas de los Estados off the tip of Tierra del Fuego, and now belonging to Argentina.

67. Colnett, 'Log', fos 51–110. Menzies to Banks, 11 February 1787, *Kew B.C.* I, 259.

68. On the health of the crews, Menzies to Banks, 14 July 1789, *Kew B.C.* I, 356.

69. Colnett, 'Log', fo. 117. Dixon, *Voyage*, pp. xix-xx. Meares, *Voyages*, pp. lv. Meares is inaccurate as to the dates on which the *Imperial Eagle* left Ostend, and arrived at Nootka.

70. Colnett, 'Log', fo. 119. He commented that Barkley had 'engrossed the whole trade & ruin'd ours'.

71. Colnett, 'Log', fo. 119. Williams, *British Search*, p. 218. W. Kaye Lamb, 'The Mystery of Mrs. Barkley's Diary', pp. 31–59.

72. Colnett, 'Log', fos 216–31. *I.O. Marine Records* 0,404, *Log of Prince Wales*,

5 August 1788 to 18 August 1788. By the terms of the agreement with the Company Etches was obliged to deposit copies of the logs with the Company.

73. Menzies to Banks, 14 July 1789, *Kew B.C.* I, 356. This copy of a New Zealand *patu* was a relic of Cook's third voyage, and as he had not landed on the coast near these islands, the club must have been obtained by trade with Nootka, or Prince William Sound or Cook Inlet to the north. Another of these clubs was found in New Zealand 30 years later; again the Maoris refused to part with it. Kendall to Banks, 10 July 1816, *Add. MSS.* 33782, fo. 111.

74. Harlow, *Founding of the Second British Empire*, vol. II, p. 436. F.W. Howay, (ed.), *The Journal of Captain James Colnett Aboard the Argonaut*, pp. 3–39 for the negotiations. The manuscript journal of the *Argonaut* is in *P.R.O. Adm.* 55/142.

75. *I.O. China, Court's Letters* R/10 vol. I, 19 January 1787. Also *Consultations* R/10, Vol. 17, pp. 138–9, 17 November 1788.

76. Howay, *Colnett Journal*, p. 18.

77. Ibid., pp. 24–7.

78. Menzies to Banks, 14 July 1789, *Kew B.C.* I, 356.

79. *I.O. Home Misc.* 494, pp. 361–2.

80. Etches to Banks, 17 July 1788 in F.W. Howay (ed.), 'Four Letters from Richard Cadman Etches to Sir Joseph Banks, 1788–1792', p. 131.

81. See below, Chapter 4.

82. Strange to Banks, 3 December 1785, *Kew B.C.* I, 215. Strange asked Banks for any instructions he might have relative to the voyage, and as this request came only a few days before the *Captain Cook* and *Experiment* sailed, Strange presumably considered staying long enough on the coast to make a reply effective.

83. Etches to Banks, 17 July 1788 in Howay, 'Four Letters', p. 132.

84. Etches to Banks, 20 July 1788, ibid., pp. 132–4.

85. Etches to Banks, 30 July 1788, ibid., pp. 135–7.

86. Etches to Banks, 20 July 1788, ibid., p. 134.

87. Meares, *Voyages*, pp. lxxxi. Etches to Banks, 6 May 1790, *Kew B.C.* II, 11. Etches to Banks, 19 May 1792 in Howay, 'Four Letters', pp. 137–8. For Broughton's expedition, see below, Chapter 4.

88. See the list of items Menzies gave to Banks in 1790, in which he suggested that ships going to the coast should take a blacksmith and forge to fashion copper and iron to the Indians' prevailing tastes, *H.O.* 42/16, 4 April 1790.

89. Colnett, 'Log', fo. 230. He was referring to the region of Queen Charlotte Islands.

90. H.B. Morse, *The Chronicles of the East India Company Trading to China, 1635–1834*, vol. II, p. 185. The prohibition was imposed on 13 March 1791, and lifted the following year. Because of this ban the *Jenny* of Bristol took her furs back to England in 1792, see below. p. 78.

91. *I.O. China Consultations* R/10, vol. 19, p. 7, 30 May 1791. Ibid., p. 8, 26 July 1791.

92. Colnett to J. Harrison &c, 3 November 1791, ibid., pp. 62–3.

93. Ibid., 25 November 1791, p. 86.

94. *I.O. China Consultations* R/10, vol. 19, p. 106, 2 December 1791.

95. Ibid., 3 December 1791.

96. Etches and Meares to R. Woodford, 24 August 1792, *H.O.* 42/21, fos 404–5. Ralph Woodford was the Commissioner appointed to negotiate a commercial treaty with Spain. See J. Ehrman, *The Younger Pitt*, pp. 481–514.

97. Woodford to Dundas, 12 September 1792, *H.O.* 42/21, 513–19.

98. Ibid., 405, 24 August 1792, *H.O.* 32/2, 3 August 1792.

99. Court of Supercargoes, 16 May 1793, *I.O. China, Court's Letters* R/10 Vol. III. That such an agreement had been reached is made clear in Grenville to

Dundas, 5 July 1792, *H.O.* 32/2. 'The parties made their acceptance of the other terms depend on this point.'

100. Meares' list of prices is in *H.O.* 42/16, 20 May 1790. Dalrymple's in *I.O. Home Misc.* 494, pp. 431–6. Dixon gives some in his *Voyage*, pp. 315–21. Meares' figures are about 15 per cent to 20 per cent higher.

101. Meares, *Voyages*, p. lxviii.

102. Portlock and Dixon to Browne &c, 1 January 1788, *I.O. China Consultations* R/10, vol. 16, pp. 300–1, ibid., 17 January 1788, p. 335; ibid., 19 January 1788, p. 346.

103. Etches and Colnett to Browne &c, 5 January 1789, ibid., vol. 17, pp. 210–11.

104. Ibid., 17 January 1789, p. 218; 2 January 1789, p. 221.

105. Ibid., 22–24 January 1789, pp. 221–3.

106. Ibid., 23 December 1788, p. 196; 26 December 1788, p. 200.

107. Ibid., 25 January 1789, p. 226.

108. Strange's furs sold for £24,000, but were left at Canton, after the ships returned to Madras, to be sold by the supercargoes. See F.W. Howay, 'The Voyage of the *Captain Cook* and the *Experiment*, 1785–1786', pp. 285–96. Hosie claims the expedition was a complete commercial failure, see J. Hosie, 'James Charles Stuart Strange and his Expedition to the North-West Coast of America in 1786'.

109. See Kaye Lamb, 'Mysteries of Mrs. Barkley's Diary'.

110. On the Russian trade, W. Tooke, *View of the Russian Empire During the Reign of Catherine the Second*, vol. II, pp. 126–35. W. Coxe, *Account of the Russian Discoveries between Asia and America*, pp. 10–15. Sauer, *Account*, pp. 170–81. S.D. Watrous (ed.), *John Ledyard's Journey Through Russia and Siberia 1787–1788*, pp. 66–8. McCracken, *Hunters*, p. 71, claimed profits from the Russian trade averaged £1,000,000 a year. S.R. Tompkins & M.L. Moorehead, 'Russia's Approach to America', pp. 55–66, 231–55.

111. On the ships in the trade, F.W. Howay, 'A List of Trading Vessels in the Maritime Fur Trade, 1785–1794', pp. 111–34. Also Howay, 'An Outline Sketch of the Maritime Fur Trade', *Canadian Hist. Assoc. Dept.*, 1932, pp. 1–14.

112. See M. Roe, (ed.) *The Journal and Letters of Captain Charles Bishop . . . 1794–1799* for the details of these voyages and the subsequent account of Bishop. I differ with Dr Roe, however, on Bishop's place in the 'swing to the east'.

4 GOVERNMENT INTEREST IN THE NORTH PACIFIC

Although merchant interest in the fur trade declined somewhat after 1790, the continuing misfortunes of the Etches-Meares consortium were to precipitate the British government into a confrontation over territorial claims in the north Pacific, leading to the voyage of Vancouver, 1791–5, and the important but less well-known voyage of the *Providence*, 1794–8. It has been customary to regard this activity as a logical extension of merchant enterprise and, therefore, as an example of empire following trade. Such a view was propagated by men like Dalrymple, Etches and Meares who, for a variety of reasons, wanted government intervention. But until the Nootka crisis of 1790 the Pitt ministry had steadfastly refused to be involved in the affairs of the merchants and this seemed to be justified by the poor reports of the maritime fur trade sent back by the supercargoes at Canton, by Portlock and Dixon, and then in 1789 by the crew of the *Prince of Wales*.[1]

Whatever its reservations, a few determined men were endeavouring to stimulate government interest in the north-west coast of America and to obtain support for the fur trade. As the various reports came back to England in the 1780s, Alexander Dalrymple, hydrographer to the East India Company, became convinced that the north-west passage to China was a reality, and he found an informed and enthusiastic ally in George Dixon.[2] Early in 1789 Dixon published *A Voyage Round the World*, which not only described the voyage of the *Queen Charlotte* and *King George*, but gave a general account of the fur trade. Later the same year Dalrymple's *Plan for Promoting the Fur Trade*, drawing heavily on Dixon's experience, stressed the possibility of a north-west passage and put forward ideas for the regulation of the fur trade.[3] Dalrymple believed the trade had been unsuccessful only because of a lack of organisation, and he advocated co-operation between the East India and Hudson's Bay Companies, in which the former would send their ships from China to collect furs on the north-west coast which had been gathered by Hudson's Bay Company agents. Above all it was necessary that the trade be kept out of Canadian hands, for if those traders, 'reach the South-Sea, it is highly probable they would, in conjunction with emigrants from the United States of America, in course of time, establish themselves on that Sea, and carry on the Trade independant of this Kingdom'.[4]

In the first half of 1789 Dalrymple and Dixon submitted a plan to the Home Office for crossing America by way of Quebec or Hudson Bay. This was a revised version of a scheme which Dixon had put to Banks in 1784.[5] In July, after discussions with Nepean and Dalrymple, Dixon conceded that it was too late in the season for a crossing of the continent from the east, but he suggested that the government send a ship via Cape Horn to make a settlement on the north-west coast so as to avoid the possibility of the fur trade being engrossed by the many foreigners operating in the north Pacific. These arguments were strengthened by Captain Duncan's return to England in the summer. According to some reports he had navigated the tiny *Princess Royal* up various inlets on the north-west coast between 48°N and 55°N, and in some cases he had sailed 50 or 60 miles without getting soundings.[6] In September a memorandum was submitted to Nepean pressing the need for a settlement on the coast to establish British control of the fur trade. The dangers of foreign competition were raised again, and it was asserted that the Russians already had a factory in Cook Inlet, and the Spanish one at Nootka. In times of war an establishment on the coast would be valuable for attacking Spanish settlements and trade.[7]

There was much speculation in the autumn of 1789, as to whether Captain Robert's expedition to the South Atlantic was actually to sail to the north Pacific, more particularly as both Banks and Archibald Menzies were known to be involved in the fitting out of the ship. On 12 September, Patrick Wilson, Professor of Anatomy at Glasgow, wrote to James Lind the physician, seeking information on behalf of a friend who had seen 'lately announced in the publick Prints a new Attempt after the *North West Passage* under the auspices of *Sir Joseph Banks*, he has begd of me to procure him, if I could do so with propriety, some information as to the reality of such an Expedition'.[8] Wilson suggested that Nootka might be a suitable place for the disposal of convicts.

So confident was Dixon that an expedition was in the offing, that he too fell prey to these rumours, and in October suggested to Banks that Roberts be accompanied by two small schooners suitable for inshore work, and that a settlement be established in the region of the Queen Charlotte Islands. The Pacific between the American coast and Japan should also come within the scope of the survey, as it was thought that some large islands in that expanse of ocean might form the breeding colonies for the sea otter. Dixon enclosed additional information on the fur trade, with notes of recent discoveries on the north-west coast.[9] Yet another plan for a convict settlement was forwarded to Banks in November.[10]

Initially, the government showed to sign of yielding to this pressure, but in 1790 events on the north-west coast of America forced a change in its attitude. Early in January a despatch from Madrid informed the ministers of the seizure of British vessels at Nootka Sound by a Spanish commodore. Two Spanish ships, the *Princesa* and the *San Carlos*, had arrived in the Sound on 5 May 1789 under the command of Don Etienne Joseph Martinez, with the ostensible purpose of forming a settlement to forestall any Russian or American occupation. In the Sound at this time were three other vessels; two American traders, the *Columbia* and the *Washington*, and a ship belonging to the Etches-Meares consortium, the *Iphigenia*, which was still flying Portuguese colours. Another ship owned by the consortium, the *North-West America*, was at the time gathering furs to the north of Nootka. During May Martinez examined the papers of the various ships and seemed initially satisfied as to their *bona fides*. Shortly after this he seized the *Iphigenia* on the pretext that she had anchored in a Spanish domain and violated Spanish sovereignty, but two weeks later, almost as though her detention was too much of a burden, he released her on the condition that she sail immediately for Macao or the Sandwich Islands. Douglas ignored this injunction by gathering furs to the northward before putting off for Hawaii. Shortly after the *Iphigenia* sailed, the tiny *North-West America* put unawares into Nootka only to be seized and have her furs confiscated. From this point onwards the actions of both sides became confused and erratic while the Americans stood by and observed events with disinterested amusement. In mid-June Captain Hudson arrived in the *Princess Royal*, but after a few questions from Martinez he was allowed to depart, apparently on friendly terms. The tactless Captain Colnett sailed blithely into the spider's web on 4 July 1789 in the *Argonaut*. At first he and Martinez observed all the common civilities, but soon the unguarded territorial assertions of the one, and the hotheaded chauvinism of the other, provoked a confrontation. On 5 July the Spaniard clapped Colnett in irons and took his ship. The *Princess Royal*, senselessly returning six days later, suffered the same ignominious fate. In mid-July the *Argonaut* and *Princess Royal* were sent with

Spanish crews to San Blas in Mexico, while the *North-West America* was used by the Spaniards for trading voyages along the coast.[11]

This sequence of events was close to comic opera, but it begs some comment. Both Martinez and Colnett seem to have been confused as to their respective rights and duties. Martinez was obviously perplexed by the Portuguese registration and English crew of the *Iphigenia*, and lacked the confidence to detain the vessel. The case of Colnett seemed more explicit. Meares had issued instructions for the establishment of a permanent settlement at Nootka, involving a treaty with a local chief and the construction of a storehouse and fortifications. To assist in this work, and in the assembling of a schooner in frame on board the *Argonaut*, 29 Chinese artificers had been included in the crew. Although Captain Hudson must have been aware that the intentions of Martinez were ambiguous, to say the least, he did little to warn Colnett of the dangers he was sailing into, and the latter entered Nootka Sound apparently oblivious to the very evident signs of trouble. To make the task of Martinez easier, Colnett made no attempt to disguise his intention to establish a settlement, although the nature of his stores and crew might anyway have aroused suspicion.

Martinez did not have clear instructions as to how to behave towards the English, and he initially told the Americans, and Colnett, that his purpose was to forestall the Russian drive down the coast.[12] It may have been significant that all the vessels involved in the seizure were small, and obviously no commander would risk his ships and men if the odds were heavily against him. The largest English vessel was the *Iphigenia* of 200 tons, which had been allowed to depart by Martinez. The *Argonaut*, according to Colnett, was only 120 tons, while the two schooners, the *Princess Royal* and *North-West America*, were both between 50 and 60 tons, and had difficulty in defending themselves against the Indians much less the Spaniards. The two Spanish ships shared only 42 guns between them, and the snow *San Carlos* seems to have been under 100 tons. Ironically, the two American vessels comprised the largest force on the coast. The *Columbia*, 300 tons, and the *Washington*, 100 tons, may have escaped seizure partly because of their size, although their commanders were more diplomatic than their English counterparts. It was not likely that the Spanish government was looking for a conflict at this time, and it appeared later that there was much confusion in the Spanish government at Mexico, and weaknesses in the chain of command from Madrid. To Spain, as to England, the whole matter was the cause of much embarrassment.[13]

Confusion and embarrassment continued to be the keynotes of the whole affair. On 1 February the Duke of Leeds sent vague details of the seizure to Home Secretary Grenville.[14] Merry, the consul in Madrid, had attempted to obtain more specific information from the Spanish Foreign Minister, Count Florida Blanca, but the latter refused to explain the particulars of the events at Nootka, and would not clearly admit that any vessels had been captured.[15] Until the arrival of John Meares from Canton in April, Britain was therefore largely in the dark about the exact nature of the happenings on the north-west coast, and relied on news filtered through from Mexico to Spain, and passed on to London by Merry: all by courtesy of the Spanish government. Operating in such a vacuum imposed its frustrations and tempted Leeds to weaken his tactical position by demanding the release of the ships before the facts were fully known.[16] Spain, on the other hand, was able to take a strong line. On 10 February Del Campo, her ambassador in London, officially notifying Leeds of the seizure, claimed prior discovery and occupation of Nootka Sound, challenged Britain's right to trade in the seas in that area, and requested that British merchant interlopers be controlled.[17]

Being thus handicapped in the diplomatic field, the Pitt ministry planned another course of action. It was decided that a force should be sent to the north-west coast of America to seek a clarification of the episode, and to establish a settlement there so as to present Spain with a *fait accompli*. This was the real genesis of the later Vancouver expedition.

Grenville was not prepared to undertake such a mission without some assurance that the Spanish claims of prior discovery could be effectively countered, and in the middle of February he approached Banks for background information on the incident. In his reply of 15 February, Banks pointed out that the Spanish voyage of 1775, referred to in Del Campo's letter, had not landed at Nootka, and in answer to the general Spanish claim to the whole coast, he noted that the narrative of the voyage described 'a grand ceremony by which the Spaniards took possession of a Harbour in Latitude 41° 7' which seems as if they did not then consider themselves as entitled to the whole Coast'.[18] Fortified by this information Grenville asked Nepean to draft a plan of an expedition which could be submitted to the cabinet.

Nepean's proposals were embodied in a draft secret memorandum to the Admiralty drawn up in the week before 23 February. He suggested that the *Gorgon*, a 44-gun ship which had been prepared to carry troops and supplies to New South Wales, and was at the time ready for sea, should sail for the north-west coast via Port Jackson. The Admiralty would be directed to prepare the ship for such a voyage, and to have her lower deck guns, which had been removed as a part of her original mission, taken on board and stowed in her hold. Because of recent rumours that two more ships had left Spain for the north-west coast, it was thought proper to give the *Gorgon* some support. The crucial question was how much? Nepean put forward a flexible proposal. As the *Discovery* was ready for sea she would accompany the *Gorgon* as far as the Cape, 'particularly as her departure will not be likely to create a suspicion of the intended operation'.[19] On arrival there the *Gorgon* would meet the frigate *Vestal*, returning from India and these two vessels would head for Nootka. In this case the *Discovery* would begin her exploration of the south Atlantic as formerly directed. If the *Vestal* had left the Cape by the time the other vessels arrived, the *Discovery* was to continue with the *Gorgon* on to Port Jackson. On arrival there another option opened up, for if the guardship on duty at Port Jackson, the *Sirius*, was seaworthy, she would accompany the *Gorgon* and some of the *Discovery*'s men and stores would be transferred to her. To assist the *Gorgon* and her consort, a surveying vessel would be sent out from England in the spring or early summer. Once on the northwest coast the commander of the expedition was to establish contact with the Spanish ships and also establish whether any British vessels had in fact been seized.

Nepean's plan presupposed a need for urgent action. The *Discovery* and *Gorgon* were immediately seized upon as they were on the point of sailing at the time, and would require little in the way of re-equipment. It was recognised that the *Discovery*'s size and firepower were insufficient to the task, and consequently her attendance was in the nature of a stopgap, should the more powerful *Vestal* and *Sirius* not be available. Before the onset of the Nootka crisis the *Discovery* was not intended, as Harlow and the various biographers of Vancouver suggest it was, to go to the north-west coast of America.[20] It is certainly not true that the 44-gun warship *Gorgon* was going as an 'armed escort' to the 10-gun sloop *Discovery*.[21]

Nepean's plan was discussed at a cabinet meeting called to review the crisis on 23 February. Leeds' reply to Del Campo was considered and it was agreed that some naval expedition was necessary.[22] But for various reasons Nepean's plan was found to be inadequate. It was found that the *Vestal* had already left the Cape on her passage to England, and the *Guardian*, a storeship going to New South Wales with provisions for the settlement and naval stores for the *Sirius*, was wrecked in December 1789, barely a week after leaving the Cape.[23] Finally, it was thought that in view of the increasing seriousness of affairs, a much larger force would be necessary. During, or as a result of the Cabinet discussions, Grenville drew up an alternative plan, substantially modifying Nepean's proposals.[24] In this scheme the *Discovery* was definitely to accompany the *Gorgon*, and Commodore Cornwallis, on station in the East Indies, was to detach one of the two frigates in his squadron to a rendezvous point in Hawaii. In the spring of 1791 these vessels would proceed to the north-west coast and establish a settlement in the most favourable position. This done, the *Gorgon* would return to Port Jackson while the other two ships surveyed the coast between 40°N and 60°N with a view to finding a communication eastwards. In most other respects the expedition would follow the lines of Nepean's draft.

Two days after the cabinet meeting orders were sent to Commodore Cornwallis, placing him under the direct command of the Secretary of State. In March the same orders were sent to Governor Phillip.[25] Secret instructions were drafted for Captain Roberts of the *Discovery*. These were not to be opened until the ship had sailed, and they announced the postponement of his original design, and his employment in 'a more distant part of the world'. Roberts himself was to convey the despatches to New South Wales and there place himself under Phillip's orders.[26]

Full instructions based on the new draft plan were drawn up in March. These instructions — to Phillip, Cornwallis, and the commander of the frigate to be despatched from the East Indies — gave detailed plans of the type of settlement to be established, and the nature of the surveying work to be carried out. Phillip was to equip the *Gorgon* with her guns and with such stores and provisions as would be sufficient to 'fulfill the object of forming such a Settlement as may be able to resist any attacks from the Natives, and lay the foundation for an establishment for the assistance of His Majesty's subjects in the prosecution of the Fur Trade from the N Wt. Coast of America'.[27] Thirty additional persons from New South Wales would be initially sufficient for this establishment, and the contingent could be placed under a discreet subaltern officer.

Should the vessels miss the appointed rendezvous with the frigate, the senior officer on the *Gorgon* or *Discovery* was to open the secret instructions and proceed accordingly. If either of these two vessels were disabled, then the *Sirius* was to be sent in place of the *Gorgon*, and 'any light vessel in place of the *Discovery*'. Almost as an after-thought, Grenville proposed that the *Gorgon* should stop at the Society Islands on her return to New South Wales in order to appre-hend the *Bounty* mutineers.

Governor Phillip would have been far from pleased with such orders. His reprobate little colony was desperately short of provi-sions, stores and men, and the *Sirius*, and the small tender *Supply*, were constantly employed in procuring provisions. Although the ministry was not to learn of it until several months later, the *Sirius* foundered on a reef at Norfolk Island on 19 March 1790.[28]

The fullest account of the proposed settlement was in the in-structions to the commander of the frigate. After the rendezvous with the other vessels, he was to proceed to Queen Charlotte Sound in 51°N where it was believed there was 'a considerable River or navigable inlet into the interior Country'.[29] If this was found to exist, the settlers were to be landed with their arms, stores and provisions. The whole coast from Cape Mendocino to Cook Inlet was then to be thoroughly surveyed, with a particular eye for any rivers or inlets likely to provide a communication with the interior. As the *Discovery*, and the vessel in frame aboard her were of a smaller class, and particularly suited to surveying, they were to be extensively used. When winter approached the *Gorgon* was to return to New South Wales, and the *Discovery* and frigate were to winter on the coast, or at the Sandwich Islands, so as to complete the survey the following summer. If the squadron should meet any Spanish vessels and establish that British ships and subjects had been seized, immediate restitution was to be demanded. If the Spaniards should become aggressive, strong resistance was to be offered and if pos-sible the Spanish vessels were to be captured.

To complement this survey by sea it was intended that two over-land parties should set out the following spring using Hudson's House and Lake Arathapescow as their bases. They were to proceed by way of the numerous rivers towards the west coast.[30] These two parties would rendezvous with the ships on that coast, giving them valuable information as to the best place for a settlement, and assisting them to complete the survey. This idea possibly developed from a plan Dalrymple put to Nepean in February suggesting that an expedition should be sent out from Hudson Bay.[31] Although the government was not prepared to finance such a venture, it was willing to supply two men to head the expedition if the Hudson's Bay Company would underwrite the scheme. At Dalrymple's insistence, the Company agreed, and Charles Duncan and George Dixon were chosen to lead the expeditions. The approach through Hudson Bay was a well-tried one, and it is doubtful whether the company really expected substantial discoveries to be made. However, they had another object in view. Their posts around Hudson Bay were being cut off from their fur supplies by the energetic Canadian trappers moving rapidly across the continent to the south. Duncan's and Dixon's expeditions would open up new routes westwards which would enable the Hudson's Bay Company to establish itself in the fur-rich Athabaska country, and to forestall the traders from Montreal. Unfortunately, when Duncan arrived at Churchill in September 1790, he found the vessel intended for his use was virtually derelict, and he was obliged to wait a further year before his voyage could get underway. Dixon's expedition was later cancelled.[32]

To assist in the establishment of a settlement on the north-west coast of America, various articles of trade were to be supplied to the *Gorgon, Discovery* and the frigate, and in March Nepean approached Banks for guidance as to what articles would be most appropriate. As has been shown, this was a difficult problem, and Banks sought the advice of his protégé Archibald Menzies, recently returned from the coast in the *Prince of Wales*. On 4 April Menzies produced a suitable list of articles and suggested that a blacksmith and forge should be taken with the expedition so that iron and copper could be fashioned into patterns according to the prevailing tastes of the Indians.[33] Banks incorporated these suggestions in a list dispatched to the Home Office. On 12 April this was sent to the Admiralty with covering notes by Grenville. It was unusual for the Admiralty to undertake such purchases, but Grenville explained: 'I mention the Admy rather than the usual form of entry to the Treasury, as I imagine the former has a *secret* department thru which such business passes.' Even if the supply of articles was arranged publicly through the Admiralty it would not arouse suspicion 'as they might be supposed to be for the use of Phillip, to enable him to open an intercourse with the natives'.[34]

Banks' calculation as to the total cost of the articles came to £6,800, and it is obvious that such a quantity would have been sufficient to satisfy the trading requirements of a moderately sized settlement for some time. Grenville observed:

> If Sr. J. Banks forms the estimate of 6800£ on any first ground of calculation it seems very desirable not to stint that part of the service as the articles in question will be so very necessary to the Settlement to be formed . . . I can see no advantage that can arise from putting any part of them into the hands of the Sailors or Petty Officers, but perhaps I am wrong in this, & if I am Sr J.B. can certainly set me right. But I should feel particularly concerned if any part of the plan should fail from an ill-judged economy in this respect.[35]

Some of these articles were to be shipped aboard the *Gorgon* and *Discovery*, the remainder were to be taken out to Commodore Cornwallis. On 27 April Grenville wrote to the chairman of the East India Company enclosing a list of 20 tons of trading articles which were to be shipped to Madras on the *Foulis*, East Indiaman, already waiting for a wind at Gravesend.[36]

But it was now two months since the crucial cabinet meeting of 23 February, and the original plan had been that the vessels should sail before the month was out. Certainly the *Gorgon* and *Discovery* seemed ready for sea, and as early as 8 February orders had been given to Admiral Roddam, on station at Portsmouth, for the *Gorgon*'s lower deck guns to be taken on board and stowed in her hold.[37] In the first week of March, however, fate overwhelmed the enterprise with a heavy, and rather pestilential hand. A violent outbreak of fever occurred among the troops on board the *Gorgon*. Roddam recounted the events in a letter to the Admiralty of 4 March.[38] Two surgeons from ships of the line lying at Spithead had immediately been sent on board, and they confirmed the outbreak, stating in their report that nine of the troops had gone down with a putrid fever, and would have to be removed. This critical situation was explained by one of the surgeons in a report of 9 March:

> The situations of a fresh levied body of Men, exposed to the Jail Fever under the circumstances of a long sea Voyage, a crowded Ship, & the little advantages which any assistance can therefore afford, requires that the necessary precautions be adopted before the Ship leaves Harbour.[39]

The ministry treated the matter very seriously, aware that a delay at this juncture could be critical. Grenville demanded frequent reports on the state of the ship, and ordered that the surgeons' requests for fresh meat and fruit for the men should be immediately complied with. But it was not until 11 April that the surgeons were able to report that the men were fully recovered, and could 'return to the *Gorgon* that she may proceed to sea'.[40]

It was too late. By early April John Meares had arrived in England with his inflated account of events at Nootka, and the Pitt ministry, previously starved of information, proved too eager to take his testimony at face value. On 30 April Meares' memorial on the events on the north-west coast of America was put into Grenville's hands, and the public clamour began.[41] At about the same time intelligence came through from the consuls at Leghorn and Lisbon that Spain was mobilising the fleet. On 1 May 1790 the government called for a general armament, the fleet was ordered to be got ready for sea, and the proposed expedition to the north-west coast of America was abandoned.[42]

There is no need to discuss in detail the events of May-October 1790. The conflict was basically over the principle of freedom of navigation in the Pacific. National honour was also involved. It was not essentially a dispute over territorial interests. In fact, it seems to have been the realisation that the piece of land under discussion was unimportant which pulled both sides back from the brink. The British government showed only a vague interest in the maritime fur trade, and little the traders themselves could do would alter this situation. From Calais on 6 May Richard Cadman Etches bewailed the course of events to Banks and asked for assistance in making good his losses.[43] Characteristically, he claimed that the fur trade had been doing particularly well at the time of the Spanish seizure. The union with Meares had eliminated competition and much enlarged the capital of the enterprise, enabling Colnett to be extensively equipped. Had only Portlock and Dixon followed their orders to establish a settlement, their efforts 'wou'd have render'd abortive the attempts of all Competitors, and made my fortune'. He then sought to curry Banks' favour by pointing out the probability of great discoveries in that region. There was also the immediate prospect of accomplishing that long hoped for object, 'the Opening an intercourse with the Japanese Islands for the Sale of our Furs and American produce'. As a 'warm and strenuous patronizer of the first Enterprize', Etches exhorted Banks to contribute his efforts towards obtaining restitution.[44]

The problems of the trade must have become apparent at the Board of Trade meeting of 27 May which Meares was called to attend.[45] Meares was nothing if not a subtle propagandist. He had followed up his presentation of the memorial to Grenville, by sending him a copy of his narrative, *Voyages Made in the Years 1787 and 1788*. A copy was also sent to Hawkesbury.[46] On 20 May Meares produced a detailed account of fur sales at Canton, as well as an estimate of the value of furs annually introduced into China through Kyakhta, and his testimony before the Board naturally presented a flattering view of the trade. As well as furs, the north-west coast of America was rich in whales, seals and ginseng, and some of these articles could be purchased from the Indians who were particularly receptive to British goods. The Committee remained sceptical, to say the least, and it was particularly reserved about the possibility of opening the Japanese market. The fur prices given by Meares were higher than those sold through the East India Company and on Meares' own testimony it was not a trade which could stand much competition.[47]

Such negative findings provided little comfort for a ministry confronted with an inflamed public opinion and an opportunist opposition. In June the situation looked particularly bleak, and Leeds grimly wrote to Pitt that war could scarcely be avoided without a disgrace to one of the parties concerned. Fitzherbert's despatches from Madrid confirmed this impression, and presented the picture of a 'King and his Ministers bent on war and only waiting for Britain's first move'. At home little progress could be made through Del Campo, for as Leeds told Robert Walpole in Lisbon, he had found how 'little calculated he is either to serve his own Court with Effect, or to conciliate the Friendship of a foreign one'.[48] Meanwhile, the dispatches flowed endlessly between London and Madrid, reaching such a level that Leeds could sardonically remark on a despatch 'not much more voluminous than Postlethwayte's Dictionary. Heaven forbid the Discussion with Spain should be long in Proportion to it.'[49]

Fortunately this was not to be the case. An agreement signed by the two powers on 24 July provided hopeful signs that things might be accommodated, and Grenville felt sufficiently confident to notify the City of this improvement.[50] From that point on the object of the negotiations was to work out a face-saving formula and an agreement to protect the rights of British seamen generally. When a

Convention was finally signed between the two powers on 28 October, the territorial arrangements about Nootka were vague to the point of being meaningless. Compensation for the injured merchants was provided for, but Spain managed to fend the matter off and the Pitt ministry was not so proprietary over the interests of the fur traders as to press the point. The 'southern whalers', as has been shown, gained much more from the Convention.

Although the Convention of 28 October provided for the restitution of the buildings and parcels of land occupied by Spain in 1789, no definite plans seem to have been made before December for an official acceptance of the restitution.[51] However, rumours were circulating to the effect that a ship would be sent to the north-west coast of America to carry through the formalities, and to follow up the work of Cook. As early as 9 November the Marquis of Buckingham asked Grenville to secure a place for young Thomas Pitt on such a ship:

> I am still very partial to the idea of sending him to the North-west coast of America, concluding that you will (immediately upon this convention, and the time of the year is particularly fit for it) send an able and proper officer to see Nootka restored, and to endeavour to push the discovery of those seas and shores as far as he can go eastward.[52]

By 11 December it was clear that planning for such a voyage was underway, for on that day the *Discovery*'s voyage to the south Atlantic was indefinitely postponed, and that ship, and its tender, the *Chatham*, were appropriated for an expedition to the north Pacific. The reasons for this change were probably those of convenience. The *Discovery* and *Chatham* were suitable vessels for such a survey, and as they were ready for sea no time would be lost in getting them under way.

As Captain Roberts was still intent upon the survey of the south Atlantic, Lieutenant George Vancouver was appointed to command the *Discovery*. Nathaniel Portlock was offered the command of the *Chatham* because of his previous experience on the north-west coast, but he declined for health reasons and the position was accepted by Lieutenant William Broughton.[53] The alteration in the destination of the ships upset Archibald Menzies, who wrote to Banks recounting the change of plan and asking whether he was to go with Roberts or Vancouver: 'I need not observe the necessity of obtaining the information soon that if I go in the latter [*Discovery*] I may have some time to equip for the voyage.'[54]

Nepean drew up a plan for the new expedition in December, guided by a draft memorandum on surveying submitted by Banks. The ships were to proceed by way of Cape Horn and the Sandwich Islands, making the north-west coast in the latitude of Nootka, where the restitution was to take place. Once the formalities were over, the Strait of Juan de Fuca 'which is supposed leads into a Sea of great extent', was to be surveyed and the River Oregon, which was thought to fall into this sea was to be traced, as it 'promises to afford the readiest communication with the Lake of the Woods, and the Western parts of Canada'. When a suitable site had been selected, the commander of the expedition was to purchase land from the local chief and form an establishment which would serve as a commercial base and a communications post with the interior. The main aim was to secure to Britain 'the possession of those parts which lye at the back of Canada and Hudson's Bay, as well as the Navigation by such Lakes as are already known or may hereafter be discovered'. Another object was to forestall American attempts to establish bases in the area. The base was to be fortified to withstand the attacks of Indians, Americans or other foreign powers.[55]

By the time this had been done, winter would be approaching and the ships would sail to the Sandwich Islands. Here they were to rendezvous with one of the Navy's 44-gun ships which would be sent out later in the year with stores, provisions, troops and women; all to be taken to the proposed settlement 'for the purposes of protecting Merchant Adventurers who may have occasion to resort to that place'. After these stores were landed the survey ships would continue their work, while the 44-gun ship loaded timber for masts and spars, with which it would return to England.

There was no guarantee that such a plan would be accepted by the whole cabinet. The expense of such an undertaking could not be justified once the Spanish threat had been removed and it was realised that the fur trade did not warrant government support. A fortified settlement was also likely to jeopardise the amicable relations with Spain re-established by the Convention. Ironically, the fear that the United States would extend its territory west along a line from the Lake of the Woods was to arise in the nineteenth century. In any case, it was decided to let the matter of the final instruction wait until the ships were fully prepared.

To make the ships suitable for the new voyage, some alterations in the fitting and provisioning were necessary. Because of the duration of the voyage and the remoteness of the area of operations, a greater quantity of victuals and stores were required, and during December and January the vessels were re-stocked. Once again the Cook model was followed with respect to the supply of anti-scorbutics. The new commander not only wanted his own crew, but wanted the ship rigged and fitted to his own preferences, and accordingly the masts and yards of the *Discovery* were altered, and adjustments were made to the sails. As no commander was appointed to the *Chatham* until the end of December, Vancouver was initially responsible for her fitting as well, and he changed her cabin accommodation, and on 20 December requested that she be re-coppered as her bottom was decaying. Indeed, it was these various repairs to the *Chatham* which delayed the sailing of the expedition, for on 24 December the brig was navigated down to Woolwich and taken into dry dock. Although she was victualled and stored while repairs were being carried out, the *Chatham* did not leave Woolwich until the middle of February.[56]

When it became obvious that the ships would not put to sea at the end of December as originally planned, the government had hopes that the negotiations pending with the whalers and the East India Company would be completed before they sailed. These discussions began at the Board of Trade offices on 20 January and continued for two months, with the Board keen to know if it would be in the whalers' interests to participate in the fur trade. This was perhaps the final irony of the Nootka crisis. Small merchant concerns involved in a precarious trade in a remote part of the world had brought two great nations to the brink of war. Now the government was benefiting from the discussions with Spain to further the interests of the 'southern whalers' and even suggested that they should take the fur trade under their wing. Total government disillusionment with the fur traders followed the examination of John Meares by Pitt, Dundas, Grenville and Hawkesbury at Privy Council meetings between 8 and 13 February. Meares constantly contradicted himself and was pulled up by his questioners. On 11 February he claimed the *Princess Royal* was copper-bottomed; two days later he was forced to retract this. Although he had earlier claimed that his house at Port Cox had an enclosure of land around it, on 13 February he admitted that this was not the case. On 11 February he stated the value of the *Argonaut* as being £8,000; by the 13th it had increased in value to £9,000, a sum Meares regarded as an underestimation as he had bought her from a friend.[57]

The failings of the fur trade were further highlighted in a memorandum by Alexander Dalrymple. He saw it as an unstable, unregulated and unprofitable trade, subject to fluctuating prices and false economies. Harking back to his memorandum of 1789, he reiterated his faith in a junction of the Hudson's Bay and East India Companies, so that supply could be effectively linked to the demand at Canton. The trade to the East Indies was a specialised one, which if opened to all merchants would mean the eastern seas would be flooded with pirates. Admittedly, the trade needed expansion, but it was vital that the East India Company should be the agent of such growth. To support his case Dalrymple produced a set of figures contradicting Meares' arguments as to the profitability of the fur trade, and renewed his long-standing plan of establishing an entrepôt somewhere in the eastern seas, possibly at Balambangan.[58] He remained a stout defender of monopoly trade.

By the beginning of February it was obvious that no bill on the extension of the whalers' limits could be brought before Parliament in time to affect Vancouver's instructions. Grenville privately expressed his belief that it would be impossible to pass anything before the beginning of March, and he seemed a little impatient with the dilatoriness of the Board of Trade.[59]. Further delays in the departure of the *Discovery* and *Chatham* were clearly inadvisable, although it was already too late to send them off in time to pass around Cape Horn. Grenville decided that the two vessels should leave as soon as the repairs on the *Chatham* were completed. The *Discovery* had sailed down to Longreach on 6 January, and she remained there for three weeks while various additional stores such as marquees, bedding, articles of trade and specialised nautical and astronomical instruments were taken on board. On 24 January Banks requested that Towerowero, the Sandwich Islander brought to England on the *Prince of Wales*, should be taken back to his homeland, and Vancouver was ordered to take him on board the *Discovery* and enter him in the books as a supernumerary. Two days later the ship left Longreach and proceeded down Channel to Portsmouth, where, after some final victualling, she lay waiting for her final instructions and the arrival of the *Chatham*, which was still at Woolwich undergoing repairs.[60]

On 11 February Grenville drew up orders for the Admiralty on which Vancouver's instructions were to be based. These new plans were a far cry from the more grandiose proposals of December 1790.

The primary object of the expedition was to survey the north-west coast of America between 30°N and 60°N in a search for the north-west passage, with particular attention paid to the Straits of Juan de Fuca and to Cook Inlet. In his first season on the coast, Vancouver was to accept the lands and buildings which were to be restored by Spain, and more detailed information on this matter was to be taken out in a storeship with which he was to rendezvous in the Sandwich Islands. While on the coast Vancouver was to study the nature and situation of settlements made by other powers, although any conflict with foreigners was to be strictly avoided. If he met Spanish vessels he was to give any assistance required, and offer to make a reciprocal exchange of charts and information. At the end of their second summer the vessels were to return via Cape Horn, but if they had sufficient time they were to explore the coast of South America below the latitude of Chiloe Island, looking for the most southerly Spanish settlement, and keeping a watch for harbours suitable for the use of the 'southern whalers'. Significantly, no mention was made of a British settlement to be established on the coast. Nor were the fur traders to be offered any assistance — in fact, the merchant adventurers did not even warrant mention in the instructions.[61]

As the *Chatham* was almost ready to leave Woolwich, Grenville was anxious that Vancouver should get away as quickly as possible, and he asked Nepean to check out the orders and discuss them with Lord Hood at the Admiralty.[62] It was at this juncture in the planning of the expedition that Banks' hand became clearly visible. On 1 January he had drawn up Archibald Menzies' conditions of appointment. The botanist was to receive £150 a year for his wages and mess and was allowed a servant to assist in the care of the plants. Vancouver was ordered to receive him on board the *Discovery* together with his servant. Four weeks later Menzies joined the ship at Spithead.[63] In the middle of February Nepean approached Banks in an effort to find a suitable astronomer, by this time a recognised element in such expeditions. Banks had lost much of the egocentricity which in Cook's time had enabled him to nominate to such positions without himself seeking advice, so he asked Dr Maskelyne, the Astronomer Royal, to suggest a suitable person and mention an appropriate allowance.[64] Maskelyne put forward the ill-fated William Gooch, who, although he missed a passage in the *Discovery*, went out to the Sandwich Islands in the storeship *Daedalus*. Banks also undertook to supply specialised nautical and astronomical instruments through the medium of Maskelyne. Because

Jesse Ramsden, the notable instrument maker was, as usual, late in his deliveries, these instruments also had to go out in the store-ship.[65]

At the time Grenville issued his orders to the Admiralty, he con-sulted Banks for more detailed information on the way the survey should be carried out, and asked him to draw up Menzies' instruc-tions. Banks complied by sending various sets of instructions to Grenville on 20 and 22 February, and together these make up the most detailed guide for scientific and marine exploration ever set out in the eighteenth century. Banks' detractors would say, and did say, that he was arrogating to himself powers of command which could have been more rightly and efficiently exercised by others. Anderson, the most recent of Vancouver's biographers, compared the drawing up of Menzies' instructions to Banks' intrusions in Cook's voyages.[66] The parallel is not a valid one. In 1769 and 1772 Banks had exhibited arrogance and presumption in a situation where his assistance was unsolicited by government. But Cook had been dead for over eleven years by 1791, and Banks had in many respects become the civilian heir to his experience and technique. The surveying instructions were a testament and tribute to Cook's abilities. Moreover, Banks was not in a direct sense interfering. From 1785 onwards, the government came to have an increasing trust in his management of imperial affairs, and it repaid this trust by giving him greater control over the enterprises with which he was concerned. In 1790 and 1791 Grenville had repeatedly sought Banks' advice on the question of the north-west coast of America, often working through the scientist's personal friend Evan Nepean, the Under-Secretary of State.

On 20 February Banks sent the first set of instructions to Grenville with a covering note to Nepean promising that he would call at the Home Office the following day to elaborate where necessary.[67] The first of these was a paper regulating Vancouver's conduct towards Menzies. The commander was to lend the botanist a boat whenever possible and to offer assistance in the collecting, carrying and care of plant specimens. To enable Menzies to obtain the aid of natives in carrying luggage, acting as guides, and giving information on the nature of their country and its natural productions, he was to have a portion of the trading articles supplied to the *Discovery*. He was to have complete custody of the greenhouse on board the ship, and to ensure that it was carefully tended. It is rather odd that such instruc-tions were necessary at all, and they hint at early warnings of the friction between Menzies and Vancouver which broke out on the voyage.

The surveying instructions were in two parts, and were covered by a letter to Grenville offering some explanation: 'Enclosd your Lordship will receive the opinions you did me the honor to require from me, concerning the mode of carrying on the intended survey of the N.W. Coast of America in the most Speedy & Effectual manner consistent with the degree of accuracy required in an undertaking intended to be of a General nature.'[68] Banks warned about the temptation of substituting conjecture for fact in determining the shores of an unknown country: a temptation some of the fur traders had fallen prey to. Charts and logs were most important and they should be made to agree in laying down a particular coastline. Banks concluded by apologising for the delay in drawing up the instructions, but they were of such a technical nature that he had been obliged to call in a friend 'whose Observations relative to that business will I am confident be found the most valuable Part of the Paper'. Much time was also spent in revising the paper to ensure that nothing had been omitted.

The first set of surveying instructions described the form of a log survey book. This was followed by a detailed technical description of taking angles and bearings, plotting a survey course, observing latitude by various methods, taking transient bearings, and the drawing up of accurate and standardised charts. In all, this lengthy paper amounted to an explorer's manual and embodied the surveying experience of Cook and his followers. This was the section which Banks referred to as having been drawn up with the assistance of a friend, in this case the Geographer, Rennell. Captain William Bligh, one of the few other men with experience in the specialised craft of surveying had also drawn up a set of instructions, but in the event these were not used.[69]

Following the technical paper was a more general set of instructions which was the work of Banks himself. The general object of the expedition was 'to obtain with all the Dispatch that is consistent with General Accuracy, a correct General Outline of the Northwest Coast of the Continent of North America; or what from the present state of European knowledge of the Subject, may appear to you to be the Coast of the Continent'. During the survey prominent landmarks and all Spanish settlements were to be marked. In the course of the ships' progress up the coast a special lookout was to be kept for any opening into the interior, and such openings were to be pursued. Vancouver was to 'consider the Investigation of its utmost Extent Eastwards as one of the principal objects of your Survey'. If such a channel led into an inland sea or any other open water, the nature of the opening, its defensibility, and its ease of navigation were all to be carefully considered. When surveying normally along a coastline, the *Chatham* was to operate inshore of the *Discovery* to observe any openings and to give a double line of soundings. The two vessels were to keep within sight of each other as much as possible. Various other tasks such as the estimation of longitude and the taking of views of the coastline were to be attended to.[70]

Banks' instructions to Menzies were complementary to the surveying instructions and are a classic statement of the empirical method in natural science. They were based on Banks' own experience and lead naturally through to the work of Darwin on the *Beagle*. But it is apparent that they were more than a guide for an itinerant dabbler in botany. They were a directive on the potentialities and value of overseas empire. Menzies was warned that diligence and perseverence, discretion and good sense were vital to a mission which included 'an investigation of the whole of Natural History of the Countries you are to visit; as well as an enquiry into the present state and comparative degree of civilization of the Inhabitants you will meet with'. Of primary importance was the nature of the soil in the regions visited; whether clay, sand or gravel; whether well-watered and fertile, and 'whether, should it anytime hereafter be deemed expedient to send out settlers from England, the Grains, Pulse, and Fruits cultivated in Europe are likely to thrive, and if not what kind of produce would in your opinion be the most suitable'. Different plants were to be described, and their environment to be recorded. Particularly interesting specimens were to be dried and brought home, and their seeds, or living plant specimens, were to be cared for. While on shore Menzies was to study the general nature of the country and in particular to examine any exposed strata, such as cliffs or river banks, for valuable deposits of coal, limestone or other valuable minerals. Rock samples were to be brought back to Banks for examination under a microscope. All animal life, especially forms valuable for food or clothing, was to be studied, and the method of its husbandry or capture to be observed. The natural history of the sea otter, wild sheep, seal and whale was to be especially noted. Lastly, the customs, language, religion and manufactures of the natives were to be inquired into. All Menzies' findings were to be entered in a well kept journal which was to be delivered to the Secretary of State at the conclusion of the voyage.[71]

Grenville sent the Admiralty a copy of the instructions stressing that 'the service Mr Menzies has been directed to perform is materially connected with some of the most important objects of the Expedition'. A further copy was to be given to Vancouver with directions that Menzies should be given every possible assistance. The letter went on to enumerate the various types of help Menzies had a right to expect, as set out in Banks' letter of 20 February.[72] This particular set of instructions was identical to that drawn by Banks except in one respect, for as Nepean pointed out 'the clause which related to ascertaining the practice of eating human flesh has been struck out, his Lordship conceiving it better that any directions to Mr. Menzies on that point should if necessary be given to him in a private letter' — delicacy prevailed over empiricism. Nepean further explained that Grenville wanted the instructions signed by Banks himself.[73] Vancouver received a copy on 8 March.

Menzies departed from London on 8 February, leaving his affairs in the hands of Banks and Francis Wilson of the Navy Board, and joined the *Discovery* at Spithead the following Sunday. Before the ships left for Falmouth on 3 March, Menzies wrote to Banks expressing his gratitude and appreciation. The letter gives some indication of the effect Banks had on men such as Gore, Bligh, Ledyard, Park and Flinders:

> From the first moment I had the honour of being your correspondent, I found within me a particular desire of traversing unknown regions in quest of my favourite pursuit, and fondly looked forward, for the enjoyment of that indulgence under your kind tuition & patronage which I am happy I now have the pleasure to possess, in being entrusted by You, with such a particular share of the present Expedition, as will, I hope, afford a free & liberal scope to its full exercise — This principle has already bore me cheerfully up under the peculiar hardship of a long & tedious circumnavigation & is by no means yet extinguished on the contrary the present opposition it meets with, serves only to add fresh fuel to the flame.[74]

Menzies promised faithfully to carry out his instructions, and send regular reports to Banks whenever opportunity offered.

The *Discovery* left the *Chatham* at Portsmouth for last minute repairs, and proceeded to Falmouth where Vancouver was to receive his final instructions. From that port he sent back an estimate of the stores and provisions which were to be taken out in the storeship later in the year, with the instructions for the restitution of Nootka. The stores were expected to last until September 1793, by which time it was hoped that the storeship might have returned from New South Wales with additional supplies. Just prior to the sailing of the *Discovery*, Grenville requested the Admiralty to provide and fit out a vessel of from 250 to 300 tons suitable for this service.[75]

Vancouver received his final instructions on 20 March, but he was obliged to wait a further eleven days for the *Chatham*. To Broughton's disappointment she had proved exceedingly crank in her passage from Spithead, and to avoid more delay Vancouver transferred the greater part of the *Discovery*'s shot into the hold of the brig to save taking on more ballast. On 1 April the two ships headed down Channel on their four-year voyage.

Although the Admiralty had hoped to despatch the storeship in the spring or early summer, it was not until 6 May that the Navy Board reported the purchase of the ship *Daedalus* of 300 tons which lay waiting at Deptford to take on stores. Nepean was so concerned at the delay that he wrote directly to the Secretary of the Admiralty concerning the loading of the vessel, thereby anticipating the official order from Grenville. The stores and provisions listed in Vancouver's return of 12 March were to be loaded, together with some additional trading articles, and the ship was to proceed to sea as soon as possible. By 26 May the *Daedalus* was ready for sea, Lieutenant Hergest, her commander, had been appointed and Nepean advised Gooch, the astronomer, to repair on board.[76]

The prompt despatch of the *Daedalus* was made impossible by delays in drafting the instructions to Vancouver on the subject of restitution, and by ministerial changes. In April Grenville replaced the Duke of Leeds as Foreign Secretary, and for the next two months negotiations were in progress to find a successor for the Home Office. After some indecision the post went to Dundas. By the Beginning of June the government must have received Florida Blanca's instructions to the Spanish commander at Nootka ordering the restitution of the land seized in 1789.[77] As these instructions were not completely straightforward they required some interpretation for Vancouver's sake and in July Dundas seems to have consulted Banks on the subject, giving him a copy of a draft to the Admiralty to read through and approve. It was apparently these instructions which Banks discussed with Nepean on 9 July.[78]

Another reason for the consultation with Banks was the continuing dissension between Vancouver and Menzies which had been evident before the voyage got under way. Vancouver objected to the intrusion of Menzies in what he regarded as a purely maritime venture and despite requests to do so, he refused to appoint Menzies as surgeon or surgeon's assistant on the belief that it was not possible to practise both botany and surgery effectively. In such a situation Menzies felt himself vulnerable, more especially as he had never seen, and Vancouver refused to show him, the instructions given to the commander regulating his conduct towards the botanist. To add to his troubles, Menzies was asked to contribute what he thought was an excessive amount towards the gun room mess, and on 14 March he had complained to Banks about his treatment. A week later he had pointed out certain deficiencies in his own instructions 'lamenting the situation in which they place me in, by not being empowered to ask for a boat at any time from the ship, or the least assistance whatever by not being empowered to claim the least article of trade to carry my instructions into execution'.[79]

For nine months Banks endeavoured to obtain a copy of the instructions relating to Vancouver's conduct towards Menzies, but he was unsuccessful. He had expected them to be among the papers Nepean had given him on 9 July, and two days later he even went so far as to offer to copy them out himself if the clerks were too busy. Immediately prior to the sailing of the *Daedalus* Banks expressed regret at being unable to obtain them, which was partly due, he told Menzies, to the 'hurry of the political business' at the time the expedition had sailed. In case he was finally unable to secure a copy, Banks outlined the heads of proposals on the subject which he had given to Grenville. In November he again approached Nepean for a copy of the instructions which 'have never been given to me, tho' you promised I should have them, which will be essentially usefull to me if the difference which existed between these gentlemen before they went to sea should continue during their voyage'.[80] Banks himself had many reservations about Vancouver's own personality, and in his letter to Menzies of 10 August he gave an indication of the extent of his authority:

How Capt. Vancouver will behave towards you is more than I can guess, unless I was to judge by his conduct towards me, which was not such as I am used to receive from persons in his situation;

but as there was no imprudence in his being civil to me & it would be highly imprudent in him to throw any obstacle in the way of your duty, I trust he will have too much good sense to obstruct it. If he does, the instances whatever they are, will, of course appear as they happened in your journal, which, as it will be a justification to you, will afford ground for implicating the propriety of his conduct, which, for your sake, I will not fail to make use of.[81]

Fortunately the dispute died down once the voyage got under way, although it was to flare up again later.

The matter of Vancouver's instructions illustrates the manner in which Banks influenced government in expeditions of this nature. Their general organisation normally fell into the hands of Evan Nepean at the Home Office and Philip Stephens, the Secretary of the Admiralty. It was through these two men that Banks worked, and he was on especially good terms with Nepean, so that when any special arrangements were in hand, Nepean drew heavily on Banks' freely available advice. Unfortunately, the greater part of the negotiations between these two was at an unofficial level and it is, therefore, often difficult to trace. Only occasionally do the transactions come to the surface. On 10 November 1791 when Nepean was about to depart for a holiday in the West Indies, and Banks was anxious to secure payment of some bills, and to obtain copies of Vancouver's instructions, he wrote:

> I am, therefore, to request that you will be so good as to leave a line upon the subjects at the office, which I conclude you will not think unreasonable, for, as the money was advanced with your sole authority, you only can be my voucher for its repayment, and as you only know the share I have had in arrangeing [sic] the outfit of the ships you can only estimate the goodness of the claim I make to these papers, and are also the only person privy to the repeated promises you made me that they should be given to me.[82]

While Nepean was away Banks' influence declined. On 31 December 1791 when Banks was approached by the contractor William Richards, seeking support for a contract to transport convicts to New South Wales, he replied: 'I cannot inform you whether there is at present any immediate intention of sending out convicts or not, having since Mr. Nepean left the office of Under Sec. of

State no acquaintance in that department. I cannot, I fear, unless I am consulted on the subject, be of any service to you.'[83] In this instance Banks was eventually consulted, and he was able to promote Richards' scheme.

Dundas does not seem to have taken any steps to despatch the *Daedalus* until 6 July, when he asked the Admiralty to have her ready for sea at the earliest opportunity. As it was unlikely that Vancouver would still be at the Sandwich Islands by the time the *Daedalus* arrived, Lieutenant Hergest was to proceed to Nootka where the letters from Florida Blanca were to be delivered to the Spanish officer in command and restitution was then to follow. This done, Hergest was to await Vancouver's arrival. After the stores had been transferred, the *Daedalus* was to go to Port Jackson, stopping at New Zealand on the way to pick up one or two Maori flax dressers. The final instructions were not issued to Hergest until 10 August.[84]

By the time the *Daedalus* arrived at Nootka in 1792, Vancouver had surveyed the Straits of Juan de Fuca and the passage behind what was to become Vancouver Island. When the *Discovery* and *Chatham* returned to the Sound in August 1792, the *Daedalus* had arrived with the instructions from Dundas, and the tragic news of the death of Hergest and Gooch.[85] Because of the imprecise nature of the instructions Vancouver found himself unable to complete the formalities of restitution. His Spanish counterpart, Quadra, felt authorised to offer only a small section of land, which has been described by Godwin as being smaller than the board room of the Admiralty, and Vancouver did not feel able to accept such a diminutive slice of territory. He left Nootka in October with the matter unsettled. Texts of the negotiations were carried back to England via Mexico by Lieutenant Broughton.[86]

While Broughton set off homeward, the *Discovery* and *Chatham* wintered in the Sandwich Islands. Two more summers were spent in surveying the north-west coast. In 1793 the ships proceeded northwards from Fitzhugh Sound to Cape Decision, taking in the continental shoreline and the Queen Charlotte Islands. That season only six days were spent at Nootka. The *Discovery* put into the Sound in May to obtain news of the *Chatham* which had preceded her to the coast, and also to forward despatches to England through Mexico. No discussions took place with Fidalgo, the new Spanish commander. At the end of the summer, Vancouver again touched at Nootka, but on finding no new despatches had come through from

Spain or England, and that the *Daedalus* had not yet returned from
Port Jackson, he continued south along the American coast, before
putting off to spend another winter in the Sandwich Islands. At
Monterey, in October 1793, the ships were joined by the *Daedalus*
which had left Port Jackson at the end of June. Again, no new
intelligence was received relative to the restitution. After two
months at the Sandwich Islands the *Discovery* and *Chatham* sailed
again for the coast in March 1794 to complete the survey. The
Daedalus returned to Port Jackson in February with despatches for
the Admiralty and livestock and fruit trees for New South Wales.

In the final summer on the coast the area between Cook Inlet and
Port Conclusion was extensively examined, taking in some of the
Aleutian Islands, Cook Inlet itself, Prince William Sound and Cross
Sound. On 2 September 1794 the two vessels anchored in Friendly
Cove, Nootka Sound for the last time. Once more Vancouver
bewailed the absence of despatches, although the Spanish
'governor', Alava, hourly expected intelligence. As the ships needed
repairs, Vancouver remained at Nootka in the hope that fresh
instructions might arrive. When by 16 October all the repairs had
been completed and no fresh information had come through, the
expedition put to sea in advance of the approaching winter, and
headed south along the American Pacific coast. After touching at
Monterey, the Cocos, Galapagos Islands and Valparaiso, the two
ships rounded the Horn and headed for St Helena to pick up a convoy. While the *Chatham* was engaged in carrying despatches to San
Salvador the *Discovery* sailed in convoy to England calling at
Shannon Harbour on 12 September 1795. Leaving the *Discovery*
there to await another convoy, Vancouver travelled on to London
with his journals and charts.[87]

Although Vancouver was unable to carry through the restitution
of Nootka, his other object, the survey of the north-west coast of
America, was thoroughly carried out. It was no easy task, and the
greater part of this work was done in small open launches which
were rowed and sailed along the indented coastline, and up the
numerous inlets and sounds. The work was accurate and the charting superb, despite the many hardships of the voyage. The Hawaiian
Islands were less arduously surveyed. As a surveyor, Vancouver was
a fine product of the Cook school of seamanship, although his less
interesting personality, and the narrower scope of his work, meant
that his endeavours were not as attractive as the seminal labours of
that earlier, more illustrious navigator. Cook was a great explorer,

Vancouver was a highly skilled surveyor. In one other respect Vancouver was a fitting heir to Cook. Despite the length and hardship of the voyage, only six of the *Discovery*'s crew were lost, and only one of those from disease. More remarkable still, the smaller *Chatham* lost not a member of its complement.

The scientific results of the voyage were considerable. As instructed, Menzies kept a full journal which revealed his constant concern for the intrinsic value of what he found. In the area of King George's Sound in south-west Australia he described forests and woodlands:

> capable of affording an excellent range & good feeding to domestic animals of every denomination. . . . In short the inland country of this part of New Holland has a delightful & promising appearance & we therefore conceive it an object well worth the attention of government in a more particular investigation of it, as it offers fair to afford an eligible situation for a settlement which on account of its nearness & easy access to our settlements in India possesses peculiar advantages not to be derived from the opposite shore.

In New Zealand he remarked upon the difficulties of clearing bush and forest for cultivation, but saw the situation as ideal for raising the flax *Phormium tenax*. Near Admiralty Inlet on the American coast he described a

> flat country of very moderate height & render'd the western side of this arm a pleasant & desirable tract of both pasture & arable land where the Plough might enter at once without the least obstruction, & where the Soil though light & gravelly appear'd capable of yielding in this temperate climate luxuriant crops of the European Grains or rearing herds of cattle who might here wander at their ease over extensive fields of fine pasture.[88]

Such observations abound throughout Menzies' *Journal* and in his many letters to Banks, reflecting the utilitarian strain of eighteenth-century science. The idea of settlement was continually in his mind.[89] Natural history was not neglected. Menzies obeyed his instructions to collect plant specimens and seeds, carefully preserving live plants in the greenhouse on the *Discovery*'s quarterdeck. These live plants were deposited in Kew gardens, while the dried specimens were later divided between the Linnean Society and the Edinburgh Botanic Garden. Menzies also brought back an assortment of other rare or valuable objects, the greater part of which were deposited by Banks in the British Museum.[90] In 1796 Menzies had an account of the anatomy of the sea otter published in the *Philosophical Transactions* of the Royal Society.[91]

During the voyage the dispute between Menzies and Vancouver had again come to a head. In his *Journal* Menzies made several criticisms of Vancouver's conduct towards native peoples, in particular recording an incident on the island of Maui in March 1793 when the commander was angered by the theft of a ribbon from one of the Hawaiian women on the ship: 'Captain Vancouver in endeavouring to recover this trifle put himself into such a passion & threatened the chiefs with such menacing threats that he terrified some of them out of the Ship with great precipitation.'[92] It was possibly because of such references that Vancouver decided to confiscate the botanist's journal at the end of the voyage, although Menzies intended to seal up his narrative and forward it to Banks. Menzies' own instructions ordered him to deliver it to the Secretary of State. Towards the end of the voyage Menzies was placed under arrest after he had complained at damage to some of his plants by the neglect of his servant. Before leaving the ships at Shannon, Vancouver formally requested that Menzies hand over his journal. The request was denied. Later, Menzies sided with Thomas Pitt, the notorious Lord Camelford, in a dispute with Vancouver which almost terminated in a duel.[93] In this instance the unfortunate commander was confronting the Establishment, and it was not surprising that he should come out of the affair rather the worse for wear. Many of his difficulties were obviously brought on by continued illness, often acute, during the voyage. His return to England did not ease the distress, and his career was tragically cut short by his death in 1798.

Even during Vancouver's voyage the number of British ships in the maritime fur trade was declining, and the Etches-Meares consortium, despite proclamations to the contrary, had no intention of sending more ships to the north-west coast of America. As late as May 1792 Etches was seeking Banks' support for the extension of the trade and making the now common complaints about Portlock and Dixon. He had not abandoned the prospect of expanding the China trade by the sale of furs:

If the China trade which is a drain to the Nation of upwards of a

Million and a half of specie annually be of importance of what consequence must that branch of Commerce be, which bids fair gradually to diminish such .drain, by substituting the returns of the Manufactures and Produce of our Country?[94]

Meares was also attempting to recoup his losses at this time, but without much luck. In June 1793 he was still unsuccessfully pressing the government for compensation.[95]

As if to ram home its lack of interest in the fur trade, the Pitt ministry, largely under the influence of Dundas, thought fit to abandon the 'settlement' at Nootka. Anticipating Broughton's arrival in England with despatches from Vancouver, Grenville in June 1793 pressed Dundas hastily to resolve the Nootka problem. On the arrival of the despatches Dundas lamented the fact that Vancouver had not accepted the parcel of land offered to him by Quadra, explaining that although national honour demanded restitution, 'The Extent of that Restitution is not of much moment'. While he now saw technical means of getting around the difficulties he thought it axiomatic that the future use of Nootka and Port Cox should be common to both parties.[96]

Subsequent negotiations with Spain were largely left in the hands of Lord St Helens, the ambassador in Madrid, but until January 1794 progress was slow and unsatisfactory. On 14 January 1794 St Helens was able to report to Grenville that Spain had accepted the proposals put forward by Britain and that great care had been taken 'to frame this Instrument so as to prevent as far as possible any future Discussions or Misunderstanding between the Officers employed on the Spot'. As the Spanish officer appointed to handle the negotiations was soon to leave for Nootka via Mexico, the Spanish government arranged that the British officer concerned should accompany him. On 17 February Dundas ordered the Admiralty to find a suitable officer.[97] On arriving at Nootka the two representatives were to exchange declarations stating that all lands seized in 1789 had been restored. The British officer was then to hoist his flag on the site and 'after these Formalities the Officers of the two Crowns shall respectively withdraw their people from the said port of Nootka'. The Admiralty chose for this service Lieutenant Pearce of the Marines, who had just returned from Tahiti with Bligh, and who spoke fluent French.[98] The relatively low rank of this officer indicated the scaling down of the whole dispute. This ceremony was duly carried out in February 1795 by Pearce and his

Spanish counterpart, Brigadier-General Alava. It is surprising that after a similar accommodation over the Falkland Islands 22 years earlier, such an obvious expedient had not come to mind more readily.[99]

British involvement in the North Pacific in this period went through an eventful and final stage. From despatches brought back by Lieutenant Broughton in 1793 Dundas deduced that because of various difficulties and shortages in carrying out the survey, the *Discovery* or the *Chatham* might not be in a fit state to complete the work. Accordingly, on 20 July 1793 he ordered the Admiralty to search for a suitable ship to be prepared for a voyage to the north-west coast to carry out instructions regarding the restitution, and to assist Vancouver in completing the survey. It was intended that this vessel should leave England in August so as to rendezvous with Vancouver in the Sandwich Islands the following spring.[100]

This was one occasion when the Navy Board did not have to scour the Thames to find a suitable ship. On 7 August Captain Bligh returned from his second breadfruit expedition in the *Providence* sloop of 420 tons. This vessel had been new at the time she was taken up for the expedition in 1791, and although originally built for the West Indian trade, she was particularly suitable for surveying, as Bligh could well testify. A week after his return, Bligh was ordered to pay off his crew as quickly as possible and leave the ship in its fitted situation, ready for repairs. By 6 September the ship had been paid off and was waiting to be taken into dock. Bligh made his last log entry on 9 September. It had originally been intended that the ship should be fitted out at Deptford, the usual yard for such tasks, but because of the existing work commitments in that yard and the exigencies of war, it was eventually decided that she should go into dry dock at Woolwich.[101]

As well as having a suitable ship, the Admiralty could also boast a well qualified commander, Robert Broughton, who had recently returned from the north-west coast, and therefore had more experience of that region than any other officer in England at the time. On 3 October Broughton received his commission, and the following day he was ordered to have the ship ready for sea at the earliest opportunity. The *Providence* was to be fitted and stored as the *Discovery* had been in 1791, indeed, along the lines upon which all vessels going on voyages of discovery had been equipped since Cook's pioneer work. Although the ship was generally thought to be in good condition considerable changes were necessary because of the change in function; the special deckings and railings fitted to accommodate the breadfruit in 1791 had to be removed and the cabins had to be altered.[102]

For the remainder of 1793 the *Providence* was berthed at Woolwich being refitted. Broughton was impatient with the speed at which work was being carried out and suggested to Stephens that the ship should be moved to Deptford, and Greenwich Hospital out-pensioners should be assigned to the sloop to prepare her rigging. Specialised nautical and astronomical instruments, marquees, tents and trading articles were supplied to the sloop to bring her into line with the equipment of the *Discovery*, and the proportion of officers was increased to facilitate the survey work which had to be carried out in open boats. Because of the death of Gooch, the astronomer, the Admiralty decided that the *Providence* should carry another astronomer as a supernumerary, and on 31 December Broughton was ordered to receive John Crosley who had been appointed by the Board of Longitude to the expedition. Because of delays in the delivery of stores, the *Providence* was not able to move down to Galleons Reach to take on her guns until 25 February, by which time the Home Office must have realised that the departure of the ship would be too late to enable her to carry through the formality of restitution. It was for this reason, therefore, that Dundas accepted the Spanish offer of a passage through Mexico for an officer able to carry out the ceremony.[103]

At the end of April the *Providence* left the Nore at the mouth of the Thames as an escort to a small fleet of merchant vessels and Navy storeships, but she remained for a further six months at Spithead waiting for a convoy. During this delay Broughton arranged with the Admiralty for the crew's pay to be brought up to date, and took on several extra crew members to make good any deficiencies in Vancouver's complement.[104] On 2 October Broughton received his final instructions but there was little hope, by this time, that the *Providence* would meet up with the *Discovery*. Doubtless, Lieutenant Pearce had instructions informing Vancouver of the Broughton expedition, but Pearce was not to arrive at Nootka until after Vancouver's departure. If Broughton did meet the *Discovery* he was to assist in completing the survey, and then proceed with Vancouver to carry out the last part of the mission — the exploration of the Pacific coast of South America below Chiloe Island. If the *Providence* failed to join up with the other expedition, which now seemed highly likely, she was to winter in the Hawaiian Islands, and then to survey the western coast of South America in its entirety, including the many offshore islands visited by the *Rattler* in 1793–4. It was thought that Vancouver would be so busy with the work on the north-west coast that he would have insufficient time to perform this latter task satisfactorily.[105]

Because of unfavourable winds, Broughton had to wait another three and a half months before he finally put to sea on 19 February 1795, as part of Admiral Parker's fleet of 400 sail, including 34 sail of the line. By this time there was practically no chance of meeting Vancouver and no doubt the appropriate alterations were made in Broughton's instructions. It is not clear what the government's objectives were at this time. The war against France was not going so well that they could afford to spare a fast-sailing sloop of war or its hand-picked crew. And yet the *Providence* was one of the most thoroughly equipped survey ships to put to sea in this period. The only conclusion must be that the government was particularly anxious to find whaling or strategic bases on the Pacific coast of South America, and that the peace with Spain was not expected to last long.

As Parker's convoy headed south it split up, part going to the Mediterranean, part to the West Indies, and a small detachment, including Broughton, heading for New South Wales. Somewhere in the south Atlantic the *Providence* passed the homeward bound *Discovery* and *Chatham*. On 27 August Broughton reached Port Jackson where essential repairs were carried out before he proceeded on to Tahiti and the Sandwich Islands. In the Sandwich Islands in January 1796, he learned from an English brig that Vancouver had left Valparaiso for England in May of the preceding year. Undeterred, Broughton followed his instructions by proceeding to Nootka, where he received letters from Vancouver, Pearce and the last Spanish commander, indicating that the settlement had been abandoned in March 1795. At Monterey in June Broughton received further letters from Vancouver, and he learned that the *Discovery* and *Chatham* had left that port 18 months earlier in good condition, and in good time to complete the survey of the Pacific coast of South America. The Spanish officers were also able to inform him that Vancouver's ships had been fully seaworthy when they left Valparaiso in May 1795. This last information was incorrect. The *Discovery* left Valparaiso with a thoroughly rotten mainmast and numerous other defects, and for these reasons Vancouver had been obliged to abandon the survey of the coast south of Chiloe Island.[106]

Broughton took the Spanish information at face value and concluded that it would be superfluous for the *Providence* to sail to
South America to cover the same ground. At this point his instructions gave him discretionary powers and after a council with his
officers he decided to survey the coast of Asia and its adjacent
islands from Sakhalin to the mouth of the Nanking River. Why had
he taken this decision? In the introduction to his *Voyage* he stated
that Captain King, in his account of Cook's third voyage, had
marked that part of the world as being the most eligible area for
further discoveries. Daines Barrington had made the same observation in the preface to his *Polar Tracts* of 1781.[107] Although
Broughton was not aware of the fact, Vancouver came to the same
conclusion in the third volume of his *Voyage*. John Crosley, the
astronomer on board the *Providence*, had instructions to make
observations at all places possible, and to ascertain the latitude and
longitude of unknown places. In fact, Broughton's decision was
well-considered. Knowledge of that part of the north Pacific was
particularly scant, even among the Russians, who knew it best.
There is no indication that this was the government view, and it
cannot be said that Broughton's voyage fits into a conscious policy
of a 'swing to the east'.[108]

The *Providence* left Monterey on 20 June 1796, and after a month
in the Sandwich Islands gathering provisions, she headed for the
coast of Japan, arriving off northern Honshu on 7 September.
Broughton sailed north along the east coast of Hokkaido and the
Kurils but by October the weather was beginning to deteriorate, and
he swung south towards Canton, surveying much of the east coast of
Japan and the Ryukyu Islands. At Macao in the winter of 1796–7 he
decided to purchase a schooner to assist with inshore surveying, and
by drawing bills on the Admiralty for £1,500 he acquired a small
rigged vessel of 87 tons. It was as well that he did. A month after the
ships left Macao in April 1797, the *Providence* struck a reef near
Miyako Island in the southern Ryukyus and she was abandoned to
the sea. Broughton jammed his crew of over 100 into the schooner
and returned to Canton.[109]

But he was not a man to give up easily. After discharging almost
two-thirds of his men he headed north in the schooner in June 1797.
Moving up the east coast of Honshu, which was thoroughly surveyed, he sailed through the Tsugaru Strait at the north of that
island and surveyed the western coast of Hokkaido and Sakhalin.
He reached his highest latitude at 52°N in the Tatarski Proliv, thus

failing to establish Sakhalin as an island. As provisions on the ship were low, he was obliged to abandon his intention of completing the survey of the Kurils and Sakhalin, but decided instead to trace the continental coast south towards Canton. In this way the coast parallel to the Ussuri River and the eastern shore of Korea were surveyed. Broughton then returned to Macao, putting into the Typa on 27 November 1797. After provisioning he sailed through the Malacca Strait to Madras, and then on to Trincomalee, recently captured from the Dutch. Here the schooner was sold. Broughton joined an East Indiaman and returned to England.

Thus ended two decades of British involvement in the north Pacific. The maritime fur trade and north-west passage had provided a certain fascination, but until the Nootka crisis of 1790 the Pitt ministry had not intended to follow up Cook's work, although there had been constant pressure on it to do so. There had been no consistent policy towards the region. In fact, the north Pacific was most notable because of its propagandists — Etches, Meares, Dalrymple and Dixon who were continually offering extravagant schemes for opening the Japanese and Korean markets, establishing convict colonies on the north-west coast of America, and the beginning of a bonanza in the whale and seal fishery. In the last analysis, with both the north-west passage and the profitability of the maritime fur trade exposed as myths in 1795, the government lost what small interest it had. For this reason the re-directed *Providence* voyage was the official counterpart of Charles Bishop's adventures. It represents in epilogue a recurrent theme in imperial development; the independence of the man at the periphery.

Nevertheless, however reluctant the government was to become involved in enterprise on the north-west coast, whenever expeditions were eventually planned and despatched, certain common characteristics emerged. The officials involved invariably sought outside advice from men like Banks and Dalrymple; the expeditions were based on the model provided by Cook's voyages in respect of their ships, crews and equipment; great concern was shown for properly evaluating new territories by the employment of trained scientific personnel; and the eighteenth-century empirical tradition manifested itself in the instructions to the commanders, natural historians and astronomers. The men who followed in Cook's wake drew on experience which went far beyond the confines of seamanship.

Notes

1. For a statement of the traditional thesis, see V.T. Harlow, *The Founding of the Second British Empire 1763-1793*, vol. II, pp. 438–41. The linkage is also stressed in Margaret Steven, *Trade, Tactics and Territory*, ch. 3.

2. On Dalrymple and the north-west passage, see G. Williams, *The British Search for the Northwest Passage in the Eighteenth Century*, pp. 221-6, 235–45; H.T. Fry, *Alexander Dalrymple and the Expansion of British Trade*, ch. 8

3. A. Dalrymple, *Plan for Promoting the Fur Trade, and Securing it to this Country by Uniting the Operations of the East-India and Hudson's-Bay Companys.*

4. Ibid., pp. 31-2.

5. Dixon to Nepean, 14 July 1789, *C.O.* 42/72, 2431. For the 1784 plan, see above, Chapter 3.

6. *H.O.* 42/13, 57, n.d. 1789, headed, 'Relative to the Discoveries made by Capt. Duncan on the N.W. Coast of America in 1787 and 1788'.

7. *C.O.* 42/21, 57–62, September 1789. The memorandum could be by Dixon or Dalrymple. The author claimed that the Spanish had a settlement at Nootka, although he could not, in September 1789, have known of the arrival of Martinez at Nootka the preceding May.

8. Wilson to Lind, 12 September 1789, in R.H. Dillon, 'Convict Colonies for the Pacific Northwest', *B.C.H.Q.* XIX, 1955, pp. 98-9.

9. Dixon to Banks, 20 October 1789, in R. H. Dillon, 'Letters of Captain George Dixon in the Banks' Collection', *B.C.H.Q.*, XIV, July 1950, pp. 168-71.

10. Dillon, 'Convict Colonies', pp. 99-102.

11. Accounts of the seizure, often conflicting, are in Colnett, *Journal aboard the Argonaut*; Meares, *Voyages Made in the Years 1788 and 1789 from China to the North West Coast of America*; Meares, memorial and enclosures in *H.O.* 28/61, 291-373; Del Campo to Leeds, 10 February 1790, *P.R.O. (Chatham)* 30/8, 341, fos 64-5; J.E. Martin-Allanic, *Bougainville Navigateur et les Découvertes de son Temps*, confuses the *Argonaut* with the *Prince of Wales*, vol. II, p. 1504. The Spanish side of the story is recounted in W.L. Cook, *Flood Tide of Empire: Spain and the Pacific Northwest*, chs. 5 & 6.

12. Martin-Allanic, ibid., vol. II, p. 1503, suggests that Martinez' first expedition along the north-west coast was prompted by information on Russian expansion which La Pérouse had given to the Spanish governor at Monterey. At Unalaska in 1788, Martinez had been told by the Russians that the governor of Kamchatka was planning to occupy Nootka Sound.

13. On the political background to the crisis see Harlow, *Founding of the Second British Empire*, vol. II, pp. 441-71; W.R. Manning, *The Nootka Sound Controversy*; J.M. Norris, 'The Policy of the British Cabinet in the Nootka Crisis', pp. 562-80; J. Ehrman, *The Younger Pitt*, pp. 553-71.

14. Burgess to Nepean, 1 February 1790, *H.O.* 32/2.

15. Burgess to Nepean, 2 February 1790, ibid., with enclosure from Merry dated Madrid, 15 January 1790.

16. Harlow, *Founding of the Second British Empire*, vol. II, p. 444.

17. Del Campo to Leeds, 10 February 1790, *P.R.O. (Chatham)* 30/8, 341, fos 64-5. It is perhaps evidence of the poor communications between Mexico and Madrid, that Del Campo's date for the arrival of Martinez at Nootka was out by two months.

18. Banks to Nepean, 15 February 1790, *H.O.* 42/16. See Cook, *Flood Tide of Empire*, p. 72. This was the Hezeta-Bodega expedition of 1775. The Spanish account Banks referred to would be Francisco Mourelle's, 'Journal of a Voyage in 1775' in D. Barrington, *Miscellanies*.

19. Sketch of a Letter to the Admiralty, February 1790, *H.O.* 28/7, 50.

20. Harlow, *Founding of the Second British Empire*, vol. II, pp. 438–41. G. Godwin, *Vancouver. A Life*, pp. 24–5. B. Anderson, *Surveyor of the Sea. The Life and Voyages of Captain George Vancouver*, p. 37.

21. Harlow, ibid., vol. II, p. 439.

22. Pitt to Leeds, 23 February 1790, *P.R.O.* (*Chatham*) 30/8, 102, 170.

23. On the *Guardian*, see *Adm*. 1/2395, 25 November 1789–22 June 1791.

24. 'Heads of Instructions', February 1790, *H.O.* 42/16, 10.

25. *Adm*. 3/107, 48, 25 February 1790. *H.O.* 28/61, 251, March 1790.

26. *H.O.* 28/61, 249, March 1790.

27. *C.O.* 201/5, 50, March 1790, marked 'Secret'.

28. An account of the loss is in ibid., 154, 10 April 1790. On the state of the penal colony at this time see David Mackay, 'Far Flung Empire: A Neglected Outpost at Botany Bay 1788–1801', pp. 125–45.

29. Grenville to Cornwallis, 31 March 1790, *H.O.* 28/61, 273, 31 March 1790.

30. *H.O.* 28/61, 276, 31 March 1790. Lake Arathapescow was the Great Slave Lake, only vaguely defined at the time. Hudson's House was a trading post on the Saskatchewan River.

31. *C.O.* 42/72, 249–56, 2 February 1790.

32. On these expeditions see Williams, *British Search*, pp. 238–48.

33. Menzies to Banks, 4 April 1790, *H.O.* 42/16, 15.

34. *H.O.* 42/16, 18, 12 April 1790.

35. Ibid.

36. Morton to Nepean, 29 April 1790, *C.O.* 77/26.

37. Stephens to Roddam, 8 February 1790, *Adm*. 2/591, 469–70.

38. Stephens to Nepean, 18 March 1790, *H.O.* 28/7, 70, enclosure, Roddam to Stephens, 4 March 1790. *Adm*. 3, 107, 59, 10 March 1790.

39. J. Trotter to Roddam, 9 March 1790, *H.O.* 28/7, 75–6. The fever was probably typhus. The *Gorgon* had been tied up alongside the hulks in Portsmouth harbour.

40. Ibid., 137, 11 April 1790.

41. Meares' memorial, 30 April 1790, *H.O.* 42/16, addressed to Grenville.

42. Cabinet Minute, *H.M.C.* (*Dropmore*) 30, i. p. 579, 30 April 1790.

43. Etches to Banks, 6 May 1790, *Kew B.C.* II, 11.

44. Harlow and Norris suggested that Etches may have introduced Meares to the ministers, but as the former was at this time returning from St Petersburg, such an introduction was not possible, see Harlow, *Founding of the Second British Empire*, Vol. II, p. 447; Norris, 'Policy of the British Cabinet', p. 569n.

45. *B.T.* 3/2, 323, 25 May 1790.

46. Meares to Grenville, 18 May 1790, *H.O.* 42/16, 23. Cf. Harlow, *Founding of the Second British Empire*, vol. II, p. 447n. It is possible that these were manuscript copies.

47. *H.O.* 42/16, 18. *B.T.* 5/6, 113–19, 27 & 28 May 1790.

48. Leeds to Pitt, 2 June 1790, *P.R.O.* (*Chatham*) 30/8 151, fo. 51. Fitzherbert to Leeds, 16 June 1790, ibid., vol. 341, fo. 150. In May 1790 Alleyne Fitzherbert replaced Merry as British Ambassador in Madrid. Leeds to R. Walpole, 29 June 1790, *Add. MSS. 28066, fo. 59 (Leeds MSS.)*.

49. Leeds to Fitzherbert, 16 August 1790, *Add. MSS.* 28066, fo. 217.

50. *H.O.* 42/16, 5 August 1790.

51. In *H.O.* 42/17, 76, November 1790, there is a list of articles with the notation 'to be shipped on *Discovery*'. This is the only suggestion before 11 December that the *Discovery* was at the time intended to go to Nootka. On the other hand the list is the same as that given to Grenville by Banks in April, and may therefore be connected with the expedition planned earlier in the year.

52. Buckingham to Grenville, 9 November 1790, *H.M.C.* (*Dropmore*) 30, i, p. 611.

53. *Adm.* 3/107, 447, 28 December 1790.

54. Menzies to Banks, 12 December 1790, in R.H. Dillon, 'Archibald-Menzies' Trophies', p. 151.

55. *H.O.* 42/17, December [?] 1790. Grenville to Lords of Adm., December 1790, *H.O.* 28/7, 392-9.

56. *Adm.* 106-2635, 20 & 27 December 1790. *Adm.* 106/2636, 4 January, 16 February 1791. *Adm.* 3/108, 11 & 22 February 1791. *Adm.* 106/3322, 113, 20 December 1790, Deptford Yard Letter Book, ibid., 24 December 1790.

57. *P.C.* 2/135, 439-51, 8, 11 & 13 February 1791.

58. *I.O. Home Misc.* 494, pp. 429-41, 23 February 1791.

59. Grenville to Westmoreland, 3 February 1791, *H.M.C.* (Dropmore) 30, II, p. 27.

60. *Adm.* 106/2636, 10 January 1791. Ibid., 24 January 1791. *Adm.* 3/108, 8, 28, 24 & 25 January, 11 & 22 February 1791. *Adm.* 106/2636, 9 & 16 February 1791.

61. *Adm.* 1/4156, 14, 11 February 1791. *H.O.* 28/8, 17-24.

62. *H.O.* 28/61, 394, 11 February 1791.

63. *H.O.* 42/17, 1 January 1791, note in Banks' hand. *Adm.* 3/108, 18, 15 January 1791. Menzies to Banks, 8 February 1791, *Kew B.C.* III, 45.

64. Banks to Maskelyne, 16 February 1791, *Kew B.C.* II, 30.

65. Gooch, along with Lieutenant Hergest, the commander of the *Daedalus*, was killed by the Sandwich Islanders in 1792. Maskelyne to Banks, 19 February 1791, *R.S. Misc. MSS.* 7, 82.9. *Adm.* 106/2636, 8 February 1791.

66. Anderson, *Surveyor of the Sea*, pp. 45-7.

67. *H.O.* 42/18, 20 February 1791, with enclosures.

68. Ibid., enclosure 2.

69. *M.L. Banks* 9, A79-2, fos 7-8.

70. *H.O.* 42/18, enclosure 5.

71. The instructions are in *D.T.C.* VII, fos 197-201, 22 February 1791; also *Add. MSS.* 33979, fos 75-8, and Grenville to Lords of Adm., 25 February 1791, *Adm.* 1/4156, 17.

72. Grenville to Lords of Adm., 23 February 1791, ibid.

73. Nepean to Banks, 24 February 1791, *Add. MSS.* 33979, fo. 80. *Adm.* 2/1344, 8 March 1791.

74. Menzies to Banks, 1 March 1791, *Kew B.C.* II, 34. The previous circumnavigation being that in the *Prince of Wales*. The 'present opposition' was a reference to his dispute with Vancouver over messing arrangements.

75. G. Vancouver, *A Voyage of Discovery to the North Pacific Ocean and Round the World*, vol. I, p. 3. Vancouver to Nepean, 12 March 1791, *C.O.* 5/187, 62-73. Nepean to Vancouver, 17 March 1791, *H.O.* 42/18. Grenville to Lords of Adm., 28 March 1791, *Adm.* 1/4156, 31. *H.O.* 28/8, 50.

76. Stephens to Nepean, 7 May 1791, *H.O.* 28/8, 66. Nepean to Stephens, 10 & 26 May 1791, *Adm.* 1/4156, 43, 46. *Adm.* 2/1344, 20 July 1791.

77. *Adm.* 1/4156, 50, 6 July 1791.

78. This summary of events is based on the unusual occurrence of a letter from Dundas to the Admiralty among the Banks Correspondence. *H.R.N.S.W.*, vol. I, ii, pp. 499-501, 6 July 1791. Also Banks to Nepean, 11 July 1791, ibid., pp. 502-3.

79. Menzies to Banks, 20 March 1791, ibid., pp. 480-1.

80. Banks to Nepean 11 July 1791, *H.R.N.S.W.*, vol. I, ii, pp. 502-3. Banks to Menzies, 10 August 1791, ibid., pp. 520-1. Banks to Nepean, 10 November 1791, ibid., p. 551.

81. Banks to Menzies, 10 August 1791, ibid., p. 521.

82. Banks to Nepean, 10 November 1791, ibid., p. 551.

83. Banks to Richards, 31 December 1791, *H.R.N.S.W.*, vol. I, ii, p. 580.

84. *Adm.* 2/1344, 10 August 1791. *Adm.* 3/108, 247, 10 August 1791.

85. Vancouver, *Voyage of Discovery*, vol. I, p. 384.

86. Papers on the negotiations between Quadra and Vancouver, including the testimony of Robert Duffin, a witness to the seizure of 1789, are in *C.O.* 5/187, 45–61, September 1792.

87. This account is taken from Vancouver's *Voyage of Discovery*, which remains the best account of the expedition. Menzies' *Journal* provides a valuable supplementary account. Some of the manuscript logs and journals of the *Discovery* and *Chatham* are in *Adm. MSS.* 17542 to 17551.

88. Menzies, ibid., fos 30–1, 119.

89. Good examples are in Menzies to Banks, 1 January 1793, *D.T.C.* VIII, fos 142–55, and Menzies to Banks, 1 October 1794, ibid., IX, fos 105–8.

90. Banks to Portland, 3 February 1796, *D.T.C.* X (i), fos 15–16.

91. *Philosophical Transactions of the Royal Society*, LXXXVI, 1796, p. 385.

92. Menzies, *Journal*, fo. 280.

93. Menzies to Banks, 28 April 1795, *D.T.C.* IX, fo. 213. Menzies to Banks, 14 September 1795, ibid., fos 288–91. Menzies to Banks, 21 October 1796, ibid., X, fos 80–2, with enclosed notes on the affair, fos 83–6.

94. Etches to Banks, 19 May 1792; F.W. Howay, 'Four Letters from Richard Cadman Etches to Sir Joseph Banks', pp. 125–39.

95. Nepean to Meares, June 1793, *C.O.* 5/187, 79–80.

96. Grenville to Dundas, 10 June 1793, ibid., 74. Dundas to Grenville, June 1793, ibid., 82.

97. St Helens to Grenville, 14 January 1794, *Adm.* 1/4160. Ibid., 17 February 1794.

98. G. Mackaness, *Sir Joseph Banks. His Relations with Australia*, pp. 136, 138, 302. Pearce brought back plants for Banks, see W. Dawson (ed.), *The Banks Letters*, p. 210.

99. The general similarities between the Nootka and Falkland Island crises were often alluded to at the time, see *Monthly Review*, New Series, vol. III, September–December 1790.

100. Dundas to Lords of Adm., 20 July 1793, *H.O.* 29/2, 217–18.

101. *Adm.* 2/124, 386, 15 August 1793. Ibid., 390, 17 August 1793. Mackaness, *Sir Joseph Banks*, p. 300.

102. *Adm.* 2/124, 506, 4 October 1793.

103. Broughton to Stephens, 10 & 15 October, 4 December 1793, *Adm.* 1/1508. *H.O.* 28/62, 391–2, 26 October 1793. *H.O.* 29/3, 24, 4 November 1793. *Adm.* 2/125, 167, 29 November 1793. The ship was allowed three lieutenants, three masters' mates and six midshipmen. *Adm.* 3/125, 247–8, 31 December 1793. *Adm.* 1/1509, 4, 11, 12 & 25 February 1794 on manning and stores.

104. *Adm.* 1/1509, 17 March, 2 April, 1 May 1794. *Adm.* 2/125, 16 April, 26 August, 19 September, 5 October 1794. *Adm.* 2/126, 487, 23 September 1794.

105. No copy of Broughton's instructions seems to have survived. This account is based on material in the Captain's log in *Adm.* 55/147, and on W.R. Broughton, *A Voyage of Discovery to the North Pacific Ocean*.

106. Vancouver, *Voyage of Discovery*, vol. III, p. 455.

107. Broughton, *Voyage*, pp. lv, 65. D. Barrington, *Polar Tracts*, p. vii, *Miscellanies*.

108. Cf. M. Roe (ed.), *Journals and Letters of Captain Charles Bishop*, p. xxiv.

109. The reef now bears the name of its victim. Strangely, the schooner is never named in Broughton's log, or his *Journal*.

PART TWO

5 FOOD FOR SLAVES

In December 1787 a most unusual vessel left Spithead and proceeded down the Channel on a voyage which was intended to take about two years. Outwardly the ship looked like a medium-sized merchant sloop, with slightly shortened masts. But below decks she looked like no other commissioned ship in His Majesty's Navy. The decks were mounted with rows of garden pots and tubs, and an elaborate system of ventilation and drainage. The pots even occupied what would normally have been the commander's cabin, and he was relegated to a small cabin to one side of the vessel. A few of the pots carried recognisable plants — mostly English fruit trees — but the majority were empty.

This ship was actually off to the South Pacific to gather living plants of the Tahitian breadfruit, Artocarpus altilis, and to carry them to the West Indian islands of St Vincent and Jamaica. This voyage has been remembered as the occasion of the most notorious mutiny in naval history, and as marking the historical debut of one of England's more controversial sea officers. But in spite of the continuing flood of literature on the voyage, there has been scant attention paid to its background or to its actual purpose. Was the British government in the habit of sending naval vessels on jaunts of 30,000 miles with the sole purpose of gathering specimens of exotic plants? Or was this the product of a collective national madness — a sentimental journey in fulfilment of some irrational dream? Had the lure of Tahiti and its lifestyle even infected the staid ranks of William Pitt's ministry? The answers to these questions involve aspects of eighteenth-century artistic taste; attitudes to empire and economic power after 1783; and the activities of that scientific imperialist, Sir Joseph Banks.

The aspect of artistic taste was part of a tradition which stretched from Pliny to Pope. The eighteenth century was, *inter alia*, an age of decorative gardens, and of gardeners. One of England's more notable contributions to the neo-classical movement was the landscape garden in which the formal, regular and ostentatious shapes of the baroque era were swept away to be replaced with no-less cultivated, but naturalistic, landscapes complemented by artificial lakes and classical ruins blended into the surroundings. The gardens at Stowe and Stourhead epitomised the quest for wilderness or Arcadian images, suggestive of virtue, harmony and sympathy with nature. The 'picturesque' in landscape, of which Kent, 'Capability' Brown and Repton were the greatest exponents, involved historical or archaeological images, of a time when man was at one with his environment. Classical ruins, grottos and temples of worthies associated the eighteenth-century landed gentry with medieval and classical predecessors, all deriving their strength from the soil and its products. The vistas from the country villa looked out through 'wild' forests to the cultivated corn fields beyond, for, in the words of Addison:

> why may not a whole estate be thrown into a kind of garden by frequent plantations, that may turn as much to the profit, as the pleasure of the owner.[1]

These associations could have geographical as well as historical dimensions. The rivalling antiquity of China began to make its effect on gardens in the form of pagodas, tea pavilions and other items of chinoiserie which began to appear after mid-century. The search for more exotic decorative plants was intensified in the new era of exploration. Eventually, with the voyages of Bougainville and Cook, the Arcadian quest encompassed the south Pacific. The perception of the explorers and the artists they carried with them was of a naturalistic landscape with lush forests, steep cliff walls, and waterfalls, instead of lakes and temples. A naïve and noble savage formed part of this imagery, as he sheltered in a protective grotto from the elemental powers of nature. This romantic prospect frequently conflated the dramatic and verdant landscape of Tahiti, with the real economy of its inhabitants. Man and environment seemed to be at one.[2]

Although nature's wild garden had had its effects on Sir Joseph Banks when he travelled with Cook, the sort of gardens in which he was interested by the 1780s were largely botanic ones. At Kew, Chelsea and Edinburgh, men were trained in the empirical processes of observation, comparison and evaluation, and they began to gather comprehensive collections of native and exotic plants for microscopic examination. Drawing on the pioneer work in plant classification carried out by Linnaeus, England despatched plant collectors to every corner of the globe, and these men sent home living plant specimens, seeds and dried samples to their patrons and employers.

From the middle of the eighteenth century onwards the utilitarian strain in natural history became more pronounced as scientists and collectors interested themselves in the practical benefits which might be reaped from their endeavours. In many respects the world of nature had not endowed equally the peoples of the earth. Botanists in particular believed that their technical skills would enable them to rectify this imbalance by transferring certain natural productions from one region to another, and acclimatising them in the new environment. There was a genuinely humane component in this train of thought. Periodic famine in India, for example, might be averted by the establishment of sago and date plantations founded on transplanted stock. However, the main objectives of those promoting plant transfer were unabashedly economic, and had as their purpose the closer integration of imperial possessions with an industrialising mother country. English cotton mills might be supplied with fine raw cotton from within the empire, following the transplantation of cotton seeds. The Navy might be supplied with hemp and flax grown in Ireland or Canada. The Dutch stranglehold over the spice trade might be broken by the production of spices in British dominions. Coffee, indigo, cochineal, tea, silk — all might be produced within the Empire.

Such schemes had the mercantilist purpose of destroying the monopolies or predominance of rival nations, and substituting Britain's own. Botany and great power rivalry became curiously intertwined, as nations endeavoured to guard their precious colonial treasures while seeking to filch those of their competitors. This competition was most intense over tropical productions, and the regions of greatest concern were South America, the West Indies, India and South-east Asia. It was in such a context that Captain Bligh's breadfruit expedition was planned and executed.

By the time of the Seven Years War it had been realised that West Indian dependence on a single crop, such as sugar, had a number of drawbacks and there were numerous attempts to diversify the Caribbean economy. In 1760 the Society of Arts had offered a premium for the encouragement of cinnamon production, and over the next 40 years such premiums were extended to a number of other tropical products including cochineal, silk, indigo, fine cotton, cloves, camphor and coffee. As a complementary step, the Society, in 1762, made available a premium to anyone establishing a nursery or botanic garden on the island of St Vincent for the propagation of useful plants and the reception of transplanted varieties from Asia.[3]

It was as a response to this offer that a garden was begun on a 20-acre site outside Kingstown in 1765 and for a few years it enjoyed moderate success. After 1774 it went into a state of decay partly, it seems, because its superintendent, Dr George Young, helped himself to its produce.[4]

Banks had been a member of the Society of Arts since 1761, and after 1770 used his influence to guide the direction of policy in the distribution of premiums.[5] At the same time he began to correspond with planters in the West Indies, offering them assistance in collecting exotic plants. It may well have been Banks who suggested to the West Indians the idea of transplanting breadfruit, for he had been introduced to the variety during Cook's first voyage and had recognised its value as a food crop. 'In the article of food these happy people may almost be said to be exempt from the curse of our forefathers;' he wrote of the Tahitians, 'scarcely can it be said that they earn their bread with the sweat of their brow when their chiefest substance, Breadfruit, is procur'd with no more trouble than that of climbing a tree and pulling it down.'[6]

To the planters of the British West Indies the advantages of such a plant as food for their slaves seemed obvious. One such planter, Hinton East of Jamaica, cogently expressed the general view:

> The acquisition of the best kind of the Breadfruit wou'd be of infinite Importance to the West India Islands in affording exclusive of variety, a wholesome and pleasant Food to our Negroes, which wd. have this great Advantage over the Plantain Trees from whence our Slaves derive a great part of their Subsistence, that the former wou'd be rais'd with infinitely less labour and not be subject to be destroy'd by every smart Gale of Wind as the latter are.[7]

Both Banks and East were oversimplifying the Tahitian economy. Breadfruit was important in the Tahitian diet, but it had been traditionally supplemented by sea foods, pork, banana and taro. In those Pacific Islands where it was the single staple, there were always problems of seasonal scarcity — problems which survive in the Marquesas and on Truk Island (in the Caroline Islands) where it remains the principal food crop.[8] It is at this point that the myth of Tahiti and the notion of the noble savage exerted their power, for Banks and East were reflecting the prevailing primitivism which looked to a natural society in which nothing is wanting and food is in abundance. In this sense the breadfruit was more than a food plant: it was a symbol of a simple and idyllic life free from worries about work or property. The scientists had lost their objectivity by idealising Tahitian society, or, at least, in assuming that if the Tahitian 'savage' was something less than noble, this was not the fault of his environment. For this reason they did not see the breadfruit in its true light — as a subsistence food — but as royal fare, freely and continuously available.

Such beliefs clearly provided a background to the schemes to transfer tropical plants, and with the advice and encouragement of Banks, the West Indian interest exerted every pressure for the introduction of the breadfruit into the British Caribbean. In April 1772 Valentine Morris, a planter with estates in the West Indies, Captain General of those islands, and a later Governor of St Vincent, strongly endorsed the introduction of the plant into the Sugar Islands and sought Banks' assistance in drawing up a plan of action.[9] Three years later, in partial response to this call, John Ellis, FRS, a friend of Banks and a correspondent of Linnaeus, published a pamphlet under the auspices of the Society of West India Merchants which described the breadfruit and mangosteen, and recommended their introduction to the West Indies as food for slaves. Citing the opinions of a bevy of travellers from the Dutchman, Rumphius, through to Cook, and including the remarks of 'a gentleman of distinction who accompanied Captain Cook', Ellis supplied advice for anybody likely to carry the plants to the West Indies. The pamphlet was appropriately dedicated to Cook's patron, the Earl of Sandwich, for his 'zeal in the field of discovery'.[10]

Interest in the transfer of plants to the West Indies was maintained throughout the early years of the war for America. Towards the end of 1776 the Society of Arts offered a prize for the successful transplantation of the breadfruit to the West Indies, and the West India Merchants, in February of the following year, offered a similar inducement, but 'in a more ample manner than is provided by the Society of Arts and Manufactures'.[11] It was even rumoured at this time that a government-sponsored expedition was to go to the Pacific to collect the breadfruit.[12] Charles Clerke, just returned from Cook's second voyage, was thought to be taking a ship to the Pacific to return the Tahitian Omai to his native land, and Lieutenant George Vancouver, in a later memorandum to Banks on the subject of breadfruit, recalled a suggestion at that time that Clerke should bring back a cargo of the plants.[13] Whatever the substance of this rumour the expedition did not eventuate and the West Indies had to be content with a promise from Banks to send a shipment of East Indian plants for the purposes of experimentation.[14]

The arrival in American waters of the French fleet under D'Estaing late in 1778 led to a postponement of the attempts to transplant the breadfruit, but with the cessation of hostilities efforts were vigorously renewed, and they gained heightened impetus from the great economic changes foreshadowed by American independence. After 1783, the Americans were placed outside the imperial economic network, and the West Indies were therefore cut off from their principal source of supply as well as from an important market for their molasses. Despite strong representations from the West India Committee, making clear the damaging effects that a rigorous interpretation of the Navigation Laws would have on the islands, the Pitt government remained adamant that except in the most calamitous of circumstances, American shipping must be excluded from the West Indian trade.[15]

Notwithstanding the impossibility of enforcing these restrictions efficiently, or the ultimate impracticability of the British policy, real fears were aroused among the planters. The exclusion of American shipping would mean expensive food for their slaves, cutting back profits and producing periodic famine.[16] Brian Edwards, the contemporary historian of the islands, claimed in 1794 that the restrictive measures had caused the death of 15,000 Negroes in Jamaica alone, and although the reliability of his statistics may be questioned, they nevertheless suggest considerable distress in the Sugar Islands in the decade after American independence.[17] Despairing of sympathy for their predicament from the British government, the planters of the West Indies looked to any feasible scheme which might provide an answer for their problems. It was in this atmosphere that plans for plant transfer were renewed after 1783, and from the outset it was Banks who provided the central direction.

Being a methodical man, Banks realised that one of the preconditions for the successful transfer of exotic plants was a network of suitable reception centres for specimens which might already have suffered the rigours of a long sea voyage. This meant the establishment of well-tended botanical gardens on the Kew model where the introduced plants could be acclimatised. Upon the peace Banks made enquiries to find what progress had been made in this direction in the West Indies. He was happily surprised. By 1784 there were two botanic gardens in Jamaica. One of these a public garden maintained by the Jamaica Assembly; the other a private one on the estate of the planter, Hinton East, which already contained the mangosteen, cinnamon and several varieties of tea plant.[18]

There had also been efforts to restore the garden on St Vincent. Banks had interested both the King and the Secretary at War, Sir George Yonge, in this project, and in February 1785 the latter ordered Governor Lincoln to appoint one Alexander Anderson as the new superintendent of the garden at a salary of 7s 6d a day. Reconstruction work on the site was to begin immediately with the specific view of cultivating introduced economic and medicinal plants.[19] Banks was consulted on organisation and expenditure, and it was thought that costs could be kept down to £300 a year.[20] Despite some initial disputes between Anderson and Lincoln over the presence of some of the Governor's livestock in the garden, the enterprise soon got under way, and by May 1785 the superintendent was able to send Yonge a catalogue of 59 plants including cinnamon, sago, gum Senegal, the oil palm and the coconut.[21]

Until its closure in 1821, the botanic garden on St Vincent remained under the control of the War Office, and at the time there were sound administrative reasons for this. Because of its comparatively recent capture from France, St Vincent was still very much a garrison island and it was, therefore, inevitable that the War Office should have more contact with it than did other government departments. Throughout his term as Secretary at War, Yonge took a personal interest in the garden and did everything in his power to promote it. For Banks it was an especially favourable arrangement. By virtue of his position as head of the army, the King had more control over the activities of the War Office than of any other branch of administration. George III was extremely interested in natural history, and in the St Vincent botanic garden in particular, and thus an immediate and valuable channel of communication was opened up.[22] As Banks was soon to discover, it was also useful to have plants carried to and from the island in the care of army officers who were not only responsible to government, but sensitive to the power of the monarch's favour.[23]

Between 1783 and 1786 momentum for the introduction of esculent exotic plants continued to grow in the West Indies. Banks despatched plants and seeds to Hinton East in December 1784, and promised to provide useful information on the cultivation of East Indian plants.[24] Planters from the various islands requested new plants and sent regular reports to Banks on the state of those already in their care. Sir George Yonge provided information on the progress at St Vincent and forwarded Anderson's annual reports to Banks for his consideration and advice.[25] In the second half of 1786 Hinton East was himself in England, canvassing support for the transplantation of breadfruit, and he discussed the matter at Banks' country house at Spring Grove.[26]

Motives other than commercial or humanitarian ones were intervening to hasten action on the breadfruit question. England was by no means the only country interested in utilising the plants of the Pacific and East Indies in her colonies. Ellis' account of the breadfruit had gone into a French edition in 1779, and the French had successfully transplanted nutmegs, cloves and the East Indian varieties of the breadfruit to Mauritius, and indeed some of these plants had been transferred from thence to the French West Indies.[27] This activity provided an element of economic rivalry which became quite intense. A West Indian planter described to Banks an incident during the war when a French ship captured in the Caribbean was found to be carrying a cargo of plants from Mauritius, including the breadfruit. On finding its capture inevitable the crew set about destroying as many plants as possible to prevent their falling into British hands.[28]

Such competition acted as a spur to the British efforts and West Indian planters were not slow to contrast French energy with the apparent lethargy of the British and Colonial governments. 'Had our good People the Attention of the French to their Colonies,' Mathew Wallen wrote to Banks, 'we should not be long without these [plants]. The only Consideration of our Masters is how they can tax our Staple high enough.' As to the Jamaica Assembly: 'I despair of their doing anything, nothing but Languor and Dispondence is here.'[29] Early in February 1787 Yonge excitedly reported to Banks the arrival in the French West Indies of a ship which reputedly had on board breadfruit and other plants to the value of £2,000. 'It must therefore be acknowledged the French are beforehand with us, and that which from our Forms and the Coldness of our Tempers, we are deliberating, Their Vivacity makes them act unencumbered with the Forms, or other Impediments.'[30]

By January 1787 Banks had convinced the Pitt Ministry of the need to send out an expedition to collect breadfruit for the West Indies. The mechanics of the decision are not obvious but Banks had regular meetings with the King at this time on the subject of Kew Gardens, and it is clear that he had interested Lord Hawkesbury,

President of the Board of Trade, in the scheme. Cheap food for the slave populations would give British sugar producers a competitive edge, and the decision conformed to the new assertiveness of the Board of Trade. Official notice of the government's determination to equip an expedition was conveyed in a letter of 13 February from Pitt to Samuel Long, Treasurer of the West India Committee.[31]

In its early stages, the breadfruit expedition was linked by the government with another enterprise in the south Pacific with which Banks was closely connected — the transportation of felons to Botany Bay. In August 1786, the government had settled upon New South Wales as a convict site, and by 12 November 1786 Governor Phillip had been given his first commission. It was initially suggested that after disposing of its cargo at Botany Bay, one of the transports should be properly fitted out, equipped with a suitable captain and crew and thus be despatched to fetch the breadfruit. In February 1787, Banks gave Pitt a plan of the voyage along these lines, together with draft instructions for Governor Phillip in fitting the vessel and drawing up instructions for her commander.[32] By this plan the vessel would sail first to New Zealand where it was to take on samples of the flax *Phormium tenax* which would be tried as naval cordage. Leaving New Zealand the ship was to proceed to Tahiti, load up with breadfruit plants, and sail to the West Indies via the Dutch East Indies, Mauritius and the Cape of Good Hope, picking up other plants on the way.

The gardener whom Banks had chosen to care for the breadfruit in transit, was to go out with the fleet to New South Wales and by early March 1787 Banks had drafted his instructions and advanced money towards his outfit.[33] David Nelson had sailed on Cook's third voyage under the patronage of Banks and had thus made contact with both the Tahitians and the breadfruit.[34] With the instructions Banks included a three-page printed document which gave the opinions of Dampier, Anson and Cook on the breadfruit and enumerated its many advantages. It also described the subscription entered into by the West India planters and merchants; a subscription which Banks was able to point out would bring Nelson financial gain in proportion to the number of plants which arrived safely in the West Indies.[35]

Sometime in the second half of March 1787 Banks' opinions on the original plan changed, for by the end of that month he had set his mind strongly against sending one of the transports from Botany Bay to collect the breadfruit. Having got a foot in the door by way of the government's acceptance in principle of the scheme, he set about replanning the expedition. On 30 March he circulated a letter stating the disadvantages of sending a ship from Botany Bay and proposing, instead, the fitting out of a vessel in England. One copy of this letter went to Lord Hawkesbury, and his support for the expedition suggests the proposal supplemented his measures on the West Indian trade and the self-sufficiency of empire. Another copy of the letter went to Banks' personal friend and companion on the voyage to Newfoundland and Labrador in 1766, Lord Mulgrave. Mulgrave was also a member of the Board of Trade, and like Banks he was involved in private trading expeditions to the north-west coast of America, and in other maritime enterprise in the Pacific. One more copy of the letter reached the Secretary of State for Home Affairs, Lord Sydney, and formed the basis of the instructions to the Admiralty of 5 May, setting up the expedition.[36]

In these letters Banks argued that the proper equipping of a vessel at Botany Bay would severely tax the resources of the infant colony. The casks needed for housing the plants would be valuable commodities in New South Wales, and the colony could ill-afford to lose other timber and provisions. Because of the specialised and difficult nature of the task, he reasoned that it would be easier to find a captain and crew in England; he obviously had doubts as to the suitability of a transport captain and was thinking of appointing a commander who had sailed with Cook. He added to this the tenuous argument that a ship leaving from England would have to traverse only 420 degrees of longitude, as against 480 from Botany Bay, making an estimated difference of four to five months in the length of the voyage.[37]

The second part of the letter gave the details of the plan. A brig of about 200 tons would be fitted out and manned with 30 seamen. Because of her small complement, the vessel should be fitted with close quarters and six four-pounder carriage guns lest the Tahitians felt inclined to take advantage of their numerical superiority.[38] The best track for the ship would be via Cape Horn to the Society Islands, returning through Endeavour Strait to Princes Island in the Straits of Sunda, where she would take on plants specified by Banks, and thence to the West Indies via the Cape of Good Hope and St Helena. As the easterly monsoons commenced in March or April, the ship should leave England in July so that she might avoid them in the passage of Endeavour Strait. This revised plan was closely related to Banks' experience on the *Endeavour*, and would have the effect of bringing the voyage more closely under his supervision.[39]

This new initiative must have thrown Lord Sydney a little out of step. The convict fleet was due to sail early in April and only last minute difficulties delayed it until 13 May. What induced the government to accept the change of plan? Banks' suggestion that the equipping of the expedition would have been a drain on the resources of the new colony was undeniably true, more especially as the first fleet itself was poorly supplied. Another pertinent consideration may have been the unwillingness of the contractors to have their vessels used for an expedition which would have been barely profitable for them, and which did not have a component of private trade.[40] But one is drawn finally to the prestige and influence of Banks himself — forces which were very much in evidence at the time of the fitting out of the breadfruit expedition.

Sydney's orders to the Admiralty of 5 May set the wheels in motion, but it seemed unlikely that a ship would be ready by July, the month reckoned as most suitable for its sailing. None the less, the Admiralty attacked the problem with vigour, and from the outset sought the guidance of Banks in equipping the expedition. The first problem was to find a suitable ship and by 16 May the Navy Board was able to report that five vessels had been put forward. Not being fully *au fait* as to the requirements of the expedition, they were anxious that Banks should help Mr Mitchell, the Assistant Surveyor, on the final choice of a ship. It was accordingly arranged by the Secretary of the Admiralty, that Banks and Nelson should accompany Mitchell to Wapping for this purpose. On Wednesday, 23 May, the Navy Board was able to inform the Admiralty that the *Bethia*, 'which has been approv'd by Sir Joseph Banks', had been purchased for £1,950 and was ready to be taken to Deptford Yard for refitting. Once the vessel was on the stocks at Deptford the Navy Board again sought Banks' advice and the Yard officers were therefore ordered by the Admiralty to fit the ship according to Banks' instructions.[41]

On 8 June Banks and Nelson went down to Deptford and suggested several changes relating to the storage and watering of the plants. The commander was to surrender the great cabin which was to be enlarged to accommodate the breadfruit. Gratings were to be provided in the decks and sides to supply the plants with fresh air, and the upper parts of the deck were to be linked with lead to drain off water used on the plants so that it might flow back to the reservoir without being wasted. Various items, such as watering cans, were to be provided and a stove was to be placed in the great cabin to keep the plants warm on the voyage round the Cape. After discussions between Banks and the dockyard officers, the ship's complement was established at 45 men, exclusive of gardeners, and she was to be registered on the lists of the Navy as an armed vessel with the name of the *Bounty*.[42]

Banks' part in the fitting out of the ship is quite remarkable. His earlier experience with the Navy had shown how sensitive a body it could be in regard to the fitting and equipping of vessels. This was normally regarded as the distinct preserve of the Navy Board whose judgement on the matter was not to be thwarted. Banks had broken through this tradition, with the encouragement of the Navy Board, and despite his own regrettable pronouncements on the sailing qualities of ships at the time of the confusion over Cook's second voyage. That he had done so suggests, not only that he had recouped the esteem of the Admiralty and Navy Board, but also that his experience in the conditions of the south Pacific, and his knowledge of botany made his direction of the enterprise invaluable and inevitable. Of course, he could not attend the dockyard officers all the time, and this task was deputised to Nelson for the duration of the fitting. But Banks remained continually in touch, even when out of town. Before leaving for his Lincolnshire estates in September, he asked Under-Secretary of State Evan Nepean if anything further was desired of him, and requested that he be informed of any new problems.[43]

By 14 August, the *Bounty* had left the dock and was ready to receive men. Here Banks' hand was also visible. Nelson, the gardener, had been appointed on 1 March 1787, and his salary and conditions of employment were established by Banks. In August, Lord Sydney, claiming to be totally unacquainted with what was required, asked Banks to write the gardener's instructions and to request that Nelson attend the equipping and victualling of the ship. Banks also drew up the instructions of Brown, the assistant gardener.[44]

Banks was directly responsible for the appointment of William Bligh as the commander of the *Bounty*. Since the end of the American war, Bligh had been on half-pay and had entered the service of his merchant uncle, Duncan Campbell, as a captain in the West India trade. But on his return from a voyage to Jamaica in August 1787 he found himself once more in Navy employ. On 6 August he wrote to Banks:

I yesterday arrived from Jamaica, and should have instantly paid my respects to you had not Mr Campbell told me you were not to return from the country until Thursday. I have heard the flattering news of your great goodness to me, intending to honour me with the command of the vessel which you propose to go to the South Seas.[45]

Ten days later Bligh received his official commission. Banks also arranged the appointment of one of the midshipmen, Hallett, on a representation from the boy's father, and he was clearly regarded as the most appropriate person to apply to for a position, as a number of unsuccessful applications makes clear.[46]

Because of the specialised nature of the task she was to undertake, the equipping and victualling of the *Bounty* differed from that of a vessel on routine service, and as Bligh himself pointed out to Banks, 'Capt. Cook's supplies are a president [sic] the different boards are govern'd by'. This was particularly the case with respect to the supply of anti-scorbutics. There, indeed, was the rub, for the provisions list of the *Bounty* revealed the chaotic thinking on scurvy which had been one of the less fortunate legacies of Cook. The special victuals included such tasty items as essence of malt, flour of mustard, portable soup, kiln dried wheat and barley instead of the usual seaman's fare of oatmeal, Muscavado sugar in place of oil, juice of wort and supplies of salt for pickling any fresh meat acquired on the voyage. None of these items contain other than the barest trace elements of ascorbic acid, and there is no reference to lemon or orange juice in the victualling records. As well as food provisions, the *Bounty* was supplied with articles of barter with which to purchase plants and necessaries at Tahiti. The list of articles was provided by Banks and was based on his own experience of Tahitian consumer tastes in 1769, with an allowance for the rising expectations fostered by Cook's second and third voyages.[47]

In early October, the sailing of the *Bounty* was delayed by a general impressment connected with the crisis in the Netherlands, but by 4 November she had taken on her guns and moved around to Spithead to await orders for sailing.[48] While lying at Spithead, Bligh received various navigational instruments and other stores through the efforts of Banks, and he pressed the latter to intercede with Earl Howe to secure his promotion. Throughout November and December, the commander had difficulty with manning and on 4 November he mentioned to his patron doubts about the drunken surgeon,

Thomas Huggan. Banks' endorsement of this letter shows eight-eenth-century patronage in action: 'I offered my interest to any surgeon's mate who would go out as able with C. Bligh.'[49]

Bligh's sailing orders were issued on 20 November, and from the beginning of December onwards he made repeated efforts to leave, but he was continually frustrated by manning problems and con-trary winds. Such delay obviously imperilled his chances of round-ing Cape Horn, and once again Bligh looked to Banks to provide a remedy in the form of discretionary orders allowing him to proceed via the Cape of Good Hope if winds made the other passage impass-able. Once again Banks prevailed on Earl Howe and the appropriate orders were despatched. On 27 December the *Bounty* finally put out from Spithead.[50]

The sad tale of that voyage is of little concern in the present context. Suffice it to say that Bligh was an extremely able sailor, and in this respect perhaps the best of Cook's disciples: the smooth voyage as far as Tahiti and the 3,500-mile journey across uncharted seas in an open, crowded 23-foot launch are clear enough indica-tions of this. Compared with a commander such as Vancouver, Bligh used the lash sparingly but he was less restrained with his mocking and abusive tongue: a sailor's pride could be just as sensi-tive as his back.[51]

At every opportunity during the voyage the commander had writ-ten to Banks giving detailed accounts of his progress. After the mutiny and subsequent launch journey, Bligh, high with fever, wrote a plaintive and anguished letter from Batavia stressing the need for an inquiry into the mutiny, and affirming his own blamelessness. His sense of responsibility to Banks was apparent:

> Had I been accidently appointed to the Command, the loss of the ship would give me no material concern; but when I reflect that it was through you, Sir, who undertook to assert I was fully capa-ble, and the Eyes of everyone regarding the progress of the Voy-age, and perhaps with more envy than delight, I cannot but say it affects me considerably.[52]

To this letter he appended a 17-page report of the voyage and mutiny, requesting that Banks should convey the account to the Admiralty since his own report to that body had been more cursory.

Despite the untimely end of the first breadfruit expedition, there was never any suggestion that the whole project should be abandoned.

The planters of the West Indies continued to press for the introduction of the species and Banks was hopeful that another expedition would be prepared. In February and March 1790, as the survey vessels *Discovery* and *Gorgon* were being readied for sea, plans were formulated for the second of these to touch at Tahiti to apprehend the mutineers. Under-Secretary of State, Evan Nepean, suggested that the *Gorgon* might be loaded with breadfruit plants for her return passage.[53] But the time for such an adventure was not propitious for the crisis with Spain intervened to forestall events. Nevertheless, by the middle of 1790 plans were once again afoot and there is perhaps no more significant example of Banks' power than that within a year of Bligh's return from the catastrophe of the first breadfruit expedition, Banks had prevailed on the government to send out a second, and that under the same luckless commander.

Bligh had returned to England in March 1790 but it was not until October that the business of his procedural court-martial for the loss of his ship was over, and he was honourably acquitted. Despite its failure, the first voyage had brought him some advantages. The Jamaica Assembly voted him £600 as a recompense for his diligence and suffering, and he had a meeting with the King. An expected promotion to post captain was not so forthcoming and in December Banks wrote to Chatham, the First Lord of the Admiralty, soliciting preferment for Bligh as the 'suspense preys grievously on his mind, tho' he tries to conceal it'. Ten days later the promotion came through.[54]

In this letter to Chatham of 10 December, Banks had referred to the fitting out of a new breadfruit expedition and in a later letter to Lord Auckland he observed: '. . . the King has already order'd a ship to be prepar'd to visit the South Sea Islands a second time in order to bring the breadfruit, to the West Indies.'[55] From the outset, it was assumed that Bligh would be in command and he was involved in the early planning stages of the voyage. For two months, however, preparations seemed to be at a standstill so that Banks, apprehensive at the loss of time, wrote to Chatham for a progress report. The First Lord replied on 9 March:

> I received the favor of your letter, and in consequence will lose no time in giving the necessary directions for preparing a vessel for the purpose of the expedition to procure the breadfruit . . . the idea you suggest of a tender to accompany him [Bligh] certainly appears highly proper.[56]

This got things moving, for by the end of March, two suitable vessels had been found and Bligh had selected Nathaniel Portlock as the commander of the tender, and Francis Godolphin Bond as his own First Lieutenant. Grenville, Secretary of State since 1789, issued the belated official orders for the preparation of the expedition on 29 March, but these differed little from those issued to the Admiralty four years earlier, save for the provision for two ships. At the same time, he ordered the two new gardeners, James Wiles and Christopher Smith, to be accommodated on board according to Banks' directions. Both men were to be borne on the books of the ships as supernumeraries and victualled along with the crew: Wiles receiving, in addition, a salary of £70 and Smith one of £60. Banks himself paid for the equipping and maintenance of the gardeners until they joined the ships in June. He also procured garden implements, pots, watering cans and presents for the Tahitians on his own account, after authorisation from Nepean. In November he was still attempting to have these bills settled.[57]

During April the fitting of the vessels went ahead rapidly and on the 18th the Admiralty ordered that they be registered as the *Providence*, sixth rate, and the *Assistance*, armed tender. Considering the fate of their predecessor, there was possibly a touch of irony in these names. Essentially, the two vessels were to be fitted and manned as the *Bounty* had been, although there were indications that the Navy had benefited from that earlier experience: two large launches were to be supplied in addition to the smaller cutters and jolly boats; orange and lemon juice appeared on the victualling lists; and the crew of the *Providence* was much larger than that of the *Bounty*, included a higher proportion of officers to men, and boasted 20 marines. By the end of July the ships were fully manned, had taken on their guns and were ready to sail.[58]

Not long before the vessels put to sea, Banks forwarded signed copies of the gardeners' instructions and information relating to the storage and care of the plants. These too followed the format of those for the first voyage, although Banks emphasised that the first duty of the gardeners was absolute obedience to the commanding officer — an injunction he had not thought necessary for the *Bounty* voyage.[59] He suggested to the government that Bligh be allowed £500 for purchasing plants in the East Indies and Ile de France and he also suggested that the ship might drop some useful plants to the isolated little outpost on Norfolk Island. On 3 August, the vessels sailed from Spithead.

Bligh's second voyage was a marked contrast to the first. Despite his continuing attacks of malaria — a legacy of the launch journey and sojourn at Batavia — relations with the crew were smooth throughout. He took much care over their health and they seemed to find him a congenial commander. As well as collecting plants, Bligh was able to make some valuable discoveries around Tasmania, the Fiji Islands and the treacherous Torres Strait. At Tahiti, where the breadfruit were collected, relations with the Islanders were cordial and the ships managed to depart without any crew members absconding.[60]

Bligh touched at St Helena on the return journey and there some plants were deposited in the botanic garden and others taken on board the *Providence* in return. Although some of the plants had perished in the heat of Torres Strait, the greater part had survived up to this point and many had propagated. At St Vincent 544 plants were put into Anderson's care and again some were taken on board for Kew: most of the remainder of the cargo was left at Jamaica. Wiles' instructions had offered him the opportunity of remaining on that island to care for the plants and before the ships left in June 1793 he had succumbed to the Jamaican insistence that he should do so. The ships themselves had been obliged to wait in the West Indies for a convoy as the war with France had begun, and it was not until 7 August that they anchored at Deptford. There the plants for Kew were off-loaded and the crew paid off. On 9 September Bligh ended his commission and the *Providence* was appropriated to another expedition.[61]

In terms of what it had directly set out to achieve, the expedition was a great success. On inspecting the plants taken to Kew, Banks reported to Chatham that he 'had never before seen plants brought home by Sea even in a small box, nearly in so flourishing a state', and he commended Bligh, Portlock and the gardeners for their diligence.[62] The planters of the Caribbean were similarly pleased. Bligh was granted a thousand guineas for his efforts by the Jamaica Assembly and Portlock received five hundred. The plants themselves continued to thrive in the West Indies, and by October 1793 Wiles was able to report to Banks that some had already been distributed from the gardens to the various parishes. To foster the spread of the trees the Jamaica Assembly had appointed a special committee for the management and distribution of the plants, and at the end of 1794 Governor Shirley of Jamaica reported to Banks on behalf of the committee. All the species delivered by Bligh were fully established and the breadfruit, in particular, were spreading vigorously. The largest of the trees were 15 feet tall and about to fruit. A similar story of success came from St Vincent despite the ever-present danger of French attack. Early in 1796, Anderson reported that the breadfruit was doing better, if anything, than it had in its native soil, and for some 18 months he had been gathering fruit of fine quality. Since the establishment of a botanic garden in the Bahamas, the breadfruit had also been cultivated there with great success.[63]

By the end of the century, the breadfruit was securely established throughout the British West Indies, but as early as 1796 Anderson had indicated one of the barriers to the full adoption of the fruit as a foodstuff: 'strange to tell, there are some people who under value such a valuable acquisition, and say they prefer a plantain or Yam'.[64] Although the breadfruit slipped into the West Indian diet, it never quite lived up to expectations or replaced other basic foods. In the event, it was unlikely that it should do so, and far too much had been demanded of it. In the 1780s the West Indians had seen their plight as truly desperate and had overstressed the need for relief. By the mid-1790s conditions were returning to the pre-1778 position, and the exigencies of war and Jay's treaty helped to restore trade with the United States. But the majestic breadfruit tree still flourishes in the West Indies as a verdant memorial to the courage of Captain Bligh and the influence and vision of Sir Joseph Banks.

Notes

1. Cited in Joseph Burke, *English Art 1714–1800*, p. 41. See also Michael Reed, *The Georgian Triumph 1700–1830*, ch. 4.

2. On European attitudes to Tahiti, see B.W. Smith, *European Vision and the South Pacific*; P.J. Marshall & Glyndwr Williams, *The Great Map of Mankind. British Perceptions of the World in the Age of Enlightenment*.

3. L.J. Ragatz, *The Fall of the Planter Class in the British Caribbean, 1763–1833*, pp. 72–4. L. Guilding, *An Account of the Botanic Garden in the Island of St. Vincent from its First Establishment to the Present Day*.

4. H. de Ponthieu to Banks, 27 September 1785, *Kew, B.C.* I, 205.

5. For example, Banks to S. More, 29 July 1783, *Royal Society of Arts, (R.S.A.) Red Book*, fo. 187. More was secretary to the Society.

6. J.C. Beaglehole (ed.), *The Endeavour Journal of Joseph Banks 1768–1771*, vol. I, p. 341.

7. H. East to Banks, 19 July 1784, *Kew, B.C.* I, 168–9.

8. See J. Barrau, *Subsistence Agriculture in Polynesia and Micronesia*.

9. V. Morris to Banks, 13 April 1772, *Add. MSS*, 33977, fo. 18.

10. J. Ellis, *A Description of the Mangostan and Breadfruit*.

11. C. Knight, 'H.M. Armed Vessel *Bounty*', p. 183.

12. J.C. Beaglehole (ed.), *The Journals of Captain Cook on His Voyages of Discovery*, vol. III, p. lxxii.

13. G. Vancouver to Banks, n.d., *D.T.C.*, V, fos 228–9.

14. R. Poore to Banks, 21 February, 18 November 1778, *Kew, B.C.* I, 71–8.

15. On the negotiations surrounding these restrictions, see V.T. Harlow, *The Founding of the Second British Empire 1763–1793*, vol. I, chs. VI–IX, vol. II, ch. V; C.R. Ritcheson, *Aftermath of Revolution*, chs. I, II.

16. See the petition of the West India Committee in *P.R.O., B.T.* 5/1, 8 March 1784.

17. B. Edwards, *The History . . . of the British West Indies*, vol. I, p. xxiv.

18. Poore to Banks, 6 May 1783, *Kew, B.C.* I, 138.

19. Sir G. Yonge to Lincoln, 2 February 1785, *W.O.* 4/334, 247–9.

20. T. Steele to Yonge, 10 February 1785, ibid., 256–7; R. Melville to R. Adair, 8 February 1785, ibid., 257–61.

21. A. Anderson to Yonge, 30 May 1785, *W.O.* 40/4.

22. On the relationship between the King and the Secretary at War, see O. Gee, 'Charles Jenkinson as Secretary at War', pp. 12–20.

23. See, for example, Yonge to Banks, 18 September 1788, *Kew, B.C.* I, 321.

24. East to Banks, 24 April 1785, ibid., 196.

25. Yonge to Banks, 29 June 1786, 11 October 1786, ibid., 235, 247.

26. East to Banks, 19 August 1786, ibid., 238.

27. J. Ellis, *Description du Mangostan et du Fruit à Pain*. Some account of the activities on Mauritius is given in J.E. Martin-Allanic, *Bougainville Navigateur et les Découvertes de son Temps*.

28. M. Wallen to Banks, 23 September 1784, *Add. MSS.* 33977, fo. 267.

29. Ibid.

30. Yonge to Banks, 3 February 1787, *Kew, B.C.*, I, 258.

31. *West India Committee Minutes, West India Merchants*, 1787, vol. 3, p. 54.

32. *D.T.C.* V, fo. 247, 9 September 1787; ibid., fos 210–16. A more complex plan involving two ships, one of which was to call at China and India, was put forward by a London merchant, Benjamin Vaughan, see *C.O.* 201/2, 224, 9 March 1787.

33. Instructions in *H.O.* 42/11, 67, pt. 1. Receipt for outfit in *M.L. Banks*, vol. 5, A78–4, 13, 8 March 1787.

34. Banks had been directly responsible for the appointment of Nelson to Cook's third expedition, see J. Lee to Banks, 24 April 1776, *Add. MSS.* 33977, fo. 56.

35. *H.O.* 42/11, 67, pt. ii.

36. Banks to Hawkesbury, 30 March 1787, *D.T.C.* V, fos 143–6; *H.O.* 42/11, 42, 30 March 1787.

37. This envisaged the vessel going via Cape Horn and not the Cape of Good Hope as it was eventually to do. Banks included the passage out to New South Wales in his calculation, making it a rather dubious argument.

38. There is a draft manning list drawn up by Banks in *M.L. Banks*, vol. 5, A78–4, 5. Close quarters were strong bulkheads between the decks of merchant ships used for defensive purposes if a ship was boarded.

39. Governor Phillip was to send a vessel from New South Wales to collect the flax as the vessel was not now to touch at New Zealand or Australia, see *H.O.* 42/11, 67, pt. 1.

40. Some of the convict ships were on hire to the East India Company and were to go to Canton and return to England in freight. On the equipping of the first fleet, see David Mackay, 'Far Flung Empire: A Neglected Outpost at Botany Bay 1788–1801', pp. 130–1, 138.

41. *Adm.* 106/2624, 14, 16, 23 May 1787; *Adm.* 2/588, 70, 19 May 1787; *Adm.* 106/2214, 23 May 1787; *Adm.* 106/3407, 23 May 1787.

42. *Adm.* 106/3321, 25 June 1787; *Adm.* 1/4152, 95, 10 October 1787; *Adm.* 2/758, 242, 11 October 1787; *Adm.* 2/263, 251, 8 June 1787.

43. Adm. 3/103, 42, 30 May 1787; Banks to Yonge, 9 September 1787, *D.T.C.* V, fo. 247.

44. *Adm.* 1106/3321, 15 August 1787; *Adm.* 1/4152, 95, 10 October 1787; Sydney to Banks, 15 August 1787; *D.T.C.* V, fo. 208-9.

45. G. Mackaness, in *The Life of Vice-Admiral William Bligh*, suggested that Bligh's appointment owed much to the fact that Duncan Campbell had sold the *Bethia* to the Navy Board. However, the ship was in fact offered by the firm of Welbank, Sharp and Brown, although Duncan did tender one vessel, the *Lynx*, in which Bligh had actually sailed, see *Adm.* 106/2624. 16 May 1787; ibid., 23 May 1787; *Adm.* 106/3364, 28 May 1787. Bligh to Banks, 6 August 1787, *H.R.N.S.W.*, vol. I, ii, p. 109.

46. *Adm.* 3/103, 103, 16 August 1787. His instructions are in *Adm.* 2/117. Luttrell to Banks, 29 August, 7 September 1787, *Kew, B.C.* I, 282, 283; Hallett to Banks, 25 August 1787, *Add. MSS.* 33978, fo. 143; B. Petry to Banks, *Add. MSS.* 8096, fo. 498; J.L.A. Reynier to Banks, ibid., fos 500-1; Lord Selkirk to Banks, 14 September 1787; *M. L. Banks*, vol. 5, A78-4, 25-6, 29-32.

47. Bligh to Banks, 15 September 1787, *M.L. Banks*, vol. 5, A78-4, 40. *Adm.* 2/117, 507-8, 18 September 1787; *Adm.* 2/758, 193, 28 September 1787; *Adm.* 111/111, 18 September 1787; *Adm.* 2/758, 169, 20 September 1787; *Adm.* 1/4152, 84a, 5 September 1787; *Adm.* 2/758, 140, 7 September 1787.

48. *Adm.* 3/103, 129; *Adm.* 2/117, 513, 20 September 1787; *Adm.* 2/118, 102.

49. Bligh to Banks, 3, 9 October, 29 November, 5, 6, 10 December 1787, *M.L. Banks*, vol. 5, A78-4, 47-8, 50, 63-4, 65-6, 68-9, 73-4; Bligh to Banks, 5 November 1787, *H.R.N.S.W.*, vol. I, ii, p. 118.

50. *Adm.* 2/118, 157-60, 20 November 1787; Bligh to Banks, 29 November 1787, *M.L. Banks*, vol. 5, A78-4, 63-4; Bligh to Banks, 17 December 1787, with note by Banks, *M.L. Banks*, vol. 5, A78-4, 76.

51. J.C. Beaglehole, *Captain Cook and Captain Bligh*.

52. Bligh to Banks, 13 October 1789, *D.T.C.* VI, fo. 243. The malaria stayed with Bligh for the rest of his life.

53. *C.O.* 201/5, 54, March 1790. For the *Gorgon* and the *Discovery*, see above Chapter 2.

54. Edwards to Banks, 26 January 1791, *Kew, B.C.* II, 28a. Bligh to Banks, 24 October 1790, *D.T.C.* VII, fos 170-1; Banks to Chatham, 10 December 1790, ibid., fos 176-7, Bligh to Banks, ibid., fo. 183.

55. Banks to Auckland, 17 December 1790, *Add. MSS.* 34434, fo. 335.

56. Banks to Chatham, 7 March 1791, *M.L. Banks*, vol. 5, A78-4, 129a-b. Chatham to Banks, 9 March 1791, ibid., 130a-b.

57. *Adm.* 106/2636, 11, 24 March 1791; *H.O.* 28/8, 62-3, 18 April 1791; Banks to Nepean, 13 May 1791, *H.O.* 28/62, 154, Banks to Nepean, 10 November 1791, *H.R.N.S.W.* vol. I, ii, p. 521.

58. *Adm.* 3/108, 118, 13 April, 5 May, 8 June 1791. Of 400 and 100 tons respectively. *Adm.* 106/2637, 3 May, 20 June 1791.

59. *D.T.C.* VII, fos 218-26a, 25 June 1791.

60. See Mackaness, *Life of Bligh*, p. 301, Bligh's log is in *Adm.* 55/152 and 153. Bligh was careful to stay at Tahiti for as short a time as possible. He stayed six months in 1788-9, three in 1792.

61. Bligh to Banks, 16 December 1792, *D.T.C.*, VIII, fo. 127; Wiles to Banks, 22 January 1793, ibid., fos 158-70. It was intended that the *Providence* should go on a voyage of exploration to the South Pacific, although its destination was later changed, see W.R. Broughton, *A Voyage of Discovery to the North Pacific Ocean*, and above, Chapter 4.

62. Banks to Chatham, 1 September 1793, *D.T.C.* VIII, fo. 249.

63. Wiles to Banks, 16 October 1793, *Kew, B.C.* II, 103; Shirley to Banks, 20 December 1794, *D.T.C.*, IX, fos 41–3; Anderson to Banks, 30 March 1796, ibid., X(i), fos 25–8.

64. Anderson to Banks, 30 March 1796, ibid., X(i), fos 25–8.

THE EMPIRE AND THE COTTON INDUSTRY

The cotton industry was the first to experience the technological and financial advances of the industrial revolution and the result was the staggering increase in its manufactured output after 1765. From 1780 onwards the boom in the home and overseas demand for cotton goods created pressing problems in the supply of raw cotton wool.[1] From 5.3 million pounds in 1781, its consumption jumped to 32.5 million pounds in 1788, and an increasing percentage came from foreign sources of supply.[2] For those still attached to mercantilist theory, the problems here were twofold. It was not

Map 3 India in the 1780s

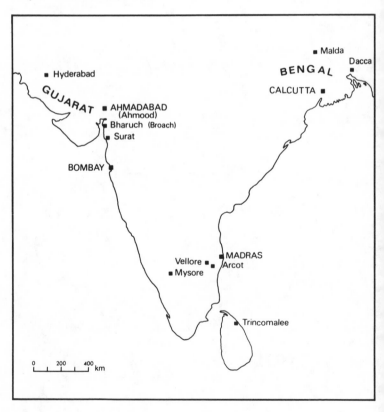

sufficient merely to increase the importation of raw cotton; greater attention also had to be paid to securing reliable sources of supply subject to firm British control, which meant the promotion of fine cottons in the British overseas dominions. The demand for higher grade staples reflected the pressure on the fustian manufacturers for cloths of intermediate quality for both the home and overseas markets. In the years of increasing demand after 1784, the manufacturers began to put pressure on the government to invigorate the cultivation of cotton in the British West India Islands.

The first government initiative was early in 1786 at the time of the negotiations on the Eden treaty with France. After representations from the manufacturers, Hawkesbury asked the Home Secretary Lord Sydney, to promote the growth of fine cottons in the West Indies. Accordingly on 10 March 1786 Sydney circulated orders to the governors of those islands explaining that they were to recommend strongly to the planters and merchants the cultivation of cotton so as 'to have from our own Islands the raw material in such perfection as we are under the necessity of drawing from other powers'.[3] Some governors were co-operative. In Dominica, for example, Governor Orde made provision for grants of up to 60 acres of unappropriated lands to anybody prepared to undertake cotton cultivation. The conditions of such grants were submitted to the Board of Trade and approved on 18 July 1787.[4]

The specialised needs of the industry, and of its market, required something more than general exhortations from the Secretary of State's office, as the West Indian varieties of cotton were not fine enough for the purposes of the fustian manufacturers. The problem became that of how best to establish sufficient supplies of the finer cottons within the Empire. There was some potential for the importation of the fine quality cotton wools of India through Bombay and Bengal, and since 1783 small consignments of wool and yarn had been offered for sale at India House. In August 1788 the East India Company surrendered to pressure from the manufacturers and agreed to ship in something more than token quantities.[5] However, this alternative was hedged with problems. Naturally the Company was loath to encourage competition for its sales of Indian piece goods in London, and the manufacturers of Surat and Bengal doubtless had similar feelings on the matter. Bad harvests and high freight costs also bedevilled the plan. Moreover, the development of a trade in fine cotton goods and cotton wool between Bombay and

China, restricted the raw material available for export.[6]

Another less direct possibility was to transplant the finer varieties of cotton plant from their country of origin to some British overseas territories, and it was this possibility which naturally attracted Sir Joseph Banks. Two courses of action occurred to him. Through his string of scientific contracts in Russia, Persia and India he could obtain sufficient quantities of seeds for transplantation in the West Indies or elsewhere. A more direct method was to despatch someone familiar with cotton, and botany in general, to secure seeds and a knowledge of their cultivation, from an area in which the finer types of cotton were produced. Banks clearly preferred the second possibility, for by this means it was feasible to utilise men with specialist knowledge, a suitable scientific training and the necessary experience of collecting plants in distant parts. Such persons could be equipped with a commission or detailed instructions, placing them under direct control of government and ensuring thereby a single-minded pursuit of the object in question. This approach was in fact being followed in the breadfruit expedition, and in another Board of Trade scheme under Banks' supervision at the time to send out a botanist to search for new varieties of useful plants in India. The similarities in method and purpose make clear that all these enterprises were being considered by Banks at the same time, and were part of a co-ordinated effort to increase the material resources of British colonies.[7]

Sometime in February 1787 Banks suggested to Lord Hawkesbury that the best response to the manufacturers' demands would be to send someone to collect seeds from a region where fine cotton was cultivated. Hawkesbury consulted both Pitt and Dundas on the plan and they agreed to try it.[8] On 26 February Banks was requested to call on Lord Hawkesbury to discuss the cultivation of cotton and give his opinion 'upon the best mode to be adopted for obtaining some Samples of that article from the neighbourbood of Bombay'.[9] As it was essential to pinpoint the exact area in which the finest cottons were produced, the Board of Trade invited Mr John Hilton, the general representative of the fustian manufacturers of Manchester, to attend a meeting on the same day.[10] In the course of the questioning Hilton confirmed that the finest cottons came from the area around Surat, in western India, and this variety of cotton wool was valued at about 3s a pound on the English market, compared to 1s 8d for the West Indian varieties. Characteristic of the optimism of the time, Hilton assured the Board that British manufacturers were capable of producing cotton goods as fine in quality as East Indian muslins if cotton wool of the Surat type could be procured. Machine spinning was constantly improving, and to maximise profits it was preferable to import raw cotton rather than yarn.[11]

These opinions concurred with those of Dundas, who had been making his own enquiries on the cotton trade at India House.[12] On the strength of the evidence produced, it was decided that a person should be despatched to the Gujarat province around Surat by the Board of Trade, with instructions from Banks to investigate the cultivation of fine cottons.

The person selected to undertake the mission was the Pole, Anton Hove, who had already acquired some experience of botany in tropical countries when in 1785 he had been appointed by Banks to an expedition to the south-west coast of Africa to search for a suitable site for a convict settlement. In July 1786 he returned from that voyage and was looking for further employment. Apparently he acquitted himself well on the *Nautilus* expedition; anyway to the extent that Evan Nepean overcame his objections to a foreigner, and suggested him for the mission to procure cotton seeds.[13]

Banks and Hawkesbury approved of the choice and by the middle of March arrangements to despatch Hove were under way. His salary for the period of service was determined by Banks and set at £60 annually, dating from 1 March 1787, with a £50 allowance for his outfit, and £50 for his mess on the passage to India. To assist him in his travels the East India Company wrote to Bombay, ordering the governor and council to furnish letters of introduction to the heads of the various districts he would pass through, and to provide him on request with no more than £300 in allowances. Hove himself was sent to India House to collect a letter for the captain of the *Warren Hastings*, the ship in which he was to travel, and to arrange for his mess on board. Hawkesbury arranged with Dundas that his passage home in a Company ship would be allowed and instructions written to Bombay to that effect.[14]

As with the breadfruit expedition, the task of briefing Hove and drawing up his instructions was entrusted to Banks. By all accounts the venture was organised with some haste so as to get Hove away on one of the last ships of the season, and the issue of his instructions suggests the possibility that the Board of Trade was merely giving an official stamp to arrangements already made by Banks. The latter was asked to draw up the instructions in a letter from William Fawkener of 2 April and on the same day Hove was ordered to 'conform yourself in all Respects to the Instructions you shall receive from Sir Joseph Banks, President of the Royal Society'. It was on 2 April, however, that Hove joined the ship at Gravesend, and when the ship sailed the following day Banks was already sending him last-minute orders not included in the official drafts, hoping to catch the ship in the Downs. Hove's official instructions are actually dated 7 January 1787 which further complicates matters. Errors on Banks' part as to the allowance to be paid Hove suggest that the instructions were drawn up at a date before 30 March when the sum of £300 was agreed upon by the Board of Trade, and it is not possible to be any more precise, unless Banks' own dating is accepted.[15]

The instructions were an interesting mixture of subterfuge, ingenuousness and scientific data. There were two sets; one marked 'Public instructions', the other 'private'.[16] The former directed Hove to proceed as he had done on the African expedition, collecting exotic plants wherever the ship would touch. His objective, it was stressed, was to collect plants for the Royal Botanic Garden at Kew, and to this end he was to proceed to the Broach district after arriving at Bombay, where he was to live among the inhabitants, and collect plants and seeds which were to be sent to Banks with accompanying lists and descriptions of the soils and climates. No mention was made of cotton. The real objectives were outlined in the private instructions which pointed out that the real purpose of the mission was to procure for the West Indies seeds of the finer sorts of cotton cultivated in the Ahmood and Broach regions. Collecting plants for Kew was merely a front and was to be regarded as strictly secondary. So that he should not attract the suspicion of the local cultivators and manufacturers, Hove was to travel as an indigent physician using his medical training to ingratiate himself with the local people and gain their confidence. On locating a suitable area he was to take up residence and remain among the planters to study the cultivation of cotton for the market. He was to note the methods of irrigation and manuring, the effects of soil, climate and cultivation on the value of the cotton, and the most profitable seed varieties. Each parcel of seeds sent back to England was to be labelled with numbers corresponding to remarks about them in a commentary sent under a separate cover. These remarks were to be written in Polish and to be transmitted to Hove's brother in India for translation, before being sent on to England. He was to stay in the cotton country for a year observing the processes of manufacture as well as cultivation, and then to return to England bringing with him large stocks of cotton seeds of all varieties, with specimens of the fibre of each for the purposes of identification. The collection of seeds was of the greatest importance for the foundation of the West Indian plantations over which Hove himself might have the opportunity to preside if the mission was successful. Four years later the same sort of inducement was offered to James Wiles, the botanist on Bligh's second breadfruit expedition.[17]

These attempts to conceal the true nature of Hove's errand require some explanation. The mission was an attempt on the part of the British government to capture a part of the commercial advantages of another country. Gujarat was a Maratha territory and although British traders did have some part in the cotton trade carried on through Surat, the cultivation and manufacture of cotton was in Indian hands.[18] Banks was far from consistent in his attitude to this sort of commercial espionage. In a letter of 15 May 1787 to Sir George Yonge he stressed in a rather high-minded way the immorality of stealing such commercial advantages from another country, while his letter to Dundas on the same subject, a month later, recommended just such an appropriation.[19] Apparently he was prepared to condone such practices, even to be involved in their implementation so long as his own name was not publicly associated with them; he had too many personal interests to safeguard.[20] The secrecy in Hove's case may also have been an attempt to prevent the Company's servants at Bombay from obstructing his progress through a fear that their interests in the area were being threatened.[21] If Hove's mission were to fail it would also be necessary to ensure that no avenues should be closed to similar expeditions to other foreign, cotton-producing countries, such as Persia or Brazil.

On 30 March 1787 Hawkesbury asked John Hilton if he had any special instructions to be communicated to Hove before he sailed. Hilton's only observations were about the fine variety of Chinese cotton cloth called nankeen, and he requested that if Hove should happen upon a type of raw cotton of the natural colour of that cloth he should collect seeds and master the culture of it. These suggestions were passed on by Banks and reached Hove while the ship was in the Downs.[22] On its passage to Bombay the ship touched at the Island of Joanna, on the coast of Africa and Hove took the opportunity to botanise and collect plants for Kew. On 29 July 1787 the vessel reached Bombay and the following day he presented himself to the Governor, Mr Boddam, asking for assistance and letters of introduction to the native powers of Gujarat. Already, it seems, he was departing from his instructions. An indigent physician would not require such letters of introduction.

In the succeeding fortnight Hove got himself equipped and gathered information on the country he was to visit. By 15 August he was ready to set out. But in preparing for his journey Hove had again gone beyond his instructions, and in doing so brought down upon himself the sort of trouble that was to dog his expedition. He had apparently thought it necessary to hire some assistants and on the day he was to leave Bombay these men complained of the badness of the weather and roads, and refused to accompany Hove unless he purchased additional carts. He had also by this time acquired an interpreter and a palanquin — hardly the sort of equipment required for the role Banks had envisaged for him — and in hiring helpers he had already caused the difficulties his instructions sought to avoid.[23]

After travelling for $2\frac{1}{2}$ months he reached Broach in the Ahmood district and began his researches, describing the cultivation of cotton and defining the finest varieties. Even at this stage he met difficulties. To enable him to travel safely from Surat to Broach, he had been obliged to hire 16 horsemen for his protection. At Broach he put himself in the hands of Mr Smith, the resident of the region, to whom he had letters of introduction. Immediately on his arrival Hove dismissed his horsemen because of the now unjustified expense — an action which was regarded by Smith as an insult to his household. The following day, 25 October, Smith invited Hove on a trip up the River Narbada, but when during the day he went off to do a little botanising, he returned to find Smith and his party drunk. Hove's request for a glass of wine was refused by Smith, who drawled out: 'Mr. Hove it is true that I am desir'd to assist you in your way, but I am not compell'd to assist you with my people, & if you wish to be more respected, keep more people and servants.'[24] Such attitudes on the part of the Company servants provided a constant dilemma for the unfortunate traveller. He was expected by his employers in England to travel on his own and as cheaply as possible, but the conditions of other Europeans in India made the task all but impossible. In the opinion of the Company employees it was a nauseating thought that a European should travel like a poor Indian, and they refused to assist or accompany a man who wished to do so.

On 26 October 1787 Hove decided to return to Surat and on the way he was raided by brigands who relieved him of his money and trading goods. This was the first of three such raids during his expedition. Inevitably he was forced to apply to the governor for more money, a request which was refused. By this stage he was in debt and as a result borrowed money from a banker in Surat at an exorbitant interest rate. From this point onwards Hove was obliged to travel in the manner of Company employees; using armed guards and armed boats; travelling in palanquins; and carrying presents for the chiefs of the various regions he passed through. Naturally the expenses of the mission spiralled as Hove was in the position of having to take more extreme measures to protect himself and as a consequence attracted more attention from friend and foe alike. By the end of 1787 he was travelling in a party that was protected by 48 coolies armed with matchlocks.

In January 1788 he returned to Bombay and attempted to secure an advance of further money from the government. He reached Surat on 7 January and by travelling overland made Bombay a fortnight later. But he had arrived too late, for the governor, Mr Boddam, had sailed for England at the end of his term on 9 January and his successor, Mr Ramsay, had no instructions to issue Hove more money. Again he was forced to rely on credit and drew bills on Lord Hawkesbury to the value of 17,000 rupees. Thus replenished, he set out for the cotton district of Ahmood again, arriving at the beginning of April. For five months he dutifully collected information on cotton, its cultivation and manufacture, information which he faithfully and accurately recorded. Aware of the general interest in propagating useful plants in the West Indies, he also noted plants likely to be of value if transplanted there.

As has been suggested, Banks conceived of two methods for obtaining fine cotton seeds for the West Indies, and while Hove was amassing huge debts in India, the second approach was not being ignored. Concluding from the last-minute instructions which Hilton had sent for Hove, that the manufacturers were interested in the nankeen variety of cotton, Banks forwarded some seeds of this type to Hawkesbury on 30 April 1787, so that the appropriate tests could be made. The following month Banks' letter and the seeds were laid before the Board of Trade which decided to send the seeds to the agent for Barbados with instructions that they should be sent to that island for experimentation.[25]

More encouraging prospects were aroused by some cotton sent to the Board of Trade for testing on 25 August. In his covering letter to

Hawkesbury, Banks remarked: 'I have ever since I had the honor of being call'd upon by the Commee of Privy Council on the subject of Cotton been particularly attentive to that article. Enclos'd is a specimen which appears to me very Fine: it comes originally from Persia & if a sufficient Price can be obtain'd for it may be cultivated in our West Indies.'[26] After being examined by the Board on the 29th the specimen was sent at Banks' suggestion to Mr Frodsham, a Manchester fustian manufacturer, for testing. If the manufacturers could give some indication as to the price it was likely to fetch, Banks promised to make enquiries to establish whether it was high enough to induce West Indian plantation owners to undertake its cultivation. On acknowledging receipt of the cotton Hawkesbury thanked Banks for his labours 'in this and other Business of the like Nature from which I have no doubt that the Publick will derive great Benefit' — a reference to the breadfruit expedition, now on the point of sailing, and the commercial enterprises in India.[27] The cotton sample was laid before a special meeting of the Manchester cotton manufacturers in September and it was agreed that its quality was extremely fine, and if quantities could be brought to market in the same condition it would reach 3s a pound, equal to the finest Surat varieties. If planted in the West Indies so as to retain its current qualities, it would be a great acquisition, but for thorough testing more samples would be required.[28]

At a Board of Trade meeting on 8 October these conclusions were discussed and Banks' advice was again sought as to whether the cotton would grow in the West Indies, and if he could 'suggest any steps the Committee can properly take for encouraging the growth of it'. Banks was at this time on his annual visit to his estate at Revesby but he promised to attend a meeting of the committee on his return in early November. In the meantime he assured the Board that they would 'be able by their Patronage to introduce the Culture of this species of Cotton into our Colonies in the West Indies without incurring any expense whatever to Government'.[29]

When he returned to London at the beginning of November some surprising but encouraging information about the origin of the Persian cotton came to light. The specimen Banks sent to the Board of Trade was apparently grown not in Persia but on the island of Barbados. The planter concerned, Langford Millington, arrived in England with a letter of introduction to Banks while the latter was still at Revesby. This obviously put a totally different complexion on the matter and caused some consternation when communicated to the Board of Trade on 16 November. Hilton and other representatives of the Manchester manufacturers were called to a meeting of the Board five days later and informed of the discovery. They were asked what inducements they were prepared to offer to encourage Millington to part with some seed. The manufacturers were disconcertingly equivocal about Banks' revelation. Speaking for them on 21 November, Frodsham reported that the specimen of cotton sent for testing was too small to enable a proper evaluation of its qualities to be made, although they believed it to be quite a good staple. They saw no point in purchasing Millington's seeds for replanting as their quality would inevitably deteriorate, and it would therefore be advisable to bring in fresh supplies from Persia for replanting. If Millington wished to send a stipulated quantity of his cotton annually, he would have to submit a written application to that effect, enclosing some samples of his wool. With this answer Frodsham included a memorandum on cotton cultivation, 'the purport of which, I have sometime since, transmitted to Sir Joseph Banks (who has been applied to by the Lords Committee of Privy Council for Trade, upon the Subject)'.[30]

This was hardly an enthusiastic reply from a body which had stressed the urgency of finding new sources of fine cotton, and it raised the possibility that the origin of Millington's cotton might have been deliberately kept from the manufacturers lest prejudice affect their opinions of its quality. Frodsham's memorandum served to dampen matters further. He believed the finest cottons came from the Malacca region and Siam, and these were followed in quality by those of Brazil and the French West Indies. He made no mention of Surat or Persian cotton. The most favourable areas for the growth of cotton he believed to be in continental situations within 15 degrees north and south of the equator. For this reason the West Indies was not the most suitable area for experiments. Instead he suggested the West Coast of Africa, in the regions of the River Gambia, Cape Coast Castle and Accra, where both the climate and the soil were suitable. A small quantity of wild cotton from that part of Africa had shortly before sold for 2s 4d a pound. He conceded that it might be worthwhile continuing experiments in the West Indies, although they should be secondary to those in Africa and it would be necessary to renew the seeds frequently to retain quality.[31]

Slightly confused by this report, the Board of Trade decided to call a meeting at which Banks, Millington and the manufacturers would be present. The manufacturers' swing in interest away from the West Indies is difficult to explain. It is strange that although Millington's cotton had been valued at 3s a pound, Frodsham should be more enthusiastic about an African product worth 2s 4d. Nor is it easy to see why he believed plants in the West Indies would need continual invigoration by supplies of seed from the parent stock in Persia — an operation which would be prohibitively expensive. The two meetings on 8 and 15 December did not substantiate Frodsham's views. At the first Banks testified that plants in similar latitudes, with similar soils and climates, and cultivated with care, would not degenerate once transplanted. A continental or insular situation did not greatly affect matters, he wrongly concluded:

> Sir Joseph is however of Opinion, that it may be worth while to try the Experiment of sowing some of Seeds of Fine Cotton in some of the British Settlements on the Continent of Africa, while similar Experiments are trying in the British West India Islands.[32]

Millington agreed in advance to provide seeds for experiments outside the Caribbean. It had been suggested to Banks some months earlier that the first ships to New South Wales should take cotton seeds as well as the cochineal insect and nopal plant to begin an industry in that colony. This proposal certainly attracted Governor Phillip, who endeavoured to obtain these articles on his passage to Botany Bay.[33]

On the day of the second meeting at the Board of Trade Millington was questioned on the origin of his cotton. It appeared the seeds had been brought from Persia by the botanist John Ellis and were introduced into Bardados by Mr Edward Jordan in 1776. In consequence of Sydney's orders to the governors of 10 March 1786, Millington had obtained seeds from Jordan in an effort to start a plantation. The plants from which the seeds were taken were ten years old at the time and in the light of the fact that they had been growing wild on Jordan's plantation, it seemed that Frodsham's point about the need for annual renewals of seed had been effectively refuted. Millington agreed to supply more cotton wool for the manufacturers so that further tests could be made. On 18 December this 26-ounce sample was sent to Hilton with a copy of Millington's testimony, and an enquiry as to whether the cotton was of a quality to make its cultivation profitable. These samples were given exhaustive tests, being spun by hand, on the jenny, and on the mule. The results proved highly satisfactory and were passed on to the Board by Hilton in March 1788. The sample spun on Arkwright's machine was suitable for fine muslins, and would reach 2s 6d a pound if bought raw. That spun on the mule or jenny could be spun much finer and would reach 4s a pound.[34]

Meanwhile Banks had been making enquiries further afield. Late in 1787 he received information that some of the finest cottons were produced in the East India Company dominions around Dacca, and in November he wrote to Sir William Jones at Calcutta asking him to obtain seeds of this type of cotton. Jones was happy to comply but was unable to procure seeds before the last ships of the season had left. He nevertheless began enquiries regarding the cultivation and processing of the cotton.[35]

Interest in cotton had generally swung around to the East Indies by the beginning of 1788, as pressure for alternative sources of raw cotton was increased by the demands of the manufacturers for a limitation of imports of white cotton piece goods and muslins by the East India Company. Despite the technological advances of the last 20 years the hand-spun Indian cloths were in general still finer in quality and they continued to dominate the market for higher grade articles. In retrospect the manufacturers' fears of being ruined by the Indian handloom weavers seem ironic, but they pictured an infant industry, employing many dependent workers, with a huge invested capital, threatened with a ruinous competition. Dundas, caught between the manufacturers and the Company, had begun enquiries in February 1787 into the state and volume of the Company imports and he reported to Hawkesbury on the subject.[36] But it was with the arrival of the new season's supply of cotton goods on the market in early 1788 that pressure really began to mount. In February the manufacturers of Paisley, Glasgow and the neighbouring districts petitioned the Board of Trade for protection against Indian cloth, and between February and May petitions from other cotton-producing regions poured into India House and the Board of Trade.[37]

On 5 May the manufacturers submitted proposals on the cotton trade to Pitt and Dundas. They suggested a swing from the Company's importation of piece goods to a concentration on raw cotton, 'and particularly the Article of fine Cotton wool called Amood [sic], also the finest Bengal Cotton, and to increase the same gradually until it extends to Six Millions of pounds — extending also the Importation of Raw Silk, Indigo, Madder Roots and other Dye Stuffs'.[38] Before the importation reached this level, the Company and the manufacturers should take an equal share of the market for cotton cloths, and there should be only two Company auctions a year. Duties on the imported cottons should be revised upwards and the importation of yarn prohibited.

These demands could hardly have come at a more embarrassing time for the Company. Despite attempts to diversify the range of East India Company exports to Britain, over 60 per cent of the investment still consisted of cotton piece goods.[39] In India itself Cornwallis had only just begun the reforms in the commercial sphere which he hoped might eventually liquidate the Company's burdensome debt.[40] Pitt and his colleagues were anxiously waiting for the financial fruits of the India Act of 1784 to materialise. To dim these prospects still further, India was going through its second year of disastrously bad harvests. In this unenviable position the Directors were asked to comment on the manufacturers' proposals.

The Company report to the Board of Trade was designed to appeal to its economy-conscious members. They claimed the plans of the manufacturers would be ruinous to the Company and the Country. The restraints proposed would divert the India trade into foreign channels and greatly reduce British revenues in Asia. Furthermore, the cutbacks suggested by the manufacturers might even prove detrimental to themselves by diminishing the export trade from England to the East Indies. To clinch the argument the Accountant General of the Company, Mr Richardson, wrote to Pitt on 14 April reminding him that at the last sales the Company made a loss on its imports of cotton goods.[41]

The gluts in the home market in 1788 and 1792 kept the issue alive, but generally the ministry was unwilling to take any measures which would damage the profitability of the Company when it was already in a delicate state. Most of the pressure fell on the unfortunate Dundas, harried on the one side by the efforts of Baring and others to explain the disaster which restrictions would bring to Indian industry, and yet forced to soothe the angry manufacturers, particularly those of Glasgow and Paisley.[42]

In August 1788 Hove's despatches began to reach Banks. Two of these were forwarded to Hawkesbury on 1 September (one addressing Banks as 'Gracious Madam'). They described the traveller's misfortunes in India, the great expense that his mission had incurred and the progress made in collecting cotton. Aware that his behaviour would not meet the full approval of government, Hove asked Banks to explain his difficulties and achievements to the King.[43]

The administration was far from pleased, and matters had been further exacerbated by the confusion as to the fineness of the Ahmood variety of cotton. In his covering letter to Hawkesbury, Banks recalled that Hove's destination had been determined by a passage taken out of a book presented to the Board of Trade by Dundas.[44] The opinions therein had been confirmed by the manufacturers. The haste with which Hove had been despatched precluded any extension of the enquiries into sources of fine cottons and by the time questions had been raised about the quality of Ahmood staple Hove had already set off from Bombay. Banks' more recent opinions were confirmed by a consignment of fine cotton seeds and samples of wool sent from Bengal by Sir William Jones. These came from the Dacca area and the Company resident there had enclosed a report on the growth and processing of this fine cotton. Banks passed these seeds on to Hawkesbury when they arrived in May 1789 and acknowledged that it was, 'universally allow'd by those who have been used to the manufacturers of India to be the only Sort from whence the Natives of Bengall Can manufacture their superfine Muslins'. This type of cotton was massseeded, like the samples of Persian cotton, but its fineness made it well worth transplanting to the West Indies.[45]

Obviously those responsible for Hove's expedition had made some grave mistakes and Banks, Dundas and the manufacturers shared responsibility. All parties had access to information which should have enabled proper decisions to be made. There remained the problem of Hove's future, and Banks suggested to Hawkesbury his immediate recall by overland despatch so as to avoid any further expense. Hawkesbury discussed the matter with Pitt and Dundas, who agreed on the recall, but no decision was reached as to what to do about his debts. As Banks had been responsible for the expedition he was asked to write the letter of recall and to consider the necessity of advancing Hove more money through the Bombay government so that he might get a passage home. Suggesting this, Hawkesbury speculated as to whether the action of the Bombay government in refusing Hove money might indicate their opinion that he had spent more than was necessary or could justify — a query, Hawkesbury added, 'you who are acquainted with Hove's character, can best determine'.[46]

Banks was quick to react to the implication that he had misjudged Hove's character by pointing out that it had originally been Evan Nepean who had recommended Hove to the Board on the basis of the work he had done under Banks supervision on the coast of West Africa. Here he had acquitted himself well and for this reason Banks had not hesitated to second Nepean's recommendation. He had stressed economy to Hove not because he had suspected the Pole of extravagance, 'but because I feared the thing which has probably been the Case that in a Country where Remittance is of such Importance, Money would be offered to him, and Persuasions used to make him take it'. There was clearly a lot of buck-passing going on. For reasons of government credit he supposed Hove's debts must be paid, but he made the surprising suggestion that on future occasions men should be sent out as his own private emissaries to avoid such troubles. In spite of the difficulties Banks thought that the mission had been fully justified, 'for as the Company have been of late so teazed by the Manufacturers to import cotton for them, they will certainly think it an Advantage to be freed from that Burthen by an increased Cultivation of that Article in the West Indies'.[47]

As Banks was at Revesby, the Board decided to leave discussion of Hove's debts until early November, but since an overland despatch was leaving for India at the beginning of October the letter of recall was to be ready as soon as possible. He wrote to Hove on 30 September, admonishing him for his extravagance and ordering that he should put himself and his collection on the first ship for Europe. Copies of the letter went to Pitt and Hawkesbury.[48] The latter was himself about to leave town at this stage and he consequently turned the whole business into the hands of William Grenville who had hitherto been lucky enough to escape the matter. Enclosing all correspondence on the subject Hawkesbury asked that Grenville confer with Pitt and then despatch the letter of recall to India House. At the same time the Company should be asked to instruct the Governor of Bombay to allow Hove a passage home in one of the Company ships.[49]

Apart from his gross extravagance Hove seemed to be faithfully carrying out the object of his mission. The first instalment of cotton seeds arrived with a letter to Banks in August and was immediately sent to the West Indies for planting. Another lot arriving in September was sent on to the Board of Trade where the seeds were examined before being despatched to the governors of the West Indies with the request that they be distributed to interested planters. Hove's account of the cultivation of cotton was duplicated and sent with the seeds.[50]

The financial side of Hove's venture again came to the fore when another letter to Banks arrived in November, and bills drawn on Lord Hawkesbury were presented for payment in London. The letter, dated 10 March was similar to an earlier one, except that it mentioned a further 17,000 rupees drawn on Hawkesbury, and it asked that the bills be honoured. Banks again attempted to defend Hove, placing most of the blame on East India Company employees who had even deceived the traveller by giving him a bad rate of exchange on his £300 allowance. While Hawkesbury discussed the matter with his colleagues, Stephen Cottrell, the Privy Council clerk, called on Banks to get his opinion on what should be done. The matter was finally decided at a meeting of the Board with Banks present on 29 November. After considering Hove's behaviour in the light of Banks' instructions it was decided that the bills drawn on Hawkesbury, now totalling £2,125, should not be accepted and that the parties in whose favour the bills were drawn should be notified. No decisions on Hove's general behaviour were to be taken until the unfortunate man was present to justify his own conduct.[51]

Hove was by now preparing to return home. On 11 September 1788 he arrived in Surat from Ahmood, and by 9 November he was in Bombay looking for a ship. Unfortunately, no British ship was due to sail before the new year and Hove decided to occupy his time by continuing his researches in the area south of Bombay. At the beginning of December he sailed to Port Victoria to study the cultivation of Daccan cotton, returning to Bombay just before Christmas. Banks' letter of recall had not by that time arrived, for when Hove attempted to get a passage home on the *William Henry* East Indiaman, its commander, Captain Dundas, asked 4,000 rupees for the journey, which Hove rightly regarded as exorbitant. When Hove eventually managed to negotiate a reasonable fare, the captain refused to take his cargo and the vessel sailed without him. He at length embarked on a Danish ship, the *Norge*, which left Bombay on 1 February 1789 and landed him at Plymouth on 18 August.[52]

If Hove thought his difficulties would end upon his arrival in England he was to be disillusioned. Banks, Hawkesbury and his creditors were all demanding some explanations. Hove's last letter to Banks had mentioned still more bills drawn on Lord Hawkesbury, and Banks met with the latter on 20 May to discuss the matter. But the immediate problem was to move Hove's huge collection of plants, seeds and impedimenta to London. While the plants were resting in a hothouse at Saltram near Plymouth the King inspected them and ordered that they should be moved to Kew as soon as possible. At Banks' suggestion the plants were taken from the custody of the customs officers, so that all official business could be left until the collection arrived in London. To further expedite matters Banks advised Fawkener to leave all negotiations with customs to his own agent Mr Maclean, the inspector of Indian goods at Customs House. After much trouble and further expense the collection was transplanted to London.[53]

Meanwhile, Fawkener and Cottrell grappled with the problem of Hove's accumulated debts. Cottrell enclosed to Banks the requisitions to the Treasury for the payment of debts and Banks expressed the hope that the bills would be honoured. Hove was none the less worried by his creditors. On 24 October Fawkener wrote to Hawkesbury: 'Mr. Hove has been here in great distress, to say that he has received a very peremptory letter from Mr. Sibbalds, the holder of the bill drawn on your Lordship for his passage home: he showed it me, & it concludes, after some uncivil language with a threat that legal means will be used, if payment is not immediately made: I advised him to see Mr. Sibbalds & to endeavour to prevail on him to wait at least a little: Sir Joseph Banks is not to be in town till the fourth of November.' In the first two weeks of September Hove's creditors had continued to petition the Board of Trade for the honouring of the bills, but after consultations with the various parties it had been resolved that only those for the ferrying of the cargo to London and for Hove's passage home should be paid. Fawkener again talked to the distressed Hove about his expenses and described the meeting to Banks: 'I am really sorry for the difficulties the poor Pole is likely to get into, as he seems a good-humoured, laborious creature, and has not, as far as I have any skill in physionomy, the countenance or manners of a knave.'[54]

Hove's collection, as described by Banks, fell into five categories. There were over 80 varieties of living plants, most of them being for food or commercial crops, and nearly all intended for the use of the West Indies. Considered most important in this group were the nutmeg of Banda, the mangosteen of Malacca, and the myrrh tree producing the aromatic and medicinal balm of Gilead. The real object of the mission had been to collect cotton seeds and there were 23 varieties of the finer sort suitable for muslins. As the cotton-sowing season in the West Indies did not begin until March and lasted until August, Banks suggested to Fawkener that the seeds should be kept at the Board of Trade so that the quality of each could be assessed by a comparison with the samples of wool that accompanied them. There were also 17 varieties of other seeds for Kew Gardens, among which were many useful plants, and as the country through which Hove had passed had not been previously explored by any man of science this group included many new species. Also important for the West Indies was the group of 14 different types of Indian grain, used for food or fodder. These Banks regarded as very important, as 'the introduction of an improved species of millet or Guinea Corn might Easily Prove a greater blessing to those Islands than the Bread Fruit for which they so long and ardently sollicited'. He advised that these be sent without delay to the governors of the Sugar Islands. Complementary to the cotton seeds was a selection of various dyes, all of which were sent to the Dyers' Company for testing. There was finally a collection of fossils and reptiles, and a catalogue of dried plants which corresponded to the seeds brought back for Kew.[55]

To distract Hove from the claims of his creditors, Banks directed him to draw up a catalogue of the collections brought from India, together with a full description of the means of cultivating those destined for the West Indies. When completed this catalogue was handed to the Board of Trade and subsequently sent on to Banks at Revesby for corrections and additions. Hawkesbury, in a letter to Banks of 3 October, expressed little faith in the Pole's ability in this respect, noting that he had not confined himself to what related to the seeds of grains and other esculent plants. He asked that Banks sift through the catalogue to extract the relevant information and put it in a digestible form for the planters of the West Indies.[56]

While Hove had been working on the catalogue, the manufacturers had been inspecting and classifying the cotton seeds and samples preparatory to their despatch to the West Indies. When this task had been completed Hawkesbury asked Banks to write a letter to the West Indies recommending that proper trials should be made of the various kinds of cotton seeds, and giving every encouragement to the planters: 'the Weight of Sr. Jos. Banks's Authority as well as of his Arguments might prove the means of inducing the Planters to avail themselves of the Advantages which are on this Occasion held out to them, and which from Indolence or Prejudice they might perhaps be otherwise too apt to neglect.'[57] Banks's advice would be sent with the second consignment of seeds which was eventually despatched in April 1790.

Banks was happy to comply with Hawkesbury's request and he produced a long paper on cotton and other useful plants. This was prefaced with a restatement of his theories on the value of transfer-ring plants: 'I hold firmly the opinion that furnishing a Countrey with Esculent Vegetables unknown to it but which will thrive there, is conferring an Obligation of the First Importance on the inhab-itants.'[58] He saw no difficulty in propagating the plants of Gujarat in the West Indies, as any plants previously transferred to places of similar climates in different parts of the world had adapted well if the methods of cultivation were adequately explained to the recipi-ents. Banks then enumerated the various plants in the collection which included types of wheat, barley, corn, pulse, rice, spinach, an East Indian indigo and other dyes, various species of timber and other productive trees.

Once approved by the Board of Trade this letter formed the basis of the reports sent to the West Indian governors and to Alexander Anderson, the superintendent of the botanic garden at St Vincent. It showed the purposes of the expedition in fields other than the pro-motion of cotton, and also how seriously the ministry took the plight of the West Indies after the conclusion of hostilities with America.[59]

There remained the investigation into Hove's conduct and the enormous expenses he had incurred. The actual date of the enquiry is almost as obscure as the result itself, but it seems likely that it was held sometime in the second half of November, after Banks returned from Revesby. The only statement that survives is a defence of Hove in Banks' handwriting apparently prepared for presentation to the Board of Trade. Despite the expense he had no doubt as to the prac-ticability of the plan as it was first conceived. Hove was supposed to travel on foot, in the cheapest possible manner, and to live with the natives of the poorest classes. There were precedents for this. A.M. Pagés had travelled in this way in the country adjoining the areas Hove had passed through. Mr George Forster, an acquain-tance of Lord Cornwallis' had travelled on foot from Bengal to the Caspian Sea. Hove had departed from these precepts and the rea-sons were obvious. He had been influenced by East India Company employees who had diverted him from the spirit of his instructions. Despite the unwarranted expenditure, in all other respects Hove had behaved with diligence, perseverance and courage in the pursuit of his object. He had made himself fully master of the processes of cultivating cotton, and had taken unwearying pains to discover how it was carded, spun and woven. Despite the antipathy of the natives he managed to bring away a loom with a weft on it and a drawing of the process of carding. Banks was convinced the money was expended in the execution of orders and that no part of it had been applied for Hove's own use. His account of expenditure, as presented to the Lords, was a fair and accurate one.[60]

After enquiries at India House about the holders of the bills on Hawkesbury, the government agreed to their payment, although no interest was allowed and the exchange was settled at 2s 3d per rupee and not 2s 6d as the holders demanded. There was no doubt that by his testimony before the Board of Trade and his defence of the Pole, Banks had rescued Hove from his difficulties.[61] Certainly Hove seemed to have felt a great debt to Banks, and to England when he left it. Two of his later letters survive. The first, from St Petersburg, described his mistreatment at the hands of the Poles and announced his decision to work as a natural historian examining the produce and fertility of the regions adjoining the Turkish border, in the service of the Empress. This letter thanked his former patron for favours received, 'while employed under your direction'. The second letter from Odessa in August 1796 again thanked Banks and enclosed some seeds from Southern Russia.[62]

As samples of various cottons grown in Africa and the West Indies came to hand they were sent to the manufacturers for evaluation. Early reports tended to be encouraging, but it is extremely difficult to assess the overall value of Banks' efforts. In March 1789 samples of cotton had arrived from Senegal and Bermuda, and the reports on these suggested that the Senegal type was extremely fine and as good as East India cotton, while the Bermuda cotton, while not of the same quality, would be suitable for fustian goods. Banks continued to make enquiries about the cultivation of fine cotton on behalf of the Board of Trade. The questions directed at Sir William Jones were partly aimed at discovering the local methods of spinning fine cotton. On Hove's return Banks asked for more information on harvesting and cleaning from Dr Helenus Scott, a correspondent in Bombay. In January 1790 Scott obliged with a long memorandum on these subjects, and added an account of the techniques of baling and loading cotton at Bombay for the China market. 'As you inform me that the cultivation of Cotton in the West Indies is become an object of so much importance,' he wrote, 'I have thought that these particulars would be worth mentioning to you.'[63]

As Edwards and Harlow have pointed out there was a startling increase in the production of raw cotton in the West Indies after

1785, but the statistics are confusing since they often include foreign cotton imported through the free ports.[64] After 1793 it becomes difficult to obtain any reliable picture of growth. The capture of the French and Dutch territories in the Caribbean, the enormous increase in the importation of American cotton, the beginnings of the export of British piece goods to India and the subsequent swing in India to the export of the raw material all confuse the situation. Certainly some West Indians believed progress had been made, and indicated their appreciation to Banks. Governor Parry of Barbados was one who sent his thanks, enclosing specimens of cotton grown from seeds which Banks had sent to the Island. Parry later arranged for a sufficient quantity to be supplied to make Banks a waistcoat. The Governor of the Bahamas, Mr Felton, believed that the cotton produced on that island from seeds procured by Hove was some of the finest he had seen.[65]

But it is the involvement, techniques and authority of Sir Joseph Banks which are the most interesting aspects of the search for cotton. As with the breadfruit expedition, he was the inevitable source to which the ministry turned for guidance, and once his advice was accepted, the Board of Trade was satisfied to leave matters in his hands. Even when a person of his choice fell under government censure, it was virtually left to him to administer that censure and enquire into the man's wrongs. Obviously, his influence in this and other matters must be viewed in the context of the ministry of the day, of his friendship with Hawkesbury and of the vigorous policy of the new Board of Trade. Finally the search for cotton suggests that the collaboration between science and industry which Musson and Robertson have effectively documented, spread also into the field of imperial endeavour. This did not perhaps occur in a way sufficiently systematic to herald a new British overseas policy: the government of the day followed rather than led in this respect. But it reveals that the vigour and purposefulness of certain industrialists, and the global scientific interest of a man such as Sir Joseph Banks, could fruitfully combine in a way which would in the nineteenth century affect the direction and purpose of British imperial policy.

Notes

1. The most recent study of the cotton trade for this period is M.M. Edwards, *The Growth of the British Cotton Trade, 1780–1815*.
2. An increasing quantity came from Portuguese South America, to the conster-

nation of the manufacturers who were unable to penetrate the Portuguese market, see V.T. Harlow, *The Founding of the Second British Empire 1763-1793*, vol. II, pp. 282-3.

3. *B.T.* 6/140, 8, 10 March 1786.

4. Ibid., 15, 18 July 1787. c.f. Edwards, *Growth of the British Cotton Trade*, p. 76.

5. H. Furber, *John Company at Work*, pp. 296-8.

6. On this trade see A. Aspinall, *Cornwallis in Bengal*, Appendix I.

7. On the breadfruit expedition, see above, Chapter 5; on Swartz's planned expedition to India, see below, Chapter 7. Both enterprises were discussed between Hawkesbury and Banks during March 1787, and Banks put official proposals on both to Hawkesbury on 31 March.

8. Nepean to Banks, n.d., 1787, *Add. MSS.* 33982, fo. 327.

9. Nepean to Banks, 22 February 1787, *Add. MSS.* 33978, fo. 106.

10. *B.T.* 5/4, 94, 23 February 1787.

11. Ibid., 26, 26 February 1787.

12. *National Library of Scotland*, [N.L.S.] *(Melville)* 1064, fos 3, 6-12, February 1787.

13. On the *Nautilus* expedition of 1785-6, see above, Chapter 2. Nepean to Banks, 22 February 1787, *Add. MSS* 33978, fo. 106. 'Perhaps my friend Mr. Au might not object to a Trip.'

14. *B.T.* 6/246, 30 March 1787. *I.O., General Correspondence* E/1/80, fo. 230, 2 April 1787. Hawkesbury to Morton, 31 March 1787, *Add. MSS* 38309, fo. 147. Hawkesbury to Dundas, 31 March 1787, *Add. MSS* 38309, fo. 148.

15. Banks to Hawkesbury, 1 September 1788, *B.T.* 6/246; 'as he was to go out on board the last ship of the season then on the point of sailing he was despatch'd with such haste as precluded all extension of enquiries on the subject.' *B.T.* 3/1, 77, 2 April 1787. *B.T.* 6/246, 3 April 1787. Banks stated the allowance as being £500, payable at Bombay.

16. These instructions are in *D.T.C.* IV, fos 122-7.

17. Banks to Wiles, 25 June 1791, *D.T.C.* VII, fos 218-26.

18. On this trade see Furber, *John Company at Work*, ch. VI.

19. Banks to Yonge, *D.T.C.* V, fo. 161 discussed in Chapter 7, below.

20. For a discussion of this point, see below, Chapter 7.

21. The behaviour of the Company supercargoes at Canton in regard to the attempts to transplant tea to Bengal; or, indeed the Bombay Government's reluctance to assist Lieutenant-Colonel Kyd, show how realistic such fears were. See below, Chapter 7.

22. *B.T.* 3/1, 76, 30 March 1787. Hilton to Hawkesbury, 3 April 1787, *B.T.* 6/246. Banks to Hawkesbury, 20 April 1787, ibid.

23. Hove's journey is recorded in a journal he kept entitled: 'Tours for Scientific and Economical Research.' A copy, presented to Banks, is in *Add. MSS* 8956.

24. Hove, ibid., fo. 26.

25. Banks to Hawkesbury, 30 April 1787, *B.T. 6/246*. *B.T.* 5/4, 142, 23 May 1787.

26. Banks to Hawkesbury, 25 August 1787, *B.T.* 6/246.

27. Hawkesbury to Banks, 31 August 1787, *Add. MSS* 38310, fo. 5.

28. Frodsham to Fawkener, 20 September 1787, *B.T.* 6/246.

29. Fawkener to Banks, 8 October 1787, *B.T.* 3/1, 129. William Fawkener was a Privy Council Clerk seconded to the Board of Trade. Banks to Fawkener, 14 October 1787, *B.T.* 6/246.

30. J. Steele to Banks, 14 June 1787, *Add. MSS* 33978, fo. 131. Banks to Hawkesbury, 16 November 1787, *B.T.* 6/246. *B.T.* 5/4, 191, 21 November 1787. *B.T.* 6/246, 30 November 1787.

31. *B.T.* 6/140, 17, 30 November 1787.

32. *B.T.* 5/4, 202, 8 December 1787.

33. *H.O.* 42/10, 5 November 1786. Phillip to Nepean, December 1786, *H.O.* 42/10. On cochineal, see below, Chapter 7.

34. *B.T.* 203/5, 15 December 1787. *B.T.* 3/1, 147-8, 18 December 1787. *B.T.* 6/246, 22 March 1788. The samples are enclosed.

35. Jones to Banks, 25 February 1788, *D.T.C.*, VI, fo. 19.

36. Dundas to Hawkesbury, 28 February 1787, *Add. MSS* 38192, fo. 45.

37. *B.T.* 6/140, 17, February 1788; 20, 26 March 1788; 22-41, 51-60. Also, *N.L.S. (Melville)* 1064, fos 20-1, 18 February 1788; fos 22-3, 13 February 1788.

38. *N.L.S. (Melville)* 1064, fos 26-8, 17 April 1788.

39. *P.R.O. (Cornwallis)* 30/11, 20, fo. 78, 25 October 1787. Grant to Cornwallis submitting order of investment for 1788/9.

40. On this see Aspinall, *Cornwallis in Bengal.*

41. *B.T.* 6/140, 54-6, 8 May 1788. Richardson to Pitt, 14 April 1788, *Add. MSS* 38223, fo. 25.

42. See H.R.C. Wright, *East-Indian Economic Problems of the Age of Cornwallis and Raffles*, ch. III.

43. *B.T.* 6/246, 10 March 1788. Banks to Hawkesbury, 1 September 1788, ibid.

44. Ibid.

45. Jones to Banks, 24 September 1788, *D.T.C.* VI, fo. 78. Banks to Hawkesbury, 5 May 1789, *Add. MSS* 38224, fo. 117.

46. Hawkesbury to Banks, 9 September 1788, *Add. MSS* 38310, fo. 24.

47. Banks to Hawkesbury, 20 September 1788, *B.T.* 6/246.

48. Hawkesbury to Banks, 27 September 1788, ibid. Banks to Hawkesbury, 29 September 1788, *Add. MSS* 38223, fos 201-2. Copies in *P.R.O. (Chatham)* 30/8, 111, fos 108-9, 30 September and *B.T.* 6/246, 30 September 1788.

49. Hawkesbury to Grenville, 2 October 1788, *Add. MSS* 38310, fo. 26.

50. *B.T.* 5/5, 78, 31 October 1788.

51. Hove to Banks, 10 March 1788, *B.T.* 6/246, enclosure. Banks to Hawkesbury, 26 November 1788, ibid. Hawkesbury to Banks, 26 November 1788, *D.T.C.* VI, fos 94-5. *B.T.* 5/5, 85-6, 29 November 1788.

52. Hove, 'Tours for Scientific and Economic Research'.

53. Banks to Hawkesbury, 19 May 1789, *Add. MSS* 38224, fo. 134. Hove to Banks, 29 August 1789, *B.T.* 6/246. Banks to Fawkener, 28 August 1789, ibid. Cottrell to T. Steele, 29 August 1789, ibid.

54. Banks to Fawkener, 1 September 1789, ibid. Fawkener to Hawkesbury, 24 October 1789, *Add. MSS* 38224, fo. 311. *B.T.* 6/246, 10 September 1789. Fawkener to Banks, 16 September 1789, *Kew, B.C.* I, fo. 360.

55. Banks' description of the collection, and his orders for its disposal, are in *B.T.* 6/246, 28 August 1789. The fossils and reptiles were given to the British Museum, see J. Planta to Fawkener, 8 January 1790, *B.T.* 6/246.

56. Hawkesbury memorandum, n.d., *B.T.* 6/246. Hawkesbury to Banks, 3 October 1789, *Add. MSS* 38310, fo. 43.

57. Ibid, enclosure.

58. Banks to Hawkesbury, 16 November 1789, *B.T.* 6/246.

59. *B.T.* 5/5, 200, 19 November 1789.

60. *B.T.* 6/246, n.d. 1790.

61. *B.T.* 3/2, 337-8, 24 June 1790; ibid., 345-7, 13 July 1790. *B.T.* 5/6, 131-2, 13 July 1790.

62. Hove to Banks, 20 September 1795, *Kew, B.C.* II, fo. 128. Hove to Banks, 15 August 1796, ibid., fo. 147.

63. Hilton to Board of Trade, 19 March 1789, *B.T.* 6/140, 92. Jones to Banks, 17 September 1789, *D.T.C.* VI, fo. 228. Scott to Banks, 7 January 1790, ibid., fos 1-21.

64. Harlow gives the following figures for the importation of cotton from the West Indies:

1761–5 (annual average)	—	3,338,346 lb
1771–5	—	2,587,204
1781–5	—	6,130,951
1791–5	—	11,602,659
1801–6	—	16,292,088

Harlow, *Founding of the Second British Empire*, vol. II, p. 290.
   65. S. Felton to Banks, 17 January 1790, *Kew, B.C.* II, 1. *B.T.* 5/6, 144–5, 6 August 1790.

7 SCIENCE AND THE EAST INDIAN EMPIRE

The East Indies reveal more clearly than any other area the inter-connection between eighteenth-century science and empire which Sir Joseph Banks promoted and exemplified. Since the time of Alexander the Great the range of climates and landforms had fasci-nated the natural historian because of its variety of plant and animal life. British interest in its natural history dated from the earliest trading voyages in the late sixteenth century. On the other hand India's large population and tropical produce seemed to offer the English people, and the East India Company as their agent, oppor-tunities for the amassing of vast fortunes through trade and tribute. The marriage of these two interests was a natural and productive one to Banks, who in the late eighteenth century sponsored attempts to increase the wealth of Britain's Indian Empire by the utilisation of scientific information and techniques.

The experimental transfer of plants within the domains of the East India Company must be seen in the context of the failing commercial system and chronic indebtedness of the Company itself, since these economic difficulties created the greatest opportunities and the greatest problems for the successful transfer of new crops. In November 1784 Lawrence Sulivan estimated the Company debts in India to be £8,000,000. Aspinall has calculated that by 1786 the home debt exceeded £11,800,000 and the Indian debt £9,770,000.[1] Some of the reasons for this situation are all too clear. The Com-pany had been leached of its funds by war, the greed of its servants, an unwieldy administrative machinery and a considerable degree of incompetence. It was able to survive partly because its outmoded accounting system prevented a revelation of the true facts, but prin-cipally because it had been able to depend on the financial bolstering of the Treasury, and of the shippers who handled its trade. To this extent it was financially circumscribed — dependent on a postpone-ment of customs dues, on the acceptance for payment of its bills of exchange, and by delays in the payment of freight and demurrage charges.

However, not even these disguised subsidies were sufficient to maintain solvency, for in 1786 and again in 1789, the Directors, pressed by Dundas, were forced to appeal to Parliament for an increase in the capital stock of the Company.[2] In spite of these accumulating debts and a regular loss on its Indian trade, the stockholders' dividends remained sacrosanct, and during the decade £3,129,155 was paid out to investors. 'In so far as its relationship to India was concerned' wrote Holden Furber, 'the Company in its corporate capacity was simply a tool used by groups of individuals who cared not a whit what the balance sheet looked like so long as their private ends were served.'[3]

In India itself the position was much the same. Both Bombay and Madras were debtor governments drawing on Bengal to balance their ledgers. Because of its smaller territorial possessions and thriving country trade, Bombay was in a slightly better position than Madras, but it was obliged to maintain small and unprofitable trading factories, and it relied for many of its purchases, sales and general finance, on Indian traders and its own servants. Madras was the bottomless pit of Indian finance; a settlement bedevilled by war and financial chicanery. Furber wrote of it:

> In order to understand the situation in which the Madras government was placed, we must think of it as a business firm hovering on the brink of bankruptcy and ill-served by a group of employees who were engaged in cheating it at every possible opportunity.[4]

Commerce was virtually at a standstill; every aspect of government activity was open to profit-making; the possibilities of financial aggrandisement through dealing in the debts of the Nawab of Arcot were as yet not fully exploited; Madras therefore stood as a model for corruption and inefficiency in the eary 1780s.

The acquisition of the *Diwani* by Clive in 1765 had ironically proved to be a financial disaster for Bengal, for it led the Directors to the erroneous conclusion that the land revenues could be used to produce a large surplus of income over expenditure. With this surplus the Company was theoretically able to purchase an investment of Indian goods which when sold in England would defray the home costs of the Indian Empire and leave a substantial profit. In fact Bengal was in a position little better than that of the other two Presidencies which relied upon it for financial solvency. Corruption existed at every level, with the additional prospect of profit in the purchase of the investment. To maintain credit the government frequently had to authorise the sale of bills of exchange on London, and to request shipments of bullion to alleviate money shortages. The Cornwallis reforms after 1786 helped to maintain the credit of the Company in Bengal, but they did not substantially improve the financial structure.[5]

The problems and misdemeanours of the Company became the concern of reformers in the 1780s, and Pitt's India Act of 1784 opened up possibilities for substantial change in India itself. The impetus came mainly from the newly created Board of Control rather than from the Directors. From the middle of 1785 onwards the Board President, Henry Dundas, was gradually drawing to himself the reins of Indian government and pressing the chairmen of the Company for wholesale financial reorganisation, starting with a drastic retrenchment of the Indian establishments. Agreements on standard reduced establishments and rigid economies in Bengal were eventually reached in April 1785, but the implementation of the reforms had to wait for the new era ushered in by the arrival of Cornwallis in Bengal in September 1786.[6]

While these obvious remedies might have halted the deterioration in the Company's financial situation, they did not offer any prospects of solving the existing debt crisis, much less invigorating the India trade. It was to these problems that Dundas turned in June 1785. On the 15th, in discussions with Pitt, he suggested that the Indian debt be funded and transferred to England. In meetings with the secret committee in July, it was decided to give Dundas' plan a trial, provided it could be done through the mechanism of the annual investment. By augmenting the investment from £1,000,000 to £1,500,000 the Company would be able to draw an increased trading profit in London, which would in turn enable it to honour the bills drawn in India on the Court of Directors. The opening up of a reliable channel of remittance for Company servants in India would check clandestine transfers to Europe, and illegal trading would consequently be curtailed.

In the long term it was apparent that augmenting the investment as it stood would bring an outcry from British manufacturers, who were beginning to mount an offensive against the Company monopoly. The Company was finding it increasingly difficult to justify at the same time the export of bullion to India and the importation into England of Indian piece goods.[7] The latter still made up the bulk of the investment, as is illustrated by the following calculation of the Company's order of investment for 1788/9:

Cloths	—	5,900,000 rupees
Raw silk	—	1,500,000
Indigo	—	500,000
Saltpetre	—	100,000

Even these figures do not tell the whole story, since their author, Charles Grant, stressed to Cornwallis that silk and indigo supplies were unreliable and therefore the balance of up to £953,279 should be held as variable.[8] But to placate the manufacturing and shipping interests, particularly of the outports, there was a need for substitutes for cotton piece goods in the investment as well as for an increase in the export of manufactures to India. Needless to say it was imperative that substitute imports should be raw materials rather than manufactured goods.

Unfortunately the promise of Dundas' scheme was not fulfilled, for by 1787 it was in troubled waters. In the first year of its operation £1,500,000 of debt was transferred to London, but only £200,000 the following year, and future prospects looked hopeless.[9] Dundas was undaunted by the setbacks and throughout the first half of 1787 he pressed the Directors for a renewal of the scheme. From the Indian end, as we shall see, he had indications that the investment could be diversified and increased, and if anything stood in the way, it was weaknesses in the financial and commercial structure of the Company itself. The fact that in March the Directors had accused various commercial residents and members of the Bengal Board of Trade of making collusive contracts in the purchase of the investment, seemed to bear out these impressions.[10] In July Dundas managed to push through another proposal for transferring the Indian debt, similar to that of 1785.

Pitt, Dundas and Hawkesbury continued to explore the possibilities for increasing and diversifying the investment after 1787. In January 1788 Dundas had the Treasury draw up a list of dyeing and medicinal drugs suitable for expanded production in India, with an indication as to the quantity currently imported into Britain, with country of origin.[11] In March Pitt drew up his own estimate of the potential profit on raw cotton, indigo, coffee and pepper, imported from India, together with the annual remittance needed to secure them at prime cost.[12] These were clearly the goods which he favoured for development, and on a remittance of £425,920 he calculated a profit, after freight, demurrage and landing charges, of £445,320. The only products which Dundas had any reservations about were spices, as he thought it unwise to threaten the Dutch monopoly thereby reducing prices and angering the Dutch. Considering England's precarious relationship with the Netherlands at the time there seemed little point in giving offence.[13]

Since the early seventeenth century there had been efforts to find new Indian exports, but in the second half of the eighteenth century these had been intensified. Warren Hastings had successfully raised several varieties of cinnamon in his own botanic garden, and during his governorship a group of merchants formed the Bengal Commercial Society for conducting experiments in sugar cane and silk with an initial capital of £50,000.[14] Although these private efforts had the support of the Directors, after 1785 the Company itself began a search for new commodities for the investment. Because of the increased output of cotton goods in England, they realistically turned first of all to the area of dyes and drugs. When indigo supplies from the Carolinas were cut off during the American War the Bengal government had encouraged some residents to fill this gap. It was at this time that future Company Chairman, Charles Grant, began his plantation while a resident at Malda, and although this particular experiment was not able to survive the renewed competition with the United States after 1783, the government continued to subsidise production through the 1780s, backing any schemes aimed at an improvement in quality.[15] With broader objects in view, the Directors in April 1786 appointed a former diamond trader, Lyon Prager, to find and purchase drugs for the European investment.[16]

The Company's concern to find new products was also seen in its attempts to find a replacement for Dr Johan Koenig, the botanist on the Bengal establishment who died in June 1785. Koenig's brief had been to search for useful plants for export, and as Sir Joseph Banks put it he had been confident of his ability 'to repay his Employers a thousand Fold in matters of investment, by the discovery of Drugs and Dying materials fit for the European market but above all by putting the Company in possession of articles proper for the Chinese investment such as that nation at present receives from other people'.[17]

Anxious that Koenig's efforts should not be wasted, the Company asked Banks to evaluate his partially completed dossier of useful plants and to report on the best way of continuing the work.[18] Banks' conclusion was that the known discoveries should be generalised by the publication of Koenig's work, and the search for other species should be continued by the appointment of a successor. On receiving this report the Company called on the assistance of the Board of Trade, hoping, no doubt, that the costs of sending a trained botanist to India might be met by the government. By the end of March Banks confirmed to Lord Hawkesbury that he had found a person willing to undertake the mission — Olof Swartz, a Swede, and like Koenig a pupil of Linnaeus with a considerable knowledge of tropical botany acquired during travels in the West Indies. Swartz was to work under Banks' direction, searching for new products and supervising a nursery of specimens in Bengal. Unfortunately, the attractive salary of £400 with travelling expenses was not enough to tempt the Swede to abandon strong family obligations and the mission was eventually called off.[19]

At the English end of these operations the East India Company generally made much use of the freely available services of Sir Joseph Banks in the evaluation of Indian products. The scientist had a number of important assets to offer in this respect. His specialist knowledge of tropical plants was a consequence of the *Endeavour* voyage, as was his faith in the plausibility of transplanting species from one part of the world to another. After 1778 his position as President of the Royal Society, his strong links with government and his valuable range of associates and contacts made him a kind of scientific entrepreneur and a collection point for scientific knowledge.

From his own point of view Banks' relationship with the Company was more satisfactory when he was on personal terms with some of its employees. The Secretary, William Morton, was always ready to pass on information and handle efficiently any administrative arrangements. During the 1780s and early 1790s Banks normally had the support of Dundas, Cornwallis and two Directors, William Devaynes and Nathaniel Smith, although the Directorate as a whole was not always unanimous in supporting his proposals. One of the difficulties in any long-term association was the nature of the Company organisation itself. Between 1798 and 1800, for example, Banks was out of sympathy with the then chairmen and had some difficulty in ensuring continuity of policy, as he pointed out to the botanist and later superintendent of the Calcutta garden, William Roxburgh: 'I am tir'd of promoting projects with a fluctuating body who are sure to be chang'd by the time I have convinc'd the first set of the propriety of any measure recommended to them.'[20]

At his peak Banks clearly wielded a great deal of power in the Company, especially in the area of patronage. In the 1780s he secured places and salary increases for Alexander and John Duncan in the factory at Canton. In 1791 he was able to get a post for a Mr Bell at the settlement on Bencoolen.[21] In various other cases he secured favours for Company personnel in India. In this area too Banks was to some extent dependent on the composition of the directorate. When he tried to get a place for William Roxburgh's talented son in 1799, he found himself butting his head against a brick wall at India House. As he wrote to the father: 'I can do little for him yet because the present Chairman does not like me but he will soon pass away & it is great odds but that he is succeeded by some friend of mine.' His accurate prediction was realised with the accession of Hugh Inglis to the directorate in 1800, when the boy finally was given a job as his father's assistant.[22]

For their part, Dundas and the Directors acknowledged Banks' ability and usefulness. Dundas referred on to him the despatches of Colonel Kyd on the Calcutta Botanic Garden and wrote back to Cornwallis:

> Wishing to give [Kyd] every aid in my power, I put the Dispatches into the hands of Sir Joseph Banks, and I send for your Lordship's perusal, and to be communicated to Colonel Kyd, a Copy of the Letter I have received from Sir Joseph on this subject; and it is unnecessary for me to say anything further on a subject which has been treated by so masterly a hand.[23]

In a similar vein in 1788 a Company Committee acknowledged the value of Banks' advice in drawing up a memorial on the cultivation of the cochineal insect in Madras: 'In their researches on the subject your Committee have been materially aided by the public spirit and communications of Sir Joseph Banks, Bart, to whom your Committee consider themselves indebted in an extraordinary degree for the information and light he has thrown on the subject.'[24]

The philosophy behind the transfer and propagation of tropical plants in the East Indies also had its origin with Banks, and various strands of his thought may be identified. He clearly perceived the changes taking place as a result of England's industrial development. The importation of Indian manufactured goods would become increasingly difficult as the pressures from home producers built up. India's best prospects were, therefore, to be looked for in areas where there could be no competition with England; principally in the production of unprocessed tropical raw materials. In a report to the Board of Control in 1787 Banks outlined his view:

> if we consider for a moment that the merchandise hitherto brought home from India have been chiefly manufactures of a nature which interferes with our manufacturies at home, that our cotton manufacturies above all, are increasing with a rapidity which renders it politic to give them effectual encouragement, & that a profit of Cent per Cent upon the importation of the raw material of cotton is to be got with certainty, can we too much encourage everything which tends to the cultivation of raw materials in India? Laborers are abundant there: Labor excessive cheap: raw materials of many sorts, dying drugs, Medecines, Spices &c sure of a ready and advantageous market and of producing a most beneficial influence upon the Commerce of the mother Country.[25]

In most commodities Banks believed that India would soon undercut the West Indies. It had a variety of climates, fertile soils, and a 'numerous race of frugal industrious & intelligent natives'[26] accustomed to working for low wages. Ultimately he saw that the government would protect the West Indian sugar interest, but cotton, coffee, cochineal and indigo could all be produced more profitably in India.

Although most of the Indian raw materials would go to England, Banks was also optimistic about the Chinese market. Many drugs and other vegetable productions in demand there could be produced in quantity in India and when exported to Canton still undersell the local product. Such a trade might diminish, and perhaps end, the immense exportation of silver from Britain. At the same time various products which the Company procured from China at great cost could be produced quite satisfactorily in parts of India — tea and silk included.

Implicit in Banks' schemes was the belief that plants from one tropical environment would flourish when transferred to another, 'few if any instances being known of Plants brought from one inter-tropical climate refusing to thrive in another'. Thus developed the idea of plant interchange: by shipping valuable plants from one hemisphere to another various natural shortcomings could be redressed, and products could be grown in regions best suited to them from a wider economic point of view. In May 1787 Banks outlined his philosophy to the Secretary at War, Sir George Yonge:

> To exchange between the East & West Indies the productions of nature usefull for the support of mankind, that are at present confined to one or the other of them, to increase by adding this variety, the real Quantity of the produce of both Countrys & by that means their population, furnishing at the same time to their inhabitants new resources against the dreadful effects of Hurricanes & droughts to one or the other of which all intertropical countries are subject, are the immediate objects. . .[27]

The breadfruit expeditions had represented one attempt to carry out such a transfer, but Banks envisaged a process involving a much wider range of products and destinations.

Integral to such a process of interchange was the establishment of properly run botanical gardens which would act as reception centres for transplanted species. Here new arrivals would be acclimatised and propagated before being distributed to interested cultivators. Another requirement was the existence of suitable staging posts so that the journey of transfer could be broken and sudden seasonal adjustments could be avoided. Lastly some regular and reliable means of transfer had to be available to facilitate interchange without damage to the plants involved. One obvious solution was to use the ships of the East India Company itself, and to offer encouragement to any of their captains who showed interest.

Between 1786 and 1791 botanical gardens were established in Company possessions at Calcutta, Madras, Bombay and St Helena, with the principal aims being the collection and propagation of useful plants. In the cases of Calcutta and St Helena it was also hoped that the gardens might assist local cultivators to establish viable food crops. All the gardens were set up by grants from the Company itself, and with the exception of that at Bombay, all had salaried superintendents to care for them.

Although Cornwallis had been introduced to the advantages of such gardens before leaving to take up his governorship, the initiative for the foundation of the largest enterprise — that at Calcutta — came from within the Presidency itself. In the middle of 1786 a former army engineer in the Company service, Lieutenant Colonel Kyd, wrote to acting Governor-General Macpherson suggesting the foundation of a botanic garden and the propagation of the sago palm as a relief for the recurring problem of famine. Kyd had been on his way home from India in 1785 for health reasons, but while in transit at the Cape he had undergone some revelatory experience and returned to Calcutta to fulfil his new mission. He explained his philosophy to Macpherson:

> Revolving in my mind the accumulated Riches which have accrued to Great Britain, consequent to the acquisition of our Territorial Possessions in India, I have sometimes been betrayed into Reflections on the comparative benefits we have conferred on the Natives of India, whom the Right of conquest has sub-jected to our Government. In this comparison I am afraid the balance will stand greatly against us.

Kyd envisaged a garden as a 'Nursery for rearing and propagating for the publick benefit the productions of other Countries & Climates, and such as may be equally conducive to increase the Commerce and improve the Culture of these provinces'. The success of the experiments in cinnamon growing in the garden of Warren Hastings pointed to the viability of the scheme, which would lead to the development of private plantations and 'ultimately may tend to the extension of national Commerce and Riches'.[28]

After receiving the approval of the Governor-in-Council, Kyd began planning work on the chosen site at the old Mogul fort of Muggah Thana, but because of his own ill health it was not until the middle of 1788 that the garden was ready to receive plants.[29] In May Kyd officially became superintendent and was provided with an assistant on a salary of 50 rupees a month. The Council drew 1,000 rupees from the Revenue Department as a setting up grant for the garden although the Directors hoped costs could be kept to 200 rupees a month. Towards the end of 1789 an assistant gardener, Hughes, was appointed at 200 rupees a month and, with a renewal of Kyd's health problems, the new man took on much of the burden of the undertaking. In spite of the lethargy of some of the other Presidencies in responding to requests for plants, by 1790 a considerable stock of useful specimens was thriving in the garden, including cinnamon, coffee, black pepper, breadfruit and the cochineal plant, nopal.[30]

The garden at Madras was the brainchild of an impulsive and erratic surgeon, James Anderson.[31] His particular botanical mission had been to wrest from the Spaniards their monopoly in the production of the expensive cochineal dye, and to this end he had been attempting to propagate species of the host plant, especially the nopal, *Opuntia cochinillifer*. Early experiments with a variety of the local salt grass as a substitute had proved unsuccessful, and on Banks' advice Anderson had committed himself to developing a more congenial host plant for the cochineal insects. Once again there was a need for a proper nursery to raise and propagate the plants, so in September 1788 Anderson suggested to the Governor that the Company should purchase some land and introduce nopals and other useful species.[32]

By January 1739 Anderson had obtained the Governor's approval and found a suitable site at Marmalon, just outside Fort St George. With official sanction he was able to appoint his own nephew, Dr Andrew Berry, to superintend the garden, and estimates of 386 pagodas for the setting up of the enterprise, with a monthly expenditure of 150 pagodas had been approved by the Madras government. 3,665 pagodas was set aside for buildings at the nursery, including the superintendent's house, and Berry himself was to have a monthly salary of 50 pagodas a month. By April the 'Hon. Company's Nopalry' (as Anderson wished it to be described) was laid out, the embankments were completed and hedges built, and the first of the nopal plants had been planted out, including some introduced specimens from Kew, Canton and Mexico. A year later the nopalry had over 800 exotic plants and many more of the indigenous variety, as well as some other useful plants.[33]

The Bombay garden was a direct response to developments in the other two Presidencies. In 1791 a correspondent of Banks, the physician and natural historian Helenus Scott, petitioned the Bombay government for the use of land on the island of Salsette, adjacent to the city. His aims were to conduct experiments in the cultivation of sugar, tobacco, indigo, coffee and a variety of other useful articles, and to provide a despatch depot for plants for other Indian gardens. After examining the rights of the existing occupants the Bombay Council acceded to his request, and between 200 and 300 acres were set aside for Scott's experiments.[34]

Although in the first two years of its operation the garden did not have any great success, in September 1792 the Council renewed the grant of land on a rent free basis for a period of ten years. Scott continued trials with sugar cane, coffee and silk, but abandoned most other experiments after a series of crop failures.[35]

The origins of the garden on St Helena were somewhat different. The strategic position of the island made it a potentially useful place for ships to refresh at on their way to the East Indies, but in fact as a supplier of provisions it was notoriously deficient and had not always been able to support its own small population. In times of peace most ships refreshed at Madeira, the Canaries, Cape Verde Islands or Rio on the Atlantic passages, touching at the Cape for further stores on their passages into, or out of, the Indian Ocean. St Helena was used mainly as a centre for despatches. In times of war this had obvious disadvantages. In 1771 both Cook and Banks had criticised the Islanders for their want of ingenuity in expanding agriculture, and Cook had been taken to task for his comments on returning there in May 1775. Banks had been so struck by the poverty of the island, that on his return to England he had despatched packets of grass seed in an attempt to establish suitable pasture land, and this had met with some success.[36]

With the development of the idea of plant interchange, other uses were envisaged for St Helena. Because of its location within the tropics, it could be a valuable resting place for tropical plants in transit from one hemisphere to another. The greatest danger to plants at sea came from the salt spray and cold weather, and it was not always possible when shipping consignments to ensure their arrival at the appropriate season. There was also a danger from cold and boisterous weather in the passage around the Cape.

For these differing reasons the East India Company, prompted by Banks, embarked on a crash programme for the agricultural improvement of the island. In January 1787 it was decided to establish a botanic garden and a Scotsman, Henry Porteous, was appointed as superintendent. Robert Brooke, the new Governor, strongly supported the scheme, and set out to arouse the interest of local planters and Company servants. Initially three separate gardens were started in an attempt to find the most suitable location, and Porteous outlined to Brooke a plan to grow mangoes, plantains and cassias in the two-acre site near the Company hospital. In May the sensitive inhabitants of the island rallied behind Porteous by establishing the St Helena Planters' Society for the encouragement of agriculture. The Society had 52 founder members prepared to pay the £10 subscription, and the body was presided over by the Governor and council. Eight captains of East Indiamen were among the founders and the Society dedicated itself to importing new products and offering premiums to anyone on the island producing new and valuable crops. Writing to a prospective donor of new species, the members outlined their intentions, which were, 'not only to increase the annual produce of this little spot, by raising a spirit of active application in the inhabitants; but as we consider the climate and soil here to be happily suited for Botanical experiment; our desire is to advance and extend this species of culture by every encouragement in our power . . . we think the situation of this Island is peculiarly well adapted to render it an intermediary nursery for the preservation of such plants as may not have strength to endure the whole course of a voyage to Europe or to the Eastern world.' From 1789 onwards St Helena was extensively used as a 'half-way House' for the trans-shipment of plants between the East and West Indies, although with the Cape in British hands after 1795 the pressure to provision passing ships was not so strong.[37]

Although Colonel Kyd's plan to propagate the sago and date palms in Bengal reflected a concern for the problem of famine and, therefore, for the indigenous inhabitants of the sub-continent, most of the crops proposed for production in India were to benefit the interest of the mother country. Even more remarkably they would have clearly augmented a philosophy of empire which did not acknowledge the work of Adam Smith. The attitudes of men such as Banks, Hawkesbury, Dundas and the Company Directors were to that extent decidedly mercantilist, although Banks in particular was concerned to buttress the old economic philosophy by the application of modern technology. Several strands of this thought are obvious. All the major crops promoted for Indian development were aimed at increasing imperial self-sufficiency in cash crops, and lessening dependence on foreign nations. In the following example of the attempts in Bengal to grow hemp for naval stores, this requirement was bolstered by strategic considerations. The revolutionary war with France had meant a renewal of the old problem of naval stores and pointed to the dangers of depending on supplies from the Baltic: hemp and flax were the Archilles heel of England's naval supremacy. From 1792 to 1794 the problem was highlighted by the deteriorating quality of the product imported from St Petersburg as a considerable quantity of White Russia's supply was diverted to the requirements of a rapidly expanding Black Sea fleet.[38]

For these reasons serious attempts were made to foster a hemp industry in Bengal after 1796. Roxburgh cultivated several varieties in the Calcutta garden and the Company itself sent a botanist, George Sinclair, to begin a hemp plantation. Banks had been involved in these enterprises from the outset and progress reports were repeatedly sent to him. In 1800 he testified before the Board of Trade on the future of an Indian hemp industry and in 1801 sent to India large quantities of hemp seed, and a team of six men from

Lincolnshire familiar with the cultivation and dressing of flax. Although these experiments were not very successful, the Indian jute industry was later to get off the ground following the interruption of Russian hemp and flax supplies during the Crimean War.[39]

Another important facet of this mercantilist thought was that if produced successfully within British dominions, many of the crops, in particular tea, silk and to some extent cochineal, would lead to a vast reduction in the export of bullion. The example of tea provides a classic statement of the case. Since Pitt's Commutation Act of 1784 English importation of tea from China had sharply increased enabling her to dominate the trade through Canton. But profitable though this trade was, it involved a considerable exportation of bullion and according to prevailing theory a consequent drain on the economic strength of England and Bengal. Of the £1,300,000 worth of tea purchased at Canton in 1786, for example, between £700,000 and £800,000 worth was paid for in silver bullion.[40] The suggestion that this valuable plant might be introduced to Bengal from Canton and then domesticated so as to found an Indian tea industry was mooted in a rather tentative way by Colonel Kyd in June 1786. But in 1788 a more significant step was taken when Lord Hawkesbury asked Banks to draw up a feasibility study on the proposal.

Banks saw no problems in introducing the tea plant into India. The most favourable areas for experimentation were between Bengal and Bhutan, where there was a suitable range of climates and an abundance of cheap labour. There would be some initial difficulties in acquiring expertise in the skills of cultivating, manufacturing and grading the teas, and these would have to be learned from the Chinese.[41] To this end the mission of Colonel Cathcart to China had instructions to gather information on the growing and blending of tea. To get the industry on its feet in India, Banks suggested that some Honanese familiar with its production should be tempted into moving to Calcutta, with some of the inferior varieties of the shrubs. These could be placed in the Botanic Garden under the direction of 'the able & indefatigable superintendent' who would nurture them under the guidance of the Chinese. Once the coarser varieties had acclimatised some of the finer types should be introduced to stock a nursery of approximately 20 acres.[42]

In spite of the active encouragement of the Directors in England, progress on the introduction of tea was slow. There were great difficulties in procuring suitable plants from Canton, although the small consignments received in 1789 and 1790 grew well in the Calcutta Botanical Garden. Samples of Bengal tea received by Banks at the end of 1790 were found to be of good quality, but the main problem remained that of getting local cultivators to adopt the new product. Although the tea experiments continued through the 1790s no commercial progress was made until the discovery of an indigenous plant variety in the nineteenth century.[43]

In so far as possible it was desirable that crops introduced into India should be raw materials, and as Banks put it, 'articles not likely to produce rivalship with the Mother Country'. The place of cotton piece goods in the investment was to be sharply reduced to avoid unhealthy competition for the expanding British industry, and necessary commodities such as indigo, raw cotton, cochineal and other dyes were to be exported instead. Natural dyes were a particularly attractive proposition for the Company. They were in the main high value, low bulk commodities of tropical origin. As the British cotton industry grew, demand for dyes rapidly increased, along with pressure to find imperial sources of supply. Indigo has already been mentioned above, and the search for finer varieties was continued by Colonel Kyd and his successor William Roxburgh. Cochineal seemed an even more profitable raw material. Culture of the insect producing the dye was limited to Central America, and because of the high Spanish duties on its exportation and the difficulties associated with limited supply, it was a substantial component in the production costs of certain cloths.

Attempts to raise the insects outside the Spanish dominions had not hitherto been successful. In 1759 the Society of Arts had offered a premium of £100 for a quantity of not less than 25 lb of Jamaican-grown cochineal, but there had been no response. By 1784 360,755 lb of the dye, worth £288,604 was imported through the port of London alone and the East India Company Committee of Warehouses estimated that £500,000 was annually paid by Europe to Spanish America for the dye. Between 1781 and 1786 cochineal averaged between 18s and 20s a pound on the London market. Hence the Company interest in the attempts of James Anderson to raise the cochineal insect in Madras Presidency. Although experiments with an insect found locally did not prove successful, Banks observed to the doctor 'that your part of India is admirably situated for the cultivation of the real Cochineal which may easily be procured and sent to you'. Because of the high labour costs the insect could not be raised in the West Indies, but in Madras sufficient cheap labour could be found for the tedious business of harvesting. The Spaniards imposed high duties on their own product, and Indian dye would thus have a great advantage on the London and European market.[44]

The Madras cochineal industry made gradual progress in the 1790s and early 1800s. The main problem was the poor quality of insects which existed locally and for this reason sustained efforts were made to smuggle the South American variety out through Mexico or Brazil. In 1794 some insects were finally procured and two years later the first commercial quantities of cochineal dye were shipped to England. In the period up to September 1797 21,744 lb of cochineal was exported from Madras. In the next two years 55,196 lb was exported, and production continued at a somewhat lower rate between 1800 and 1810. In the last two years of the eighteenth century Madras cochineal sold in London at an average price of 8s $8\frac{3}{4}$d per lb, lower than the corresponding figure for the Spanish product, but not low enough to compensate for the greater quantity needed to dye cloth satisfactorily.[45]

Anderson was also at the centre of attempts to produce silk in Madras and the surrounding area, the object again being to supply British manufacturers and replace foreign imports. Once again the Court of Directors, local Board of Revenue and Sir Joseph Banks encouraged this enterprise. An instruction centre for the winding of silk was set up at Fort St George, and the Company set up a number of mulberry plantations, including a large one at Madras itself. Various surgeons were appointed as advisers on the production of silk at factories throughout the Presidency and rewards were offered to successful growers. By 1794 there were Company plantations at six centres throughout the Presidency, including one of near 4,000 acres at Vellout, and these incurred a total monthly charge of 402 rupees. Interest in the developments even spread to the princely state of Hyderabad where the Nizam asked for an adviser to assist in the establishment of a silk industry.[46]

Although the theory of intertropical plant interchange was sound enough, Banks and his associates often underestimated the difficulties involved. Personal prejudice and jealousy, negligence and incompetence, misfortunes at sea and extremes of climate all contributed to the practical problems of establishing new crops. Colonel Kyd was forever complaining about the difficulties of procuring plants for his garden. Commanders of factories and other Presidencies were slow to respond to his call, or that of the Directors, and he complained of the 'feeble and ineffectual assistance' he had received in this respect. The Canton supercargoes drew the bulk of his criticism, and it is clear that they were something less than enthusiastic in their attempts to procure plants, and endeavoured to discourage the experiments in tea and silk production in India. Kyd speculated on the possibility of the 'Thraldom imposed by the Chinese Government on the free Agency of their Bodies having also reached that of their intellectual faculties'. Banks too was suspicious of the supercargoes in connection with the tea proposal, as he believed them to 'have an interest in its failure'; for this reason he believed it would be better if some trained person were sent to Canton to arrange shipment. Even when a Company servant, W. Mackintosh, was commissioned by one of the chairmen to bring back tea plants from Canton, secrecy was urged on Governor General Cornwallis, lest 'the circumstances might give some umbrage to the supercargoes'. Although Banks thought it possible that the inactivity of the supercargoes might 'originate in the very harsh expressions made use of in speaking to those gentlemen', Kyd's distrust remained strong and he went so far as to try and recruit a Frenchman to bring back tea plants from Canton. In November 1789 he suggested to Cornwallis that another Frenchman from the Ile de France be requested to gather plants from Bombay and the Persian Gulf that he had 'in vain applied for to our several Presidencies'. The intimation that this particular man was probably a spy working for the French Ministry of Marine did not make him attractive to Cornwallis and the plan was never adopted.[47]

In obtaining plants from outside the Company's dominions, diverse and often precarious methods were tried. Because of his range of scientific contacts throughout the world, Sir Joseph Banks frequently acted as an organising and collecting agent for the Calcutta and Madras botanic gardens. Captains of East Indiamen were sometimes interested enough to gather specimens on their passages to and from the East Indies. In 1791, for example, the Company ordered Captain Parker of the *Bridgewater* to call at Rio de Janeiro on his passage to India to collect cochineal insects. In this case Banks drew up instructions for the care of the insects at sea, and these were later distributed to the commanders of other ships. In the same year the Secret Committee of the Company allotted £2,000 for the purposes of procuring insects, and the bulk of this sum was to be made available as bounties for ships' captains.[48]

Later in the 1790s Banks managed to interest the principal of the whaling firm of Enderby and Son in the scheme to produce cochineal at Madras, and orders were given to the commanders of various whaling vessels to try and procure insects in Brazil. The first convict fleet to Botany Bay also gathered insects and nopal plants at Brazil on its passage out, and a supply of these was left at the Cape of Good Hope for trans-shipment to Madras.[49]

In the 20 years after 1793, when William Roxburgh was superintendent of the Calcutta garden, more direct methods of obtaining plants were used. After the fall of Amboina and Banda into British hands in 1795 the Bengal government sent Roxburgh's assistant, Christopher Smith, to the Spice Islands to gather nutmeg and clove plants. By 1797 a steady supply of plants from south-east Asia was arriving in the Calcutta and Madras gardens, and by his own calculations Smith distributed 127,520 nutmeg and clove plants and 29,000 other valuable species during his period as a collector.[50]

In spite of these efforts, the correspondence of the various superintendents of botanic gardens in India reveals much frustration at the slow development of the enterprises in their care. Recurrent complaints were made about the slowness of the delivery of plants and the poor state they were in upon arrival. Often plants were poorly packed or neglected during their passage, and their survival clearly depended on the whims of the various commanders. A rough passage around the Cape could wipe out a whole consignment, and the assortment of monkeys, dogs, cats and other animals on board East Indiamen could make short work of delicate species if they were accessible. Samuel Enderby lamented the failure of one attempt to procure cochineal insects, which had been 'kill'd by the Villainy of one of his Crew in throwing Salt Water on them'.[51]

Such failures drove men like James Anderson to extreme measures. Many attempts to procure plants clearly threatened the economies of foreign colonies, and in such cases great delicacy and secrecy was necessary. Banks in particular had built up a delicate but productive network of relationships with foreign scientists and governments; a network which was a principal source of information, of plants and of seeds. As with his political disinterestedness within England, he relied on remaining *persona grata* to ensure a continuous flow of material, no matter what Britain's relations with foreign powers happened to be at the time. This did not put him above dabbling in plans to filch the commercial products of other countries for propagation within the empire, but it did imply a need for discretion. In 1789 all this was threatened when Anderson chose to print and distribute copies of the secret instruction on the care of plants and insects which Banks had drawn up for the Captain of the *Bridgewater*, as well as confidential correspondence between Banks and himself. Anderson went so far as to have the instructions translated into Spanish and prepared for shipment to Manila. Banks and the Company were furious over this rash move, and the former angrily expressed his feelings on the matter:

> the Dr. actuated by a degree of absurdity wholly above comprehension immediately Printed these instructions circulated them as much as he possibly was able both in India & at home & actually sent a Copy of them to a person whom he calls the King of Spain's botanist at manilla — if the spaniards be found to have taken new precautions to Prevent the insect from being brought out of their internal american dominions where alone it is at Present to be Found the cause of them must be sought for in the doctor's incredible imprudence.[52]

More than the enterprise immediately in hand was at stake here, for Anderson had unwittingly threatened to undermine a botanical *imperium* which was Banks' purpose and interest in life. He refrained from writing to the impetuous botanist until he ceased publishing their correspondence.

Ultimately Banks' plans for the economic welfare of the empire in India succumbed to more general and sustained pressures. The Directors in London were not uniform in their support for these measures, many seeing little possibility for change in the general pattern of the India and China trade. On several occasions Banks drew up reports for the Company only to have them pigeon-holed or sent on to India without recommendation or comment. This happened in 1789, for example, and Banks took it as a sign that they 'hesitate on the propriety of carrying [the propositions] into execution'. Two years later he chastised the Directors for calling on his expertise and then failing to keep him up to date on Indian developments.[53]

In India as well there were those who were sceptical. Cornwallis encouraged the botanic garden and efforts to find substitutes for cotton piece goods in the investment, but he believed the experiments in tea were doomed to failure, and he had no faith that the pattern of the Bengal-China trade would change. In some respects Cornwallis had a more realistic idea of the conservatism of the local producers and the great difficulties of introducing new crops.

Indigo had been very slow to catch on in Bengal in spite of the profitability and promise it showed. Most plantations were in fact European run. At the end of 1789 the Bengal Board of Trade reported in a rather negative way on the experiments, although they claimed to be 'extremely desirous to second the Views of their Hon'ble Employers to introduce new Articles into the Investment'. Certain products, such as ginger, cloves, brimstone and rice had proved unsuitable because Bengal costs and charges provided financial obstructions to their exportation. A succession of floods, droughts and high winds in 1787, 1788 and 1789 had made things more difficult, but in spite of this the Board believed that pepper, sugar, tobacco and wax were worth continued efforts.[54]

In January 1791 the Board reported again on the progress made in diversifying the investment. Although numerous experiments had been conducted only 30,000 rupees had been allotted for drugs and it was feared that there would be little profit on this. There was continued optimism about the export of sugar and indigo in spite of the strong competition, and from 1789 onwards a variety of new spices and drugs appeared in the investment order.[55]

The greatest single cause for the Company's declining interest in these schemes was the onset of the third Mysore war late in 1789 which led to an immediate draining of revenue from Bengal and the beginnings of an acute money shortage. Although the war facilitated an increased importation of bullion from England, little concern was given to supplementing the investment, much less the subsidising of a botanic garden and experiments in new crops. As Furber has observed, many Company servants saw the war as a form of release from the financial strait-jacket imposed by the need to produce an investment from a surplus in revenue. Once the bullion was flowing again all attempts to live up to the financial expectations of the Court of Directors could be shelved and life became much easier.

James Anderson in Madras attempted to shift the centre of his silk industry away from the war zone, but the constant draining of officers to the front lines and the consequent neglect of plantations already established were the main causes for subsequent failures. The effects of this depletion were still being felt four months after the signing of the peace treaty with Mysore, when Anderson sent 100 skeins of silk from his own garden to General Medows, claiming that production would have been much greater but for the war. The silk was forwarded to England for tests.[56]

In the short term, the attempts to use scientific knowledge to change the pattern of agricultural production in India were not very successful. Famine remained an Indian problem; spices never became a source of great profit to the Company and generally declined in value as imports to Europe. The Madras cochineal experiments which continued into the nineteenth century did not succeed in producing a high quality product, and the importance of cochineal declined as cheaper and more reliable synthetic dyes were discovered. Production of Madras silk went into a slow decline after 1798, faced with competition from Italy, the Near East, China and even Bengal. The quality of the Madras thread could not be maintained, and with the increasing competition of fine cottons, silk of variable quality could not find a market.

In spite of these failures the observations of Banks on the India and China trade were substantially correct. Cotton piece goods did not hold their own in the investment, and the reversal of the cotton trade with India undermined aspects of the traditional economy. In imperial terms India was to end up as a supplier of raw materials for the manufacturers of the metropolitan power. The solution to the export of bullion to China was only found with the illegal export of opium, and the subsequent development of the Indian tea industry in some senses justified Banks' view that perseverance and the application of science could work to India's benefit. It was unfortunate that the conservatism of the Company and Indian producers prevented a proper application of these ideas.

In the present context the most interesting aspects of these experiments are those which throw light on the relationship between science, exploration and empire in the late eighteenth century. The discoveries of Cook and his successors had broken down barriers of distance and inaccessibility, making possible the freer movement of men and materials within an imperial framework. There was a sense in which the revelation of a finite world suggested the more efficient and rational exploitation of existing imperial resources, and to facilitate this process the empirical sciences could be employed to suggest the best possible methodology. And yet this attitude did not betoken a general change of direction in imperial thinking. The traditional mercantilist imperatives remained strong in the early years of the industrial revolution although men such as Sir Joseph Banks showed how vitality might be restored to the comforting old imperial philosophy.

Notes

1. C.H. Philips, *The East India Company: 1784-1834*, p. 46. A. Aspinall, *Cornwallis in Bengal*, p. 5.

2. Philips, ibid., p. 47. The increase was by £800,000 in 1786 and by £1,000,000 in 1789.

3. H. Furber, *John Company at Work*, p. 269.

4. Ibid., p. 195.

5. For corruption in the purchase of the investment, see A. Embree, *Charles Grant and British Rule in India*, pp. 60-1, 67-94. On the Cornwallis reforms see Aspinall, *Cornwallis in Bengal*.

6. Philips, *The East India Company*, p. 46.

7. See above, Chapter 6, also Furber, *John Company at Work*, ch. VIII.

8. Grant to Cornwallis, 25 October 1787, *P.R.O. (Cornwallis)* 30/11, 20, fo. 78.

9. Philips, *The East India Company*, p. 47.

10. Embree, *Charles Grant*, pp. 108-12. Grant himself was among those accused.

11. *N.L.S. (Melville)* 1064, fos 18-19.

12. Ibid., fos 39-40, March 1788.

13. *N.L.S. (Melville)* 1068, fos 20-37, October 1787.

14. *D.T.C.* IX, fo. 59, 16 June 1786. Extract, Bengal Public Consultations. P.J. Marshall, 'The Bengal Commercial Society of 1775: Private Business Trade in the Warren Hastings Period', pp. 173-87.

15. Embree, *Charles Grant*, pp. 83-6. *I.O. Home Misc.* 393, pp. 23-5, Bengal Board of Trade, Report on Indigo.

16. *I.O. General Corres.* E/4/45, Bengal Letters Received, 13 November 1786. *Home Misc.* 393, pp. 240-1, 9 March 1789.

17. Banks to T. Morton, 22 February 1787, *I.O. General Corres.* E/1/80, 169-b.

18. *I.O. General Corres.* E/1/80, 103, 26 January 1787.

19. Banks to Hawkesbury, 30 March 1787, *D.T.C.* V, fos 139-42. Swartz to Banks, 29 August 1787, *Add. MSS.* 8096, fos 519-20.

20. Banks to Roxburgh, 9 August 1798, *Add. MSS.* 33980, fo. 160.

21. J. Duncan to Banks, 18 January 1784, *Add. MSS.* 33977, fo. 258. N. Smith to Banks, 12 March 1790, *Kew B.C.* II, 6. Home to Banks, 17 February 1791, ibid., 31.

22. Roxburgh to Banks, 24 April 1798, *Add. MSS.* 33980, fos 137-8. Banks to Roxburgh, 9 August 1798, ibid., fo. 160. Banks to Roxburgh, 7 January 1799, ibid., fo. 170. Roxburgh to Banks, 28 November 1800, ibid., fo. 255.

23. Dundas to Cornwallis, 23 July 1787, *N.L.S (Melville)* 3387, fo. 19.

24. Report of Committee of Warehouses, in Morton to White, n.d. 1788, *L.C.C.* p. 3.

25. Banks to Dundas, 15 June 1787, *D.T.C.* V, fos 184-91. This report also appears in *P.R.O. (Chatham)* 30/8, 361, fos 34-7; *P.R.O. (Cornwallis)* 30/11, 112, fos 75-82; and the *Windsor Royal Archives*, 6262 + 6263, suggesting the involvement of Pitt, Cornwallis and the King.

26. Banks to W. Devaynes, 27 December 1788, *D.T.C.* VI, fo. 109.

27. Banks to Yonge, 15 May 1787, *D.T.C.* V, fos 159-66.

28. Extract Bengal Public Consultations in *D.T.C.* V, fo. 29, 13 April 1786. Kyd to Macpherson, June 1786, ibid., IX, fo. 57.

29. *I.O. Home Misc.* 799, pp. 29-36, 30 August 1786. Ibid., pp. 37-8, 21 August 1786. *D.T.C.* IX, fos 57-67, 16 June 1786.

30. *I.O. Home Misc.* 799, pp. 43, 65-7, 92, 12 March, 16 March, 1 May 1787. *D.T.C.* VII, fos 45, 46-8, 21 March, 16 April, 18 May 1787.

31. On Anderson, see H.D. Love, *Vestiges of Old Madras, 1640-1800*, Vol. III,

p. 331; D.G. Crawford, *Role of the Indian Medical Service, 1615-1930*. He was another product of the University of Edinburgh, and had served at the siege of Manila in 1762.

32. Anderson to Banks, 3 December 1786, *D.T.C.* V, fos 115-17. Anderson to Banks, 20 February, 26 April, 27 May 1787, *L.J.B.*, pp. 2-10. Banks to Anderson, April 1788, *L.C.C.*, pp. 2-4.

33. Anderson to Campbell, 19 September 1788, 6 January 1789, 17 January 1789, ibid., p. 16. A Madras star pagoda was worth about 7s 6d at this time.

34. Scott to Banks, 7 January 1790, *Add. MSS.* 33979, fos 1-13. Scott to Bombay Council, 1 June 1791, *I.O. Home Misc.* 210, pp. 187-96. Scott to Banks, 19 January, 26 April 1792, *Add. MSS.* 33979, fos 127-30, 135-6.

35. *I.O. Home Misc.* 210, pp. 199-202, 203-4, 207, 28 August, 12 September, 18 September 1792.

36. J.C. Beaglehole, *The Endeavour Journal of Joseph Banks*, vol. II, pp. 265-7. H. Porteous to Banks, 8 June 1790, *Kew B.C.* II, 13a. Porteous states that the seeds were sent by Banks 23 years earlier, i.e. 1767, but it is more likely to have been after the *Endeavour* voyage.

37. W. Forsyth to Court of Directors, 3 January 1787, *I.O. General Corres.* E/1/80, 5-6. Brooke to Banks, 17 June 1787, *Kew B.C.* I, 275. Planters Society to J. Anderson, 14 June 1788, *C.I.C.* pp. 4-11.

38. *B.T.* 5/4, 1-47, 7 November-1 December 1786. *B.T.* 5/9, 54-61, 12 December 1793-3 January 1794. On the Black Sea fleet and Russian Naval Stores, E.P. Zakalinskaya, *Votchinnye Khozyaystva Mogilyovskoy Gubernii vo vtoroy polovine XVIII veka* [The Economy of Patrimonial Estates in the Mogilyovskoy Gubernii in the Second Half of the Eighteenth Century], Mogilyov, 1958 (manuscript translation by Professor I.R. Christie).

39. Morton to Banks, 13 April 1785, *Add. MSS.* 33978, fo. 9, J. Goodhall to Banks, 22 December 1800, *Kew B.C.* II, 241. Sinclair to Dundas, 7 April 1798, *N.L.S. (Melville)* 1065, fos 125-6. Sinclair to Banks, 2 May 1799, *Kew B.C.* II, 218. Lady Spencer to Banks, 5 October 1800, *Add. MSS.* 33980, fos 249-50. *B.T.* 5/12, 89-94, 98-106, 113-15, 16-22 December 1800. Inglis to Banks, 6 January 1801, *Add. MSS.* 33980, fo. 260. *D.T.C.* XII, fos 194-6, n.d. 1801.

40. V.T. Harlow, *The Founding of the Second British Empire 1763-1793*, vol. II, pp. 532-4. Banks to Hawkesbury, 29 September 1788, *Add. MSS.* 38223, fo. 203.

41. Banks to Hawkesbury, ibid., fos 202-6. Cf. Lucile H. Brockway, *Science and Colonial Expansion. The Role of the British Royal Botanic Gardens*, pp. 27-8. First attempts to transplant tea antedated the efforts Brockway describes by 50 years.

42. Banks to W. Devaynes, 27 December 1788, *D.T.C.* VI, fo. 109. Memorial on Tea, ibid., fos 103-8.

43. N. Smith to Banks, 27 April 1789, *Kew B.C.* I, 343. Kyd to Smith, 10 November 1789, *D.T.C.* VII, fo. 70. Mackintosh to Cornwallis, 24 November 1790, *P.R.O. (Cornwallis)* 30/11, 39, fo. 330. Extract Bengal Public Consultations, in *D.T.C.* VII, fos 68-9, 23 September 1789. C. Boughton-Rouse to Banks, 7 May 1790, *Add. MSS.* 33979, fo. 31. Banks to Boughton-Rouse, 9 May 1790, ibid., fo. 32. Banks to Morton, 15 October 1790, *I.O. General Corres.* E/1/86, 57c. P. Griffiths, *The History of the Indian Tea Industry*. Brockway, *Science and Colonial Expansion*.

44. L.J. Ragatz, *The Fall of the Planter Class in the British Caribbean*, p. 72. *Add. MSS.* 38346, fo. 98. T. Morton to C.N. White, 10 April 1788, *L.C.C.*, p. 4. Campbell to Dundas, 3 December 1786, *N.L.S. (Melville)* 3837, fos 50-1. Anderson to Banks, 3 December 1786, *D.T.C.* V, fos 115-17. Banks to Anderson, April 1788, *L.C.C.*, pp. 2-4.

45. Banks to Morton, 17 November 1791, *Kew B.C.* II, 55, c.f. W. Dawson (ed.), *The Banks Letters*, where this letter is incorrectly catalogued. Report of Committee

of Warehouses, n.d. 1788, *L.C.C.*, p. 3. Campbell to Browne &c, 11 October 1788, *I.O. China Consultations* R/10, vol. 17, p. 231. Smith to Banks, 30 April 1789, *Kew B.C.* I, 344. Banks to Anderson, 6 June 1790, *D.T.C.* VII, fos 113–15. R. Neilson to Anderson, 8 May 1795, *A.I.C.*, p. 3. Berry to Hobart, 20 July 1796, in Anderson, *Letters &c*, III, pp. 8–9. G. Watt, *A Dictionary of the Economic Products of India*, vol. II, p. 408.

46. Anderson to Oakley, 18 April 1791, *C.I.C.*, pp. 19–20. Anderson to Sir W. Jones, 13 May 1791, ibid., p. 28. J. Ferguson & Co. to Anderson, 3 May 1792, *A.L.C.*, p. 11.

47. *D.T.C.* VII, fos 42–4, 12 March 1787, List of plants received. Kyd to Cornwallis, 23 January 1788, *I.O. Home Misc.* 799, pp. 173–9. Kyd to Banks, 6 March 1788, ibid., pp. 185–201. Banks to Hawkesbury, 29 September 1788, *Add. MSS.* 38223, fo. 203. Mackintosh to Cornwallis, 24 November 1790, *P.R.O. (Cornwallis)* 30/11, 39, fo. 330. Kyd to Haldane, 24 November 1789, ibid., 29, fos 536–7.

48. *D.T.C.* VII, fo. 52, 13 August 1787. Banks to Morton, 17 November 1791, *Kew B.C.* II, 15. White to Anderson, 23 August 1788, *L.C.C.* p. 1.

49. S. Enderby to Banks, 16 February 1793, *Kew B.C.* II, 91.

50. Roxburgh to Banks, 19 December 1795, *Add. MSS.* 33980, fos 41–2. Roxburgh to Banks, 13 July 1797, ibid., fos 101–4. Banks to Roxburgh, 29 May 1796, 9 August 1798, ibid., fos 66, 159. Smith to Banks, 9 February 1803, ibid., 33981, fos 80–1. A.M. Coats, *The Quest for Plants*, p. 205.

51. *D.T.C.* VII, fos 50–1, 13 June 1787. Enderby to Banks, 16 February 1793, *Kew B.C.* II, 91.

52. Anderson to Campbell, 10 October 1788, *L.C.C.* pp. 7–8. Anderson to Hollond, 13 July 1789, ibid., pp. 32–3. Banks to Morton, 17 November 1791, *Kew B.C.* II, 55. The Spanish botanist was probably Don Juan de Cuillar, botanist to the Royal Company of the Phillipines.

53. *D.T.C.* VII, fo. 68, 23 September 1789. Banks to Morton, 17 January 1791, *I.O. General Corres.* E/1/86, 57c.

54. Kyd to Smith, 10 November 1789, *D.T.C.* VII, fo. 70. Dundas to Cornwallis, 3 April 1789, *P.R.O. (Cornwallis)* 30/11, 114, fos 45–6. *I.O. Home Misc.* 393, pp. 324–8, 9 November 1789. Ibid., pp. 333–5.

55. Ibid., p. 520, 25 January 1791. Furber, *John Company at Work*, pp. 294–5.

56. Anderson to Oakley, 6 June 1791, *C.I.C.*, pp. 43–4. Anderson to Medows, 25 July 1792, *A.L.C.*, p. 8.

CONCLUSION

There is some irony in the fact that when the rapid industrial progress of England gave some point to the territorial expansion and economic integration of the empire, a large chunk of that empire broke free from the mother country, while at the same time the opportunities for further expansion seemed to be reduced by Captain Cook's revelation of an apparently finite world. Of late this particular area of study has been the subject of considerable debate, the terms of which were set by V.T. Harlow's formidable work, *The Founding of the Second British Empire 1763-1793*. Playing down the significance of the American War of Independence as a turning point in imperial policy, Harlow traced the change of direction back to an earlier period — the Seven Years War — where the second empire had its genesis. The progenitors of this empire had policies and aims markedly different from those of their predecessors. In the age of Adam Smith statesmen such as the Earl of Shelburne and William Pitt the Younger redirected their attentions from the Atlantic colonies to the potential markets of the East and the Pacific; markets which could be serviced by a string of entrepôts and factory bases. The new empire was not to be founded on formal settlement, but to be an empire of trade regulated by the more subtle ties of informal control. In this way the voracious demands for raw materials and markets which had been created by England's burgeoning industries could be satisfied.

In several respects this book has attempted to qualify Harlow's interpretation of events. By examining some aspects of imperial endeavour after the American War of Independence, it has suggested some ways in which the loss of those colonies disoriented and disturbed imperial 'policy', although this disturbance did not amount to a new direction in imperial thinking. Indeed in the first ten years after the ending of the war the traditional mode of thought persisted as an almost instinctive fall-back position for a nation traumatised by the victory of colonial nationalism. The old imperatives and priorities were more the product of intuitive responses than of clear policy formulation, but they were operative and even reinforced. Where the loss of the American colonies had created gaps in the rather idealised economic network, a haphazard search for

192

alternatives was initiated. Breadfruit trees transplanted to the West Indies would help replace supplies which were formerly imported from the mainland colonies. A new southern whale fishery would supply the valuable oil which energetic Nantucketers had previously exported to England. West Africa, Madagascar or New South Wales would become the new depositories for England's convict waste. In the Southern Continent, the Pacific or Africa, would be found the alternatives to the American market. India would become a vast new supplier of raw materials for England's burgeoning industries. All these enterprises would in addition bolster the navigation system which was still revered as the major safeguard of Britain's imperial hegemony.

In the years after 1782, therefore, England sought to overcome the sense of dislocation created by American Independence by a policy of consolidation and imperial stocktaking. As a consequence of this process the discoveries of Captain Cook began to appear in a more favourable light. He had, after all, lifted something of a psychological barrier. His ships had always returned from their arduous voyages. Scurvy, long the fatal deterrent to such expeditions, became less of a barrier to the penetration of the Pacific. Published accounts of his voyages were widely read and appreciated, becoming standard manuals for the exploring navigator. Cook had opened up the world in a geographical sense, making its most distant corners seem accessible and even familiar. There slowly developed the notion, always strictly qualified in practice, that the new lands and seas should be investigated more thoroughly with utilitarian ends in view, as though the discovery itself was an investment which could not be wasted. The men who followed in the wake of Cook wished to do homage to his memory by fully exploiting the discoveries he had made. The report of the Commons Committee on Transportation in July 1785, observed that, 'all the Discoveries as well as great Commercial Establishments now existing in distant Parts of the Globe have been owing to the enterprise and persevering Exertions of the Individuals who at great personal Risks frequent Losses and in some Cases total Ruin have opened the way to the greatest National Advantages'.[1] This same philosophy influenced the development of the southern whale fishery, the foundation of the New South Wales colony and the inception of the breadfruit expedition. Captain William Bligh observed of the *Bounty* mission: 'The Object of all former voyages to the South Seas, undertaken by command of his present majesty, has been the advancement of

science, and the increase of Knowledge. This Voyage may be reckoned the first, the intention of which has been to derive benefits
from these distant discoveries.'[2]

The voyage of the *Investigator*, with which this book began, was
clearly in the Cook, Thomson, Colnett and Vancouver tradition of
empirical observation and evaluation, and was another example of
the inter-relationship between exploration, science and empire which
has been at the centre of this study. In England in the second half of
the eighteenth century the ethos and methodology of experimental
science was contributing to the industrial revolution. Because of
their inclusion of scientific personnel, Cook's voyages had ensured
that practical knowledge of newly discovered parts of the world
would match scientific progress in England. The natural historians
and draughtsmen who accompanied later explorers continued to
ensure that the growth of scientific knowledge would go hand in
hand with the growth of geographical knowledge.

Because the scientific personnel working at the frontiers of empire
adopted an empirical and utilitarian approach to nature, it was to be
expected that they would develop views of empire which were in
concert with their method. They were natural scientists, and the
plants, animals and rocks which were the objects of their study, were
evaluated in terms of their raw material potential. To such men it
was axiomatic that overseas territories should provide sustenance
for the rapidly expanding industries of England. The inclusion of a
miner in the party on board the *Investigator* was therefore a new but
also a logical development. By putting remote parts of the world
within reach, Cook had facilitated the sort of imperial economic
unity which these scientists almost by instinct envisaged. The breadfruit expeditions, the search for finer types of cotton and the
attempts to foster various products in India were all aimed at
creating a self-supporting empire geared to metropolitan industrial
expansion. Within this imperial unit the new scientific methods were
available to shuffle resources from one sector to another to make up
deficits, or to promote efficiency. The techniques of navigation and
exploration were employed to secure this movement after 1780. The
voyages of exploration had also revealed a new range of natural
resources which scientists could evaluate, and by drawing on these
resources it became possible to compensate for some of the effects
of the loss of the American colonies.

While the industrial expansion in textiles, coal and iron, and in the
application of steam power went rapidly ahead after the American

War of Independence, English manufacturers became more confident and assertive, and they too demanded that the individual parts of the empire should fall into line in a combined effort to boost production. In 1784 the Navigation Acts were enforced against American shipping and the West Indian islands were obliged to face the effects of shortages consequent upon this attempt to protect British industry. In their concerns for the costs of production, the manufacturers urged that raw materials should be produced within the imperial framework, lessening dependence on foreign sources of supply. They selfishly insisted that India should swing from exporting manufactured cotton goods to exporting raw cotton so that the home industry might be further encouraged. They became generally impatient with monopolies and restrictions, and pressed for access to markets in Asia, Africa and the Americas.

The government reaction to such demands was usually controlled but encouraging. In contrast to the preceding and following decades, the first ten years of the younger Pitt's administration were relatively quiescent politically. Falling between the two great revolutionary wars, it was perhaps necessary and desirable that this should be the case. It was Pitt's good fortune to have a personality and political tone geared to the needs of the period. Economy, and sound and efficient administration were the preoccupations of his early years of office. The country gentry, with the country at large, were impressed with the good sense of such attitudes, and opposition strength waned as a consequence. As he became more secure in office, Pitt managed to bring into the centre of government men such as Hawkesbury, Dundas and Grenville who were attuned to his own political thinking. These were not colourful men; they were not in any real sense original thinkers; they were not great innovators in terms of imperial policy, for their main concerns were economy and regulation. Although they were fully prepared to utilise new discoveries and techniques which had become available since Cook's voyages, their natural predilection was to use them to affirm and consolidate the traditional view of empire which they understood best. The breadfruit expeditions are a case in point: they were supported by Hawkesbury because they supplemented his efforts to enforce the Navigation Acts against American shipping.

The government then, was not a substantial formulator or initiator of imperial policy, but it could, of course, be directed by outside pressure, often from men and institutions of more vision. In this manner the Pitt ministry was able to respond in a pragmatic way, viewing each case on its merits and seeking further outside advice where appropriate. The re-formed Board of Trade under Lord Hawkesbury was the critical agency in this sphere; listening to, and promoting, forward-looking ideas, and acting as a focal point for scientists, manufacturers and merchants who had schemes to offer. Ably assisted by clerks such as William Fawkener, Thomas Cottrell and George Chalmers, Hawkesbury turned this body into an effective custodian of imperial economic affairs, so that it was able to take under its wing projects as different as the interchange of tropical plants and the promotion of the 'southern whale' fishery.

In the period after 1780 the scientific knowledge and experience of Joseph Banks was at the disposal of government to assist in promoting these enterprises. His estates in Lincolnshire and Derbyshire had given Banks two invaluable commodities; an independent income, and its by-product, the leisure time which allowed him to follow the whims of an active scientific mind. In his earlier years these assets had enabled him to indulge his curiosity in Newfoundland, the Pacific, Iceland and Holland. After 1778, however, Banks assumed responsibilities which restricted his activities and in the 1780s there began those attacks of gout which put a limit on further global meanderings.[3] For the rest of his life he remained a frustrated traveller. That his own pride and vanity were responsible for his withdrawal from Cook's second voyage must have been a reflection which chafed badly. But this frustration also accounts for his continued zeal for exploration and plant gathering in different parts of the world; for the enthusiasm he generated in those men he sent to fulfil his missions; and for the vast network of overseas correspondents who plied him with plants, dried specimens and information which he could no longer harvest himself.

In the period after 1782 he was somewhat diverted from his own scientific pursuits and drawn increasingly into an administrative and organisational role. This did not always please him as he explained in 1791 to a French scientist: 'I have also myself been for some time more than I ought diverted from the study of Botany my favourite occupation by having undertaken other occupations Chiefly of a public nature.'[4] It was none the less something he had increasingly to accept. Banks was not always obviously to the fore in the enterprises with which he was concerned, partly because the channels through which he worked were often unofficial and unorthodox. Nowhere is this more obvious than in his connections with the New South Wales colony. One reason for this was his determination to eschew connections which could give his activities a partisan flavour. In 1789 he was offered some official position of superintendence over the colony but he turned it down since a change of administration would prejudice his position and perhaps destroy his worth to the colony.[5] This did not prevent him from wielding enormous power for the benefit of New South Wales, indeed he became quite indispensable. In January 1802 the mineralogist C.F. Greville wrote to Robert Brown: 'the confinement of S. Jos. B to his bed for this month past has prevented him from setting the new department of State, to which the colonies are since Mr. Addington's administration alotted, to work. . .'[6]

Outside his legitimate sphere of interest in Lincolnshire, therefore, Banks was not overtly political, and his opinions, in so far as they are discernible, are those of the independent country gentry — Brougham described him as 'high Tory'.[7] He did have some significant political friends. The Earl of Sandwich was important in the period before his fall from office in 1782. Hawkesbury, Mulgrave and Auckland were acquaintances of a different sort; of the type of political careerist Pares described as, 'fascinated by the details of policy and administration; especially by those most business-like kinds of business — trade, revenue, and the reform of administrative machinery' — in short, the political counterparts of Banks himself.[8] Avenues such as these clearly gave Banks access to government and administration, as did his contacts with 'civil servants' such as Nepean, Fawkener and Cottrell. There was another source of power. Banks' friendship with the King dated from his return on the *Endeavour* and his assumption of control over Kew Gardens. The relationship was strengthened by their mutual interest in farming and plant interchange.

Banks' ideas on plant interchange and scientific expeditions, which had been in gestation since 1772, had by 1786 crystallised into a coherent philosophy.[9] By that time too, he had the power, prestige and influence to effectively press his arguments. To some the scale of his enterprises seemed rather ambitious, but when put in the proper perspective they appeared to him but logical. He was an administrator and entrepreneur; a dissemination point for scientific ideas. His were the methods of the scientific, industrial and managerial revolutions in which efficacy was the touchstone and utility the justification. In the Kent Record Office there is a note in Banks' hand which explains his *raison d'être*:[10]

I have taken the Lizard, an Animal said to be Endow'd by nature with an instinctive love of Mankind, as my Device, & have Caus'd it to be Engrav'd as my Seal, as a Perpetual Remembrance that man is never so well Employ'd, as when he is laboring for the advantage of the Public; without the Expectation, the Hope, or Even a wish to derive advantage of any Kind from the Result of his exertions.

Jos: Banks

Notes

1. 'Private Report of the Committee of the House of Commons relative to the Transportation of Felons', July 1785, *H.O.* 42/7.

2. W. Bligh, *A Voyage to the South Sea*, p. 5.

3. Perhaps it was this the King referred to in his consolatory letter: 'The King is sorry to find Sir Joseph Banks is still confined; and though it is the common mode to congratulate persons on the first fit of Gout, He cannot join in so cruel an etiquette.' *D.T.C.* V, fo. 283, 19 November 1787.

4. Banks to A.L. de Jussieu, 15 October 1791, *Kew*, B.C. 3, fo. 2.

5. *H.R.N.S.W.* vol. I, ii, p. 229, February 1789.

6. Ibid., vol. IV, p. 677.

7. Henry, Lord Brougham, *Lives of Men of Letters and Science, who Flourished in the Time of George III*, p. 375.

8. R. Pares, *George III and the Politicians*, p. 29.

9. There is a letter from Banks to his sister, Sarah Sophia, dated 26 April 1773, setting out his views on interchange of plants between tropical countries. *M.L. Banks* A 80/4, fos 15–18.

10. Quoted in A. Lysaght, *Sir Joseph Banks in Newfoundland and Labrador 1766*, pp. 58–9.

BIBLIOGRAPHY

I. Manuscript Collections

A. Public Record Office

i. Admiralty.

Captains' Letters. *Adm*. 1/1508, 1617–19, 2395, 2574, 2594–5, 2804.
Letters from Secretary of State. *Adm*. 1/4152–60.
Orders and Instructions. *Adm*. 2/117–19, 124–6, 1342–8.
Lords' Letters. *Adm*. 2/263–9.
Secretary's Letters. *Adm*. 2/588–92, 757–8.
Admiralty Board Minutes. *Adm*. 3/103–8.
Logs and Journals.
 Nautilus log and journal. *Adm*. 51/627, *Adm*. 55/92.
 Argonaut journal. *Adm*. 55/142.
 Prince of Wales log. *Adm*. 55/146.
 Providence log (Broughton). *Adm*. 55/147.
 Bounty log. *Adm*. 55/151.
 Providence logs (Bligh). *Adm*. 55/152–3.
 Rattler log. *Adm*. 55/100.
Navy Board Out-letters. *Adm*. 106/2214–16.
Navy Board Minutes. *Adm*. 106/2624–38.
Deptford Yard Letter Books. *Adm*. 106/3321, 3407, 3365.
Commissioners for Victualling. *Adm*. 111/111.

ii. Board of Trade.

In-letters. *B.T.* 1/1–6, 14–15.
Out-letters. *B.T.* 3/1–5.
Minutes. *B.T.* 5/1–8.
Miscellaneous, whale fisheries. *B.T.* 6/93, 95.
Miscellaneous, cotton. *B.T.* 6/140, 246.

iii. Colonial Office.

Papers relating to Vancouver's voyage. *C.O.* 5/187.
Quebec. *C.O.* 42/72.
East Indies. *C.O.* 77/25–6.
New South Wales. *C.O.* 201/2–5.

iv. Home Office.

Admiralty Correspondence. *H.O.* 28/5–8.
Admiralty Supplementary. *H.O.* 28/61–2.
Admiralty Entry Books. *H.O.* 29/2–3.
Foreign Office Correspondence. *H.O.* 32/2.
Domestic, George III. *H.O.* 42/7–21.

v. Privy Council.

Register. *P.C.* 2/135.

vi. War Office.

Papers concerning the Botanic Garden on St Vincent. *W.O.* 4/334, *W.O.* 40/4.

vii. Private Collections.

Chatham Papers. *P.R.O.* 30/8, 102, 111, 122, 151, 341, 361, 363, 368.
Cornwallis Papers. *P.R.O.* 30/11, 13, 18, 20, 29, 39, 112–14, 150.

B. British Library

i. Private Papers.

Auckland Papers. *Add. MSS.* 34434, 34466.
Banks Papers. *Add. MSS.* 8094–7, 33272, 33977–82.
Leeds Papers. *Add. MSS.* 28064–6.
Liverpool Papers. *Add. MSS.* 38192, 38222–4, 38309–10, 38346–9, 38390–1, 38409, 38414.
Rose Papers. *Add. MSS.* 42772, 42774, 42776, 42780.
South Sea Company Papers. *Add. MSS.* 25521–3, 25546–7, 25558, 25578.

ii. Logs and Journals.

F. Buchanan, 'An Account of a Journey undertaken by order of the Board of Trade through the Provinces of Chittagong and Tiperah', *Add. MSS.* 19286.
J. Colnett, 'A Voyage for Whaling and Discovery', *Add. MSS.* 30369.
A.P. Hove, 'Tours for Scientific and Economical Research', *Add. MSS.* 8956.
A. Menzies, 'Journal of Vancouver's Voyage', *Add. MSS.* 32641.
Logs and Journals of the *Discovery* and *Chatham, Add. MSS.* 17542–51.

C. British Museum (Natural History)

Collection of copies of the correspondence of Sir Joseph Banks made for Dawson Turner, FRS, in 1833–4, 20 vols.

D. Royal Botanic Gardens, Kew

Correspondence of Sir Joseph Banks in the Herbarium Library, 4 vols.

E. India Office Library

General Correspondence. E/1/80, 82, 86, 89. E/4/45.
Home Miscellaneous Series. 190, 210, 393, 494, 799, 800. Volume 800 contains the journal of James Strange in the ship *Captain Cook*.
China Consultations. R/10, 15–19.
China: Court's Letters. R/10, I.
Board of Control Letter Book. F/2/1.
Marine Records. Log of the *Prince of Wales*, 0, 404.

F. National Library of Scotland

Melville Papers. 1064, 1068, 1075, 3385, 3387, 3837, 3845, 3847.

G. Scottish Record Office

Melville Castle Muniments. *G.D.* 51/2–3.

H. Linnean Society of London

A. Menzies, 'Journal of Vancouver's Voyage'.

I. Royal Society of Arts

Banks letters in the Society's Red Book.

J. West India Committee Library

West India Committee Minutes, Vol. 3.

K. Mitchell Library, the State Library of New South Wales, Sydney

Brabourne Collection, Banks papers. A78/1-6, A79/2-3, A81, A82, A83.

L. Sutro Library, San Francisco

Banks correspondence.

II. Pamphlets, Treatises and Contemporary Journals

A. Correspondence and Official Records

James Anderson. Collections of Letters concerning natural history, being in part reprints from the *Madras Courier*, 1787-1800. All published at Madras.
  Letters to Sir Joseph Banks, 1788.
  Letters on Cochineal, 1788.
  Letters on Cochineal Continued, 1789.
  Correspondence on the Introduction of the Cochineal Insects from America, the Varnish and Tallow Trees from China, etc., 1791.
  Letters for Extending the Manufacture of Raw Silk, 1793.
  Some Additional Letters Principally Regarding the Culture of Raw Silk, 1793.
  Letters for Promoting the Silk Manufacture, 1794.
  Letters for the Culture of Bastard Cedar Tress on the Coast of Coromandel, 1794.
  An Account of the Importation of the America Cochineal Insects, 1795.
  Miscellaneous Communications, 1796.
  Letters, etc., 4 vol., 1796.
  The Conclusion of Letters on Cochineal, 1799.
Fort William-India House Correspondence (P.C. Gupta, ed.), XIII, XXII, New Delhi, 1959.
Historical Manuscripts Commission, *Report on the Manuscripts of J.B. Fortescue, Esq., preserved at Dropmore*, 30, I-II.
Historical Records of New South Wales, I-IV.
Journals of the House of Commons, XXXVII.

B. Newspapers and Periodicals

The Gazetteer
The Gentleman's Magazine
Madras Courier
The Monthly Review
Philosophical Transactions of the Royal Society
The Public Advertiser

C. Contemporary Works

Adams, J. *Modern Voyages*, London, 1790.
Anonymous, *Observations Relative to the Resources of the East India Company for*

Productive Remittance, London, 1788.

Banks, Sir J. *The Propriety of allowing a Qualified Exportation of Wool, discussed historically*, London, 1782.

—— *A Short Account of the course of a Disease in Corn, called by farmers, the blight, the mildew and the rust*, London, 1805.

—— *Some circumstances relating to Merino Sheep*, London, 1809.

Barrington, D. *Miscellanies*, London, 1781.

Bligh, W. *A Voyage to the South Sea*, London, 1792.

Broughton, A. *Hortus Eastensis or a Catalogue of Exotic Plants in the Garden of Hinton East, Esq., in Jamaica*, Kingston, 1792.

Broughton, W.R. *A Voyage of Discovery to the North Pacific Ocean*, London, 1804.

Brulles, Abbé *The Mode of Cultivating and Dressing Hemp*, London, 1790.

Buée, W.U. *A Narrative of the Successful Manner of Cultivating the Clove Tree in the Island of Dominica*, London, 1797.

Burney, J. *A Chronological History of the Discoveries in the South Sea or Pacific Ocean*, London, 1803–17.

Collins, D. *An Account of the English Colony in New South Wales*, London, 1798.

Coxe, W. *Account of the Russian Discoveries between Asia and America*, London, 1804.

Dalrymple, A. *An Account of the Discoveries Made in the South Pacific Ocean Previous to 1764*, London, 1767.

—— *An Historical Collection of Several Voyages and Discoveries in the South Pacific Ocean*, London, 1770–1.

—— *A Collection of Voyages Chiefly in the Southern Atlantick Ocean*, London, 1775.

—— *Plan for Promoting the Fur Trade and Securing it to this Country by Uniting the Operations of the East-India and Hudson's-Bay Companys*, London, 1789.

—— *A Catalogue of the Extensive and Valuable Library of Books late the Property of Alexander Dalrymple, Esq., F.R.S.*, London, 1809.

Dancer, T. *A Catalogue of Plants, Exotic and Indigenous in the Botanical Garden, Jamaica*, St Jago la Vega, 1792.

—— *Some Observations Respecting the Botanical Garden*, Jamaica, 1804.

Dixon, G. *A Voyage Round the World; but more Particularly to the North-West Coast of America*, London, 1789.

Edwards, B. *The History, Civil and Commercial of the British Colonies in the West Indies*, London, 1794.

Ellis, J. *A Description of the Mangosteen and Breadfruit*, London, 1775; also published as *Description du Mangostan et du Fruit à Pain*, Paris, 1779.

Fothergill, J. *Directions for taking up Plants and Shrubs and conveying them by sea*, London, n.d.

Goldson, W. *Observations on the Passage between the Atlantic and Pacific Oceans*, Portsmouth, 1793.

Hawkesworth, J. *An Account of Voyages Undertaken for Making Discoveries in the Southern Hemisphere*, 3 vols., London, 1773.

Hill, J. *The Usefulness of Knowledge of Plants illustrated in various instances*, London, 1759.

Meares, J. *Voyages Made in the Years 1788 and 1789 from China to the North West Coast of America*, London, 1790.

Portlock, N. *A Voyage Round the World; but more Particularly to the North-West Coast of America*, London, 1789.

Sarytschew, G. *Account of a Voyage of Discovery to the North-East of Siberia, the Frozen Ocean, and the North-East Sea*, London, 1806.

Sauer, M. *An Account of a Geographical and Astronomical Expedition to the Northern Parts of Russia*, London, 1802.

Society of Arts, *Premiums Offered by the Society Instituted at London for the Encouragement of Arts, Manufactures and Commerce*, London, 1765–70.

Thunberg, C.P. *Travels in Europe, Africa and Asia*, London, 1795.

Tooke, W. *View of the Russian Empire During the Reign of Catherine the Second*, 3 vols., London, 1759.

Vancouver, G. *A Voyage of Discovery to the North Pacific Ocean and Round the World*, 3 vols., London, 1798.

Walker, D. *Essay on the Translation of Plants from the East and West Indies*, London, n.d.

D. Modern Works

Alekseev, A.I. 'Joseph Billings', *The Geographical Journal*, vol. 132, no. ii, June 1966, pp. 233–8.

Allen, M. *The Hookers of Kew*, London, 1967.

Anderson, B. *Surveyor of the Sea. The Life and Voyages of Captain George Vancouver*, Seattle, 1960.

Arber, A. *Herbals*, Cambridge, 1938.

Armytage, W.H.G. *The Rise of the Technocrats*, London, 1965.

Ashby, Sir E. *Technology and the Academics*, London, 1958.

Ashton, T.S. *The Industrial Revolution*, London, 1940.

—— *An Economic History of England: the 18th Century*, London, 1955.

Aspinall, A. *Cornwallis in Bengal*, Manchester, 1931.

Austin, K.A. *The Voyage of the Investigator, 1801–1803*, Adelaide, 1964.

Baker, N. 'Changing Attitudes towards Government in Eighteenth Century Britain' in A. Whiteman, J.S. Bromley & P.G.M. Dickson (eds.), *Statesman, Scholars and Merchants*, Oxford, 1973.

Banks, Sir J. *Inventory of Sir Joseph Banks's Library as Received by The British Museum*, London, 1827.

Barrau, J. *Subsistence Agriculture in Polynesia and Micronesia*, Bernice Bishop Museum Bulletin 223, 1961.

Barrow, Sir J. *Sketches of the Royal Society and the Royal Society Club*, London, 1849.

Baugh, D.A. *British Naval Administration in the Age of Walpole*, Princeton, NJ, 1965.

Beaglehole, J.C. (ed.) *The Journals of Captain Cook on His Voyages of Discovery*, 3 vols., Cambridge, 1955–6.

—— *The Endeavour Journal of Joseph Banks*, 1768–1771, 2 vols., Sydney, 1962.

—— *The Exploration of the Pacific*, London, 1966.

—— *Captain Cook and Captain Bligh*, Wellington, 1967.

—— *The Life of Captain James Cook*, London, 1974.

Biswas, K. 'Original Correspondence of Sir Joseph Banks Relating to the Foundation of the Royal Botanic Garden', *Asiatic Society Monographs*, vol. IX, Calcutta, 1950.

Blainey, G. *The Tyranny of Distance*, Melbourne, 1966.

Brockway, Lucile H. *Science and Colonial Expansion. The Role of the British Royal Botanic Gardens*, New York, 1979.

Brougham, Lord H. *Lives of Men of Letters and Science, who Flourished in the Time of George III*, London, 1846.

Brown, P. *The Chathamites*, London, 1967.

Burke, Joseph. *English Art 1714–1800*, Oxford, 1976.

Cameron, H.C. *Sir Joseph Banks*, London, 1952.

Carter, H.B. *His Majesty's Spanish Flock. Sir Joseph Banks and the Merinos of George III of England*, London and Sydney, 1964.

Christie, I.R. *Myth and Reality*, London, 1970.

Clow, A. & Clow, N.L. *The Chemical Revolution*, London, 1952.

Coats, A.M. *The Quest for Plants*, London, 1969.

Cook, W.L. *Flood Tide of Empire: Spain and the Pacific Northwest*, New Haven, Conn., 1973.

Cox, E.G. *Reference Guide to the Literature of Travel*, Washington, DC, 1935.

Crawford, D.G. *Roll of the Indian Medical Service, 1615-1930*, 2 vols., London, 1930.

Crouse, N.M. *The Search for the Northwest Passage*, New York, 1934.

Crowther, J.G. *Scientists of the Industrial Revolution*, London, 1962.

Dakin, W.J. *Whalemen Adventurers*, Sydney, 1938.

Dawson, W. (ed.) *The Banks Letters*, London, 1958.

De, B. 'Henry Dundas and the Government of India, 1773-1801', Oxford DPhil thesis, 1961.

de Beer, Sir G. *The Sciences Were Never at War*, London, 1960.

Dermigny, L. *La Chine et L'Occident. Le Commerce a Canton ou XVIIIe Siecle, 1719-1833*, 3 vols., Paris, 1964.

Dillon, R.H. 'Letters of Captain George Dixon in the Banks Collection', *B.C.H.Q.*, vol. XIV, July 1950, pp. 93-7.

—— 'Archibald Menzies' Trophies', *B.C.H.Q.*, vol. XV, July-October 1951, pp. 151-9.

—— 'Convict Colonies for the Pacific Northwest', *B.C.H.Q.*, vol. XIX, January-April 1955, pp. 92-102.

Dodge, E.S. *Northwest by Sea*, New York, 1961.

Duncan, A. *A Short Account of the Life of Sir Joseph Banks, K.B.*, Edinburgh, 1821.

Dunmore, J. *French Explorers in the Pacific*, 2 vols., Oxford, 1965-9.

Edwards, M.M. *The Growth of the British Cotton Trade 1780-1815*, Manchester, 1967.

Ehrman, J. *The Younger Pitt*, London, 1969.

Embree, A. *Charles Grant and British Rule in India*, London, 1962.

Fisher, R. & Johnson, H. (eds.) *Captain Cook and His Times*, Vancouver, 1980.

Frost, A. *Convicts and Empire: A Naval Question*, Melbourne, 1980.

Fry. H. 'Early British Interest in the Chagos Archipelago and Maldive Islands', *'Mariners' Mirror*, vol. 53, 1967, pp. 343-56.

—— 'Alexander Dalrymple and New Guinea', *The Journal of Pacific History*, vol. IV, 1969, pp. 83-104.

—— *Alexander Dalrymple and the Expansion of British Trade*, London, 1970.

Furber, H. *John Company at Work*, Cambridge, Mass., 1948.

—— *Rival Empires of Trade in the Orient 1600-1800*, Minneapolis, Minnesota, 1974.

Gee, O. 'Charles Jenkinson as Secretary at War', Oxford BLitt thesis, 1949.

Gillen, Mollie. 'The Botany Bay Decision, 1786: Convicts and Empire', *English Historical Review*, vol. XCVII, no. 385, October 1982, pp. 740-66.

Godwin, G. *Vancouver. A Life*, New York, 1931.

Griffiths, Sir. P. *The History of the Indian Tea Industry*, London, 1967.

Guilding, L. *An Account of the Botanic Garden in the Island of St. Vincent from its First Establishment to the Present Day*, Glasgow, 1825.

Hall, A.R. 'Science, Technology and Utopia in the Seventeenth Century' in P. Mathias (ed.), *Science and Society 1600-1900*, Cambridge, 1972.

Hallet, R. *The Records of the African Association, 1788-1831*, London, 1964.

—— *The Penetration of Africa*, London, 1965.

Hallward, N.L. *William Bolts. A Dutch Adventurer under John Company*, Cambridge, 1920.

Harlow, V.T. *The Founding of the Second British Empire 1763-1793*, 2 vols., London, 1964.

Harlow, V.T. & Madden. F. *British Colonial Developments, 1774-1834*, Oxford, 1953.

Hawkins, C.W. 'His Majesty's Armed Tender *Lady Nelson*', *Mariners' Mirror*, vol. 55, November 1944, pp. 417–34.

Hermannson, H. *Sir Joseph Banks and Iceland*, Ithaca, NY, 1928.

Hewson, J.B. *A History of the Practise of Navigation*, London, 1951.

Hill, J.W.F. *Letters and Papers of the Banks Family of Revesby Abbey, 1704–1760*, Lincoln, 1952.

Hoare, Michael E. *The Tactless Philosopher, Johann Reinhold Forster, 1729–1798*, Melbourne, 1976.

—— *The Resolution Journal of Johann Reinhold Forster 1772–1775*, 3 vols., London, 1982.

Hosie, J. 'James Charles Stuart Strange and his Expedition to the North-West Coast of America in 1786', *British Columbia Historical Association*, 4th Report and Proceedings, 1929, pp. 43–54.

Hoskins, H.L. *British Routes to India*, London, 1967, repr.

Howay, F.W. (ed.) *The Dixon-Meares Controversy*. Toronto, 1929.

—— 'A List of Trading Vessels in the Maritime Fur Trade, 1785–1794', *Proceedings and Transactions of the Royal Society of Canada*, 3rd Series, vol. xxiv, 1930, pp. 111–34.

—— 'An Outline Sketch of the Maritime Fur Trade', *Canadian Hist. Assoc. Dept.*, 1932, pp. 1–14.

—— *The Journal of Captain James Colnett Aboard the Argonaut*, Toronto, 1940.

—— 'The Voyage of the *Captain Cook* and the *Experiment*, 1785–1786', *B.C.H.Q.*, vol. V, 1941, pp. 285–93.

—— 'Four Letters from Richard Cadman Etches to Sir Joseph Banks, 1788–1792', *B.C.H.Q.*, vol. VI, April 1942, pp. 125–39.

Hudson, D. & Luckhurst, K. *The Royal Society of Arts, 1754–1954*, London, 1954.

Hyams, R & Martin, G. *Reappraisals in British Imperial History*, London, 1975.

Ingram, E. *Commitment to Empire: Prophecies of the Great Game in Asia 1797–1800*, Oxford, 1981.

Innes, H.A. *The Fur Trade in Canada*, New Haven, Conn., 1930.

Johnson, G.W. *A History of English Gardening*, London, 1828.

Kaye-Lamb, W. 'The Mystery of Mrs. Barkley's Diary', *B.C.H.Q.*, vol. VI, April 1942, pp. 31–59.

King, Sir G. 'A Brief Memoir of William Roxburgh', *Annals of the Royal Botanic Garden Calcutta*, vol. V, 1895.

Knight, C. 'H.M. Armed Vessel *Bounty*', *Mariners' Mirror*, April 1936, pp. 183–99.

Koyré, A. *From the Closed World to the Infinite Universe*, New York, 1958.

Landes, D. *Cambridge Economic History of Europe*, vol. VI, Cambridge, 1966.

—— *The Unbound Prometheus*, Cambridge, 1969.

Lloyd, C. & Coulter, J.L.S. *Medicine and the Navy: 1200–1900*, 4 vols., London, 1961; vol. III, *1714–1815*.

Love, H.D. *Vestiges of Old Madras, 1640–1800*, 4 vols., London, 1913.

Lyons, Sir H. *The Royal Society, 1660–1940*, Cambridge, 1944.

Lysaght, A. *Sir Joseph Banks in Newfoundland and Labrador 1766*, London, 1971.

—— 'Joseph Banks at Skara Brae and Stennis, Orkney, 1772', *Notes and Records of the Royal Society of London*, vol. 28, no. 2, April 1974.

McCracken, H. *Hunters of the Stormy Sea*, London, 1957.

McKie, D. 'The Scientific Periodical from 1665 to 1798' in A. Ferguson (ed.), *Natural Philosophy through the Eighteenth Century*, London, 1948.

McNab, R. *Murihiku: A History of the South Islands*, Wellington, 1909.

Mack, J.D. *Matthew Flinders, 1774–1814*, Melbourne, 1966.

Mackaness, G. *Sir Joseph Banks. His Relations with Australia*, Sydney, 1936.

—— *The Life of Vice-Admiral William Bligh*, Sydney, 1951.

—— *Sir Joseph Banks, Bart*, Sydney, 1962.

Mackay, D.L. 'British Interest in the Southern Oceans, 1782–1794', *The New Zealand Journal of History*, vol. 3, no. 2, October 1969, pp. 124–42.

206   *Bibliography*

—— 'Banks, Bligh and Breadfruit', *The New Zealand Journal of History*, vol. 8, no. 1, April 1974.

—— 'Direction and Purpose in British Imperial Policy, 1783-1801', *The Historical Journal*, vol. XVII, no. 3, 1974, pp. 487-501.

—— 'Far-flung Empire: A Neglected Outpost at Botany Bay 1788-1801', *Journal of Imperial and Commonwealth History*, vol. IX, no. 1, January 1981, pp. 125-45.

Maiden, J.H. *Sir Joseph Banks: the 'Father of Australia'*, Sydney, 1909.

Mander-Jones, P. *Manuscripts in the British Isles Relating to Australia, New Zealand and the Pacific*, Canberra, 1972.

Manning, W.R. *The Nootka Sound Controversy*, American Historical Association Annual Report, 1905.

Markham, C.R. *Major James Rennell and the Rise of Modern English Geography*, London, 1895.

Marshall, P.J. 'Private British Investment in Eighteenth Century Bengal', *Bengal Past and Present*, vol. LXXXVI, no. ii, 1967, pp. 52-67.

—— *Problems of Empire: Britain and India 1757-1813*, London, 1968.

—— 'The Bengal Commercial Society of 1775: Private Business Trade in the Warren Hastings Period', *Bulletin of the Institute of Historical Research*, vol. XLII, no. 106, November 1969, pp. 173-87.

Marshall, P.J. & Williams, Glyndwr *The Great Map of Mankind. British Perceptions of the World in the Age of Enlightenment*, London, 1982.

Martin, G. (ed.), *The Founding of Australia*, Sydney, 1978.

Martin-Allanic, J.E. *Bougainville Navigateur et les Dècouvertes de son Temps*, 2 vols., Paris, 1964.

Mathias, P. 'Who Unbound Prometheus? Science and Technical Change, 1600-1800' in P. Mathias (ed.), *Science and Society 1600-1900*, Cambridge, 1972.

Mills, L. 'The Real Significance of the Nootka Sound Incident', *Canadian Historical Review*, vol. VI, pp. 110-22.

Minchinton, W.E. *Politics and the Port of Bristol in the Eighteenth Century*, Bristol, 1963.

Mingay, G.E. *English Landed Society in the Eighteenth Century*, London, 1963.

Mitchell, B.R. & Deane, P. *Abstract of British Historical Statistics*, Cambridge, 1962.

Morse, H.B. (ed.) *The Chronicles of the East India Company Trading to China, 1635-1834*, 5 vols., Oxford, 1926.

Musson, A.E. & Robinson, E. *Science and Technology in the Industrial Revolution*, Manchester, 1969.

Newcombe, C.F. 'Menzies' Journal of Vancouver's Voyage', *Archives of British Columbia*, vol. V, 1923.

Norris, J.M. 'The Policy of the British Cabinet in the Nootka Crisis', *English Historical Review*, vol. 70, October 1955, pp. 562-80.

Pares, R. *George III and the Politicians*, London, 1953.

Parry, J.H. *Trade and Dominion*, London, 1971.

Phillips, C.H. *The East India Company: 1784-1834*, Manchester, 1940.

—— (ed.) *The Correspondence of David Scott*, London, 1951.

Ragatz, L.J. *The Fall of the Planter Class in the British Caribbean, 1763-1833*, New York, 1928.

Rainaud, A. *Le Continent Austral*, Paris, 1890.

Reed, Michael *The Georgian Triumph 1700-1830*, London, 1983.

Ritcheson, C.R. *Aftermath of Revolution*, Dallas, 1969.

Robinson, E. & McKie, D. *Partners in Science*, London 1970.

Robinson, J. *A Catalogue of the Books, Maps, Prints, Drawings and Tracts belonging to the Society for the Encouragement of Arts, Manufacturers and Commerce*, London, 1804.

Roe, M. *The Journals and Letters of Captain Charles Bishop on the North-West Coast of America, in the Pacific and in New South Wales 1794–1799*, Cambridge, 1967.

Rohde, E.S. *The Old English Herbals*, New York, 1971.

Rostow, W.W. *The Stages of Economic Growth*, Cambridge, 1960.

Russell, Colin *Science and Social Change 1700–1900*, London, 1983.

Rydén, S. *The Banks Collection. An Episode in Eighteenth Century Anglo-Swedish Relations*, Stockholm, 1963.

Schofield, R. *The Lunar Society of Birmingham*, Oxford, 1963.

Scoresby-Jackson, R.E. *The Life of William Scoresby*, London, 1861.

Scott, E. *The Life of Matthew Flinders, R.N.*, Sydney, 1914.

Semmel, B. *The Imperialism of Free Trade*, Cambridge, 1970.

Sharp, A. *The Discovery of Australia*, Oxford, 1963.

Shaw, A.G.L. 'The Hollow Conqueror and the Tyranny of Distance', *Historical Studies. Australia and New Zealand*, vol. XIII, no. 50, April 1968, pp. 195–203.

Smith, B.W. *European Vision and the South Pacific, 1768–1850*, London, 1960.

Smith, E. *The Life of Sir Joseph Banks*, London, 1911.

Stearns, R.P. *Science in the British Colonies of America*, Urbana, Illinois, 1970.

Steven, Margaret *Trade, Tactics and Territory*, Melbourne, 1983.

Suttor, G. *Memoirs of Sir Joseph Banks*, London, 1855.

Taylor, E.G.R. *The Haven-Finding Art*, London, 1956.

Thomas, P.D.G. *The House of Commons in the Eighteenth Century*, Oxford, 1971.

Tomlinson, C. *Sir Joseph Banks at the Royal Society*, London, 1844.

Tompkins, S.R. & Moorehead, M.L. 'Russia's Approach to America', *B.C.H.Q.*, vol. XIII, 1949, pp. 55–66, 231–55.

Turner, L.C.F. 'The Cape of Good Hope and Anglo-French Rivalry, 1778–1796', *Historical Studies. Australia and New Zealand*, vol. XII, no. 46, April 1966, pp. 166–85.

Villiers, A. *Captain Cook, the Seaman's Seaman*, London, 1967.

Ward, J.M. *British Policy in the South Pacific, 1786–1893*, Sydney, 1948.

Watrous, S.D. (ed.) *John Ledyard's Journey Through Russia and Siberia 1787–1788*, Madison, Wisconsin, 1966.

Watt, G. *A Dictionary of the Economic Products of India*, 6 vols., Calcutta, 1889–96.

Weld, C.R. *History of the Royal Society*, 2 vols., London, 1848.

Wheelwright, E.G. *The Physic Garden*, London, 1939.

Williams, G. *The British Search for the Northwest Passage in the Eighteenth Century*, London, 1962.

Wright, H.R.C. *East-Indian Economic Problems of the Age of Cornwallis and Raffles*, London, 1961.

Zakalinskaya, E.P. *Votchinnye Khozyaystva Mogilyovskoy Gubernii vo vtoroy polovine XVIII veka* [The Economy of Patrimonial Estates in the Mogilyovskoy Gubernii in the Second Half of the Eighteenth Century], Mogilyov, 1958 (manuscript translation by Professor I.R. Christie).

INDEX